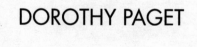

DOROTHY PAGET

Standing to attention. Slimline Dorothy holds the head of one her hunters, while her friend Daisy Walker perches sidesaddle.

DOROTHY PAGET

THE ECCENTRIC QUEEN
OF THE SPORT OF KINGS

Graham Sharpe and Declan Colley

RACING POST

To Georgia Joy Sharpe, Kiwi grand-daughter and inspiration.

First published in Great Britain in 2017 by
Racing Post Books
27 Kingfisher Court, Hambridge Road, Newbury, Berkshire, RG14 5SJ

10 9 8 7 6 5 4 3 2 1

ISBN 978-1-910497-35-7
Cover designed by Jay Vincent
Text designed by Soapbox, www.soapbox.co.uk

Printed and bound in the UK by CPI Group (UK) Ltd,
Croydon, CR0 4YY

www.racingpost.com/shop

CONTENTS

FOREWORD

by Martin Pipe CBE

15 times Champion National Hunt Racehorse Trainer, and
bestselling author of *Martin Pipe: The Champion Trainer's Story*

During my thirty-plus years as a racehorse trainer I was able to experience the 'Sport of Kings' first hand. I trained the winners of over 4,000 races, including 34 Cheltenham Festival winners as well as the Grand National winner, Miinnehoma, in 1994. In the process I was fortunate to meet many fascinating people and to train plenty of great horses, but I would have dearly loved to meet and train for the colourful and enigmatic Honourable Dorothy Wyndham Paget.

When I was approached by Graham Sharpe to write a foreword for a book about Dorothy Paget I was both flattered and hugely excited. Sadly, she and I were a generation apart, but I have spent many years researching the life and times of this pioneering lady, her horses and her eccentricities, and to now be in a position to contribute to a book about her is an enormous privilege.

My interest started when I was holidaying on the Isle of Islay, the southernmost island of the Inner Hebrides in Scotland. In the library of the cottage where we were staying I found a book, published in 1973; it was called *Queen of the Turf: The Dorothy Paget Story*, and I found it very interesting.

Later, I found some memorabilia for sale and my interest burgeoned. The items included private letters, photographs, receipts for parties and entertaining, copies and records of bets and trainers' reports – all of which were typed meticulously up to seven times by her seven secretaries.

I fell in love with Dorothy Paget, and would get up in the middle of the night to look through some of her fascinating artefacts – I have now acquired so many items that I will never get through them all, but they provide a first-hand insight into this amazing woman. Fortunately, I have a wonderful and understanding wife, Carol – and it hasn't escaped her notice that, while I am busy reading through my Dorothy Paget memorabilia, she is afforded a little welcome peace and quiet.

A renowned gambler, Dorothy Paget owned some of the most famous horses in racing history, from the amazing Golden Miller – five times a Gold Cup winner and also the winner of the Grand National (becoming, in 1934, the only horse ever to win both in the same season) – to the likes of Champion Hurdle victors Insurance and Distel, while she was also the proud owner of a Derby winner in the shape of Straight Deal. Through these horses she forged relations with other legends of the turf including Fulke Walwyn, Basil Briscoe and Sir Gordon Richards, all of whom would recount intriguing tales of a very complex, fiery character.

Dorothy was certainly a trailblazer for the big-spending owner/breeders we have become so familiar with in modern times – the likes of Sheikh Mohammed bin Rashid Al Maktoum, Robert Sangster and John Magnier all spring to mind. She would always purchase the most expensive horses at the sales, put them with the best trainers her money could buy, and employ the finest jockeys. Consequently, she would expect great results, and woe betide the trainer and jockey should these expectations not be met!

Martin Pipe surveys his treasure trove of Dorothy Paget memorabilia, which made an invaluable contribution to the authenticity of this book.

Of course, this philosophy could have been construed as rather simplistic and naïve. After all, money does not always guarantee success. Horses are not machines, and they do get headaches, just like you and I – and it must have been a challenge trying to educate this extremely intelligent, yet stubborn and powerful lady in the unpredictable ways of the turf. Even so, it is a challenge I would have relished. During my time as a trainer I dealt with many difficult owners, and I feel she would have responded well to my own revolutionary regime.

Back in Dorothy's racing days, the modern techniques I was able to introduce to the sport in the 1980s with such spectacular success were not available. There were no blood tests, tracheal washes, weighing machines, and I am sure she would have appreciated my scientific approach to training.

My methods meant I was able to detect potential problems with the horses before they ran, rather than after they had disappointed on the racecourse, while interval training meant that the horses were fitter than ever before.

As such, I would have been able to provide cold, hard facts based on science rather than guesswork – and I am certain this is something she would have embraced. As far as I am concerned you can never have too many facts on which to base an informed decision, especially as it benefits our – Dorothy Paget's – great friend, the racehorse.

Graham Sharpe has paid me a number of visits at home to enhance and authenticate the copious amounts of information he and co-writer Declan Colley have amassed between them. I am sure they will have found them of use when adding the finishing touches to this excellent book.

Graham has spent over 40 years working in the betting industry and is the author of more than 30 books – the majority of them featuring horse racing or gambling – while Declan Colley is also steeped in racing, with two books on the sport to his credit. It is hardly surprising, therefore, given their passion both for horses and betting, that Graham and Declan chose to write a book about one of racing's most fabled gamblers in Dorothy Paget.

Dorothy Paget has been written about in the past and I have read most of it, but over the following pages Graham and Declan deliver what I believe is an unparalleled look at the life and loves, winners and losers, of this amazing woman. Meticulously researched, insightful and gripping, I wasn't able to put it down, and I hope you will enjoy reading it as much as I have.

Martin Pipe CBE
Wellington, Somerset

PROLOGUE

She was perhaps the most reclusive person in Britain, yet also, for the best part of thirty years, one of its most instantly recognisable individuals. She hated drawing attention to herself in public, but the champion jump jockey Terry Biddlecombe was 'astounded at her vast size'. She inherited enormous wealth, courtesy of her American mother's family, and had little inhibition about spending it, on fast cars, and fast horses – she owned the most prolific Gold Cup winner, and a Derby winner – though often they were not quite fast enough. After her superstar racehorse Golden Miller, who already boasted four Cheltenham Gold Cups and a Grand National on his CV, had landed his record-breaking fifth victory in the 1936 Gold Cup, according to one source Dorothy celebrated in the most bizarre manner: she relieved herself twice in his horse box on the way back from Cheltenham – causing a traffic jam in the process.

She enabled her bookmakers to live in a manner they had not thought possible. When she was in a bad mood her spectacular betting habits often spiralled out of control – in 1952, she lost a six-figure sum in just one afternoon. When she died she left an estate so huge that selling it off caused the stock market temporarily to fall. Often referred to as the richest unmarried woman in the land, Dorothy Paget was legendary for her eccentricity.

'I think Dorothy was widely accepted as a complete eccentric,' said the late Sir Peter O'Sullevan,

> *and I don't think she was begrudged enormously that eccentric element in her character, or the fact that she embodied eccentricity, if you like. There was nothing arresting about her presence. She was a shadowy figure, very reclusive and incommunicative. She was dowdy, dumpy and pale. She was the antithesis of charismatic. She didn't appear to be someone it would be a great deal of fun spending an afternoon with. But you couldn't help wondering what lay behind the implacable public façade. What drove her, what made her tick?*

She would assign her members of staff different colours, and speak or write to Blue, or Pink, or Yellow, instead of their names. But never green: she had a lifelong aversion to the colour. She had a footstool called Tootsie. Her unofficial racing manager was also a concert pianist, who claimed to have taught his horses to count to ten backwards. She slept all day, stayed up most of the night, and managed to persuade a bookmaker to let her bet on races that had already taken place while she was asleep.

When one of Dorothy Paget's most trusted aides came to collect her from the cottage she had hired near Cheltenham racecourse for the duration of an important meeting, she was alarmed to see flames emerging from the building. The previous night Dorothy had built up a huge fire on the open hearth, and it had now set fire to a beam, which was smouldering and smoking fiercely. Warned of the danger, Dorothy announced, 'I have no intention of getting up until the flames are licking my pyjama legs.' Eventually making her stately progress down the smoke-obscured stairs, she told her staff, '*Now* you can send for the fire brigade.'

Newspapers were desperate to run exclusive interviews with her. None succeeded. Her hard-worked yet unfailingly loyal and devoted secretaries would accompany her everywhere she went – even to the lavatories of the racecourses and theatres she visited. So the papers would regularly feature photographs of a distinctively dowdy, almost completely covered-up figure, portlier by the year, who would accompany her Gold Cup, Grand National and Derby heroes back to the winner's enclosure.

Yet she hadn't always been so unconcerned about her appearance. She 'came out' as a debutante, was photographed in her finery by one of the most fashionable photographers of the day, and wore expensive jewellery. For no immediately apparent reason she took up with a glamorous national sporting hero, the motor racing driver and renowned 'Bentley Boy', Sir Henry 'Tim' Birkin. She poured money into his dream of creating a team of impossibly fast, supercharged cars that would revolutionise the sport, and was seen around the country's racing circuits getting up close and personal with the dashing, divorced driver.

The popular view of Dorothy Paget has portrayed a shabby, man-hating, uncaring figure who often slept through the day and worked or played through the night, ate constantly and excessively, and lived an entirely self-obsessed, joyless life. Scratch a little deeper, though, and you'll find she could also display entirely opposite characteristics. Like most of us she was a bundle of contradictions, one thing to one person, someone entirely different to another. Yet she would never deign to dispel the myths, or reveal the truth. But who wouldn't have loved to meet the woman revealed in the little-known glimpses into her life revealed in this book?

'I was there at Folkestone racecourse when Dorothy appeared with a tremendous entourage of secretaries', recalled the late racecourse commentator, Cloudesley Marsham.

*Imagine the scene as she was walking briskly along, clad in her
usual 'Speckled Hen' overcoat and fur boots with staff struggling
to keep up, only for her knickers to fall down around her ankles
as she strode along.*

*Her secretaries immediately bustled all around her, like a rugby scrum,
and the offending bloomers were duly hauled back into position. I always
wondered who the lucky one would have been if they couldn't get them back
up and someone had to stuff them into a convenient pocket.*

In 1948 Dorothy found herself up before Feltham magistrates,
accused of 'Paying no attention whatsoever to a red light, thus forcing
three cyclists into the kerb. Taking bends in a straight line and clearing a
hump-backed bridge at 50 mph.' Her excuse? She had needed to get to
the racecourse to give instructions to her trainer.

Then there was the time in the early 1930s when Dorothy asked Anne
Rolinson's father, who owned a livery yard in Newmarket, to ride out
with her during the night across Newmarket Heath, not something
allowed without prior authorisation.

*They were riding across the Limekilns special gallops and were spotted
by one of the Heathmen, who reported them to the Jockey Club. My
father was duly rung up and told they had better come in and explain
themselves. Father went down – Dorothy, of course, didn't – and they
asked father what he had been doing.*

"Trying to cope with Dorothy Paget," he answered. "I couldn't stop her."
"No," they said, "neither can we."

But one almost throwaway comment by Dorothy herself may point
to a strength of character she rarely allowed to show itself, but which
underpinned the way she conducted her life. She had lost her mother
when she was just eleven; then had to deal with the death of the one

man we know she became close to who was not a family member; add to this her inability to transform her relationship with her long-time friend Olili into living together permanently. So upon hearing herself called, by her long-time jockey, trainer, betting partner and friend, Sir Gordon Richards – with whom she remained on very amicable terms for longer than most – 'the world's best loser', Dorothy is said to have replied, 'I ought to be. I've had plenty of practice.'

One

ANCESTRY AND BIRTH

Dorothy's all-action great grandfather, the ultimately one-legged Henry William Paget, First Marquess of Anglesey, K.G. (1768–1854) demonstrating the family's equine leanings.

Eccentricity is a not uncommon character trait in the history of the Paget family.

'By God, sir, I've lost my leg!' was the stiff-upper-lipped manner in which Field Marshal Henry William Paget reportedly greeted the consequence of being hit by cannon shot in the right leg, even as he was telling his commanding officer the Duke of Wellington of the success of the heavy cavalry charge he had just led against the Comte d'Erlon's column at the Battle of Waterloo in June 1815. Wellington, something of a master of understatement himself, responded, 'By God, sir, so you have.'

Paget's action had helped rout the French army, resulting in one of the nation's greatest victories, and he was subsequently made 1st Marquess of Anglesey and a Knight Grand Cross of the Order of the Bath. During the operation to amputate the leg above the knee, without antiseptic or anaesthetic, he was heard to remark, 'The knives appear somewhat blunt.' Many years later, his great-grand-daughter Dorothy was undergoing a minor operation at a clinic when she awoke during proceedings, sat up, and declared, 'Is this an operating theatre? It looks like a kitchen to me.'

Paget's right leg now began a new life of its own, subsequently becoming a tourist attraction in Waterloo, Belgium, buried under an inscribed tombstone, with the bones reportedly becoming exposed one day after a violent storm. Paget himself was fitted, according to one report, with the first hinged wooden leg, and was able to return home almost in one piece. Today the cork leg he wore is on display at the Household Cavalry Museum in London.

Other parts of Paget's anatomy remained in good working order, however, and just over a year after Waterloo, in June 1816, his second wife, Lady Charlotte Cadogan, gave birth to the boy (one of a total brood of eighteen children) who became Lord Alfred Paget. In due course Alfred, who went on to own a Classic-winning horse and enjoy a modest flutter, married Cecilia Cadogan, and amongst their own more modest team of fourteen children was Almeric Hugh Paget, Dorothy's father.

The 5th Marquess of Anglesey, Dorothy Paget's second cousin, was also a little unconventional. Henry Paget, nicknamed 'Toppy', was a British peer notable during his short life for squandering his inheritance on a lavish social life and accumulating massive debts. The 'black sheep' of the family, he was dubbed 'the Dancing Marquess' for his habit of performing 'sinuous, sexy, snake-like dances'. His marriage to his cousin Lilian Chetwynd was annulled due to non-consummation: 'The closest the marriage ever came to consummation,' notes the historian Christopher Simon Sykes, a distant relative, 'was that he would make her pose naked, covered top to bottom in jewels and she had to sleep wearing the jewels.'

Dorothy's passion for horse racing probably came down to her via a combination of her father Almeric's interest, and her maternal grandfather's significant love of the turf. Her American grandfather, William Collins Whitney, was corporation counsel for New York City from 1875 to 1882, 31st United States Secretary of the Navy from 1885 to 1889, a force in street railway affairs until his retirement in 1902, and one of those who created the New York Loan and Improvement Company, which developed the Washington Heights section of New York City.

But in 1898, when he was already 57 years old, he became interested in horse racing – in a big way, perhaps due to his son-in-law's influence, hiring the leading trainer Samuel Hildreth to acquire for him 'almost instantaneously' a full stable of top-quality horses. He would come to bask in his American nickname, 'The King of the Turf', bestowed because, as a US newspaper explained in late 1898, 'His horses are the finest on the turf, and the private racetrack on his Long Island country seat' – which would become the famous Belmont Park racecourse – 'is the most complete in existence.' Fittingly, his grand-daughter would come to have her own nickname, 'The Queen of the Turf'.

Whitney invested substantial sums into his racehorses, and in 1901 became the leading owner in the States. On 5 June that year he also made a big impression on the British turf, winning the Derby at Epsom with Volodyovski. Dorothy would eventually become desperate to emulate this achievement. The horse was led in to universal acclaim by Whitney's son Harry, a famous polo player of the day, and himself thoroughbred racing's leading owner of the year in the US on eight occasions, and the breeder of almost two hundred stakes race winners. He also had two Kentucky Derby victories.

William Collins Whitney married Flora Payne, a senator's daughter, and they had five children in all – Harry's younger brother by four years, William Payne Whitney, always known as Payne, married Helen Hay, and together they operated the Greentree Stables, whose horses won the American Grand National four times, the Kentucky Derby twice and the other US Classics the Preakness once and the Belmont Stakes four times. Their children, John Hay Whitney, known as Jock, and Joan Whitney, also became involved.

Jock Whitney, Dorothy's cousin, became US Ambassador to Britain from 1957 to 1961 and an honorary member of the Jockey Club.

As a racehorse owner himself he enjoyed many big wins in the UK, in 1976 landing the 'Autumn Double' when his Intermission won the Cambridgeshire and John Cherry the Cesarewitch. His Easter Hero was a dual Cheltenham Gold Cup winner. He tried, unsuccessfully, numerous times, to win the Grand National – Dorothy would go one better than him. Little surprise, therefore, with such ancestry, that Dorothy should grow up to exhibit eccentricity, a strong personality and a love of horse racing.

Her father, Almeric, went to Harrow and became a Fellow of Corpus Christi College, Cambridge, although he did not study there, then went to work in the fitting shop at the Midland Railway in Derby. But by 1880 he was in Iowa in the United States, where he had 'arrived penniless', according to one source, to become a cattle farmer. 'They wanted me to be a parson,' he subsequently explained of his departure from England: 'I didn't feel it was my job.'

Once settled in America, Almeric developed a talent for making contacts at the highest level. 'The most interesting of all Mr Paget's friendships,' writes Robert E. George in *Heirs of Tradition*,

> *had been formed on the prairie, as he was riding round the cattle with a stock-whip in the burning sun. He found that, engaged on the same task, was an American with a personality and strong ideas; a man who feared for the result of forests destroyed, land exploited and money made too quickly – a man, too, with a passionate admiration for England and the English. This man was no other than Theodore Roosevelt, who, in 1901, became the 26th and, at 42, the youngest, US President.*

Almeric also became, he later explained in a speech to celebrate his elevation to the peerage, 'the best runner in the ranches at Iowa', with local cowboys backing him 'against any who could be found to run against their kid from England'. When they arranged for him to run a hurdle race in Miles City, the great cattle centre of the West, they set up tables and chairs dragged out from houses as hurdles in the main street. Young Paget duly 'romped home; many a dollar changed hands that day', writes Robert E. George, who first met Paget in 1930 and remembered another indication of Almeric's love of a gamble which he definitely would pass on to his daughter Dorothy: 'When I drove down to Cannes with Lord Queenborough to put him into the "Blue Train" on his way home, he found he had half an hour to spend. "Don't tell anyone," he said as he took me with him to the Casino for a last flutter – it was not, I fear, successful.'

In 1893 Almeric joined the American industrialist Henry Melville Whitney in establishing the Dominion Coal Company – a move significant in more than business terms, because Henry's younger brother, William C. Whitney, was the father of the woman who was to be his future bride.

Almeric married Pauline Whitney in New York in November 1895; he was 34, she 13 years younger. So well connected was the Whitney family that amongst the 400 guests was another American president, the only man to serve two non-consecutive terms of office, Grover Cleveland, who had appointed Pauline's father as Navy Commissioner. Two detectives guarded the 'large, two-handled silver centrepiece' President Cleveland and his wife brought with them as a wedding present, along with an amazing array of other valuable gifts including the tiara set with diamonds, the chain of diamonds, the diamond-studded comb and the diamond necklaces, one with 250 pearls and 250 diamonds, diamond earrings and diamond brooch in the form of a cluster of roses, all gifted to Pauline by her father.

But with Pauline, wearing a full-trained dress of ivory-white satin, entering the church on the arm of her father, the ceremony got off to an inauspicious start when the rector, the Reverend Dr John Wesley Brown, announced, 'I am the Resurrection and the Life' – before remembering that he was not officiating at a funeral. Following the marriage, the *New York Times* would later report, Almeric would have 'an interest in the management of Mr Whitney's interests, first in the turf, and then in the Metropolitan Street Railway.'

By early 1896 Pauline was expecting a baby, but it proved a difficult pregnancy, and her delicate health was to dog her for the rest of her life – in 1904 the *New York Times* would describe her as 'more or less an invalid', and 'suffering from an affection [sic] of the heart' – and she was unable to be matron of honour at her brother Harry's wedding in August to her friend Gertrude Vanderbilt, who had been one of her bridesmaids. The baby, Flora Payne, was born in the November, only tragically to die the very next day.

Meanwhile, in the September of that year her father William married for a second time, his first wife Flora, Pauline's mother, having died two years earlier. The wedding provoked a family revolt, with Oliver Payne, who had doted on Flora, distraught that his brother-in-law should take a second wife, immediately breaking off cordial relations and urging William's children to do likewise. Pauline and Payne Whitney followed suit, whereupon Oliver, hugely wealthy himself, made them his heirs.

Almeric and Pauline tried again for a baby, and Olive (named in honour of her mother's sister and also her brother, Oliver) Cecilia (in honour of Almeric's mother, Lady Cecilia Paget) was born in New York on 24 September 1899. She would grow up to marry three times, and be mother to three children, Pauline, Susan and Gawaine, become Lady Baillie, and to buy the romantic Leeds Castle in Kent.

In 1902 the Pagets moved to England (some sources put it a year earlier). 'They came over and took a small shooting in Norfolk and later a house in South Audley Street before taking one in Berkeley Square', writes Robert E. George, suggesting that the reason for the move was because 'his wife was highly strung and her doctors advised her to try the milder air of England.' Presumably the move was also connected to a story in the *New York Times* of 27 October 1902, which reported that Almeric 'has been accidentally shot by a friend while shooting in the country. After the accident Mr Paget was hurriedly brought to London, where it was found necessary to take out one of his eyes. It is believed that the sight of the other eye will not be affected.' This did not prevent him becoming a highly successful, trophy-winning yachtsman.

William C. Whitney was taken unwell in January 1904 in his box at the Metropolitan Opera House, and died the following month. Pauline was in Rome, but set off for New York as soon as possible, only to find when she arrived that the funeral had already taken place. His estate was valued at a reported $23 million. He left half of it to his son Henry, aka Harry, who had never become estranged from him, but only 10% each of what was left to Pauline and his son Payne, who had joined their uncle Oliver in objecting to his remarriage. As a result they both received a large fortune from Colonel Payne.

Ironically, given her lifelong aversion to the colour, Dorothy Paget, the last of Almeric and Pauline's three daughters, came into this world on Tuesday, 12 February 1905 at 32 Green Street, Mayfair, a large neo-Georgian mansion that would later house the Brazilian Embassy, with nearly twenty rooms, including a 42-foot drawing room, and a white marble staircase. The first mystery of Dorothy's life is why she should have been born there at all – possibly the family had rented the property, or had been visiting when Dorothy decided to make an unexpected arrival. She was named in honour of her mother Pauline's youngest sister, with her middle name, Wyndham, a reference to her father Almeric's maternal grandfather's surname.

Two

GROWING UP AND COMING OUT

Dorothy (right) with older sister Olive. (Photograph courtesy of Amber Bailee's private collection)

By 1910 Almeric Paget was reputed to be the wealthiest man in Britain, at least by taking into account his wife's wealth from the various parts of her fabulously rich family. At the start of the year he and his wife moved into a 'beautiful London house' at 39 Berkeley Square in Mayfair. Visitors entering through the front door would immediately notice a tall gilt chair used by Queen Victoria at the opening of the Royal Exchange, while the drawing room featured displays of porcelain and items from her late father's collection. In the dining room valuable paintings hung on gold brocade. The entire upper storey, a suite of seven rooms, was given over to their daughters' exclusive use, and here their mother would give much time to developing their education. Pauline's health was again fragile, but the *Onlooker* was in no doubt that 'as soon as her health is restored she will again dispense the hospitality with the same tact and distinctiveness which gave her dinner parties a cachet of their own during several London seasons'.

One indication of how large this issue loomed in the family's life might be the record of the young Dorothy's first appearance as a bridesmaid, when she was just six, at her aunt Dorothy Whitney's wedding in Switzerland, whose air was regarded as beneficial to Pauline's delicate constitution. Another is the racing writer Clive Graham's claim that Dorothy's father 'sternly forbade Dorothy, then eight years old, and presumably worried about her mother's health, to cry – under the threat of severe penalties – in case her tears might make his wife worse'.

Dorothy had been just a year old when Almeric had launched his political career by contesting the Cambridge constituency for the Conservatives, losing to the Liberal candidate. But in 1910 he managed to win the seat, holding on to it until his resignation in 1917, and now he purchased a substantial residence in nearby Newmarket as well. Soham House was an outstanding Arts and Crafts property with seven bedrooms and four bathrooms, originally built for the racehorse owner Sir Wallace Johnstone, who retained a trainer at Newmarket for his 25 horses and had won the 1898 2,000 Guineas with Disraeli. Dorothy would occasionally take up residence at the property up until 1952, some years after Almeric had died, and at least one nearby road, Paget's Place, was subsequently named in her memory.

On top of this, the Pagets were in the habit of renting grand houses for the summer season. The Deepdene in Dorking was one of them, and Almeric had also acquired a lease on Claremont, a country house at Esher in Surrey that belonged to the Duchess of Albany, the widow of Victoria and Albert's fourth son Leopold. But their most frequent choice was the Desboroughs' magnificent Panshanger in Hertfordshire, situated between Hertford and Welwyn Garden City. In the summer of 1914 they held a garden party there for over a thousand guests, including former Conservative Prime Ministers Balfour and Bonar Law. Pauline was photographed in the *Tatler* happily pushing Olive and Dorothy around the grounds in a bath chair. The very next month, however, the girls were shipped off to New York on the American Line's liner *St. Louis*. Possibly this was just to visit their American relatives – but also there was now a war on.

Dorothy would have been just nine when the First World War broke out. Almeric and Pauline became deeply involved in the war effort and Almeric sponsored the formation of a 1,350-strong volunteer Cambridgeshire Battalion, which would quickly become known as the Cambs Suffolks. He and Pauline also set up a corps of trained masseuses, originally out of the Pagets' Berkeley Square home, to work with the wounded. The women in the Almeric Paget Massage Corps (APMC) – during 1918 their numbers reached 2,000 – wore a simple uniform with its badge on their left arm, and treated wounded soldiers with a combination of massage and electrical stimulation. Soon the Corps had opened a Massage and Electrical Outpatient Clinic in London, which treated over 200 patients daily and subsequently became the model for hospital massage and electrical departments throughout the UK.

Pauline also established a well-equipped convalescent hospital with twenty beds at Panshanger, based in a nearby army hospital hut. 'Mrs Paget looks after [the patients] with a maternal care,' local media reported, 'and treats them as gentlemen. Frequently she takes the boys to the cinematography theatre in Hertford.'

The Pagets opened Summerdown Camp as well, a convalescent home for wounded soldiers in Eastbourne, and early in 1916 they took a lease on Compton Place, the Eastbourne residence of the Duke of Devonshire nearby, so that Pauline could be closely involved with the running of the Camp, where she was spoken about as the 'Angel of Summerdown'. At its height 3,500 wounded men stayed there, known locally as 'Blueboys' because of the uniforms they had to wear.

But by the summer of 1916 it was Pauline herself who was in need of care. She had suffered from mitral disease, afflicting the mitral valve which keeps blood flowing properly in the heart, for fifteen years; now her condition worsened, necessitating periods confined to a wheelchair. Following three weeks of illness at Panshanger, Pauline died at Claremont on 22 November 1916, at the age of just 42.

Queen Mary sent a letter of condolence. In New York the Whitney family cancelled all of their social engagements, and mourning continued until the following April. The funeral took place at midday, on Monday, 27 November. Only immediate family attended. The coffin, covered with a white pall bearing the Almeric Paget Massage Corps crest, was carried on the shoulders of wounded soldiers from Eastbourne, watched by convalescents from Panshanger and Esher. She was buried at nearby St Mary's Church in Hertingfordbury. Her estate was valued at some $5 million, though she had already previously made a $4m shared gift to her daughters.

Almeric wrote to his sister-in-law Gertrude Vanderbilt, a gifted sculptress who had married Harry Payne Whitney, asking her to 'prepare a fitting monument in stone for her last resting place. You could make me a "sketch of a design" to commemorate her massage work and devotion to wounded soldiers to which she gave over two years of her life and which undoubtedly hastened the end'.

Dorothy was still only 11 when her mother died, and the tragedy of her mother's passing did not improve the already wayward behaviour of the sub-teenage girl struggling to cope with the discipline of school, and to form a harmonious relationhip with her older sister and father. She had been almost unmanageable, other than by her mother, and was reportedly expelled from as many as six schools, including Ascot's Heathfield, effectively for refusing to be taught. Her first biographer, Quintin Gilbey, believed Dorothy to have been her mother's favourite, as the youngest of a family so often seems to be: indulged and doted on. According to him she 'grew into a spoiled, unlovable child, close to her mother, distant from her father'. 'Unhappy, moody, rebellious', is how Clive Graham describes her at this time. The death of her mother at such a young age, combined with her father's instruction not to cry in her mother's presence, may well have resulted in feelings of guilt that in some way she might have been responsible for her mother's passing.

Already in her teens, however, records George Quest of the *Express*, Dorothy 'was good with the ponies', and also 'played a sturdy game of tennis'. She also seems to have been interested in ornithology, having enrolled in the Avicultural Society – later she would become a Fellow of the Zoological Society.

In July 1919, the year after the war ended, Dorothy's sister Olive got married, with her 14-year-old younger sister as one of the bridesmaids. Their father Almeric, meanwhile, had resigned his parliamentary seat after his wife's death and in 1918 became Baron Queenborough, of Queenborough in Kent, a small town on the Isle of Sheppey. The various suggestions as to why Queenborough was chosen include his donation of a new Freemason's Temple to the Lodge there.

Five years after Pauline's death, in 1921, the Baron suddenly married again. At 33 his new wife, Edith Starr Miller, the daughter of a retired Fifth Avenue lawyer, was virtually half his age, and their marriage in New York shocked and scandalised American society. There had been no rumour even of their engagement. According to Clive Graham the Baron 'desperately wanted a son to carry on his new title'.

Dorothy must have felt thoroughly isolated and unloved. By now she was aware that her father would have preferred her to have been born a boy, capable of extending the family line. The only other person likely to have appreciated her plight, her sister Olive, had married and left home. Now her father was taking up with a woman young enough to be his daughter. Dorothy would have seen this as partly a quest for that elusive male heir. Almeric had shown little enough interest in Dorothy as she grew up, packing her off to a series of schools she hated. Soon he would send her out of the country altogether – inadvertently providing her with a number of long-lasting friends and companions, along with a passionate cause to believe in. She could have had few real friends and confidantes, and would have had to rely on her own resources for enter-tainment. Having been unable to create lasting relationships inside or outside her immediate family she would become unwilling – unable, perhaps – to allow herself to get close to anyone, for fear that she would soon be deprived of them again.

Nevertheless, at the age of 16, Dorothy began to appear on the social scene. She went to Ladies' Day at Doncaster racecourse, and the following year a dance was laid on for her benefit at the family town house in Berkeley Square in London. 'Miss Paget is really making her debut next season as she has not quite finished her education', explained the *Star*.

That formal entry into London society as a debutante seems to have happened in 1923 when her stepmother Edith organised a dance for her, preceded by a dinner party attended by, among many others, Mr and Mrs Winston Churchill and a variety of earls, countesses, duchesses and other members of the aristocracy. She was also dancing in public, participating in a pavane at Sunninghill Park in Ascot, and even singing, with her first performance in front of a literally captive audience – hundreds of prisoners in Wormwood Scrubs. Dorothy's singing career had begun when Princess Mestchersky, the Russian owner of the Paris finishing school where she had ended up, had arranged for her to have lessons with a well-known singing teacher of the day, Madame Ciampi. Back in England she continued her studies under Madame Fernandez-Bentham and Olga Lynn, and made an appearance with Mme Bentham at 'a soirée musicale' at London's American Women's Club. The London *Evening Standard*'s music correspondent judged Dorothy 'a dramatic soprano of more than usual merit'.

Despite introductions to the most eligible bachelors in British society and beyond, however, Dorothy seems to have formed no lasting relationship with any of them. Biographer Quintin Gilbey ascribes this bluntly to 'her aversion to the close proximity of men and her suspicion that she was not like other girls. It was a suspicion that became a certainty before the end of her season as a debutante, though there is no evidence that it depressed her unduly'.

Neither is there any evidence, however, that it did *not* depress her. Still a teenager, with little in the way of male influence in her home, school or wider life, she was probably extremely shy and unconfident of her social skills – unless she was on horseback, on stage or at the tennis court, where she could project her own identity. Also, aware that she would inherit great riches when she came of age, she may have been concerned that potential male suitors were more interested in her wealth than her womanly attractions. She may already have decided to confine her social relationships to female company. She did, though, form a long-term friendship with one man, Francis Cassel, a somewhat eccentric, apparently gay concert pianist with independent wealth, who would become an integral, unpaid, part of the team supporting her horse racing and gambling interests.

Three

HUNTING FOR
A GOOD TIME

Appropriately and immaculately turned out, Dorothy with one of her hunters, the prize-winning Bloodstone.

On 21 February 1926, Dorothy came of age, and into a decent, some would say indecent, amount of money. 'She was never the same woman after the morning of her 21st birthday,' reflected one of her trainers, Owen Anthony, a shrewd Welshman. 'On coming down to breakfast that day she opened a letter containing a cheque for £1 million, token payment of the legacy she had inherited from her American grandfather. You might say,' added Anthony, 'in a manner of speaking, that that cheque ruined her.' A year later her accounts show that the annual interest on her investments alone was over £53,000 (£2.9m at today's prices).

Dorothy's father, meanwhile, gave her a Rolls-Royce. Maybe this was an attempt to heal the breach between them caused by their disagreement over a hunting lodge Dorothy had wanted to take in Leicestershire, for which, not yet having come into her fortune, she had needed his financial support. Lord Queenborough had declined uncompromisingly, feeling it would not be 'ladylike for a girl of her tender years'. The new Roller doesn't seem to have worked; father and daughter would rarely, if ever, be seen together in public again until Golden Miller's Grand National triumph in 1934.

Dorothy's American grandfather, William Collins Whitney, who had died before she was even conceived, hadn't, of course, expressly left his unborn grand-daughter a million pounds, or even dollars. However, his wealth had enabled Dorothy's mother to divide $4 million between her and her sister Olive, when all three of them were alive.

One of the first things Dorothy did with her money was to send Princess Mestchersky a cheque. It had been shortly before Dorothy's debutante season, according to Clive Graham, that, 'slim and fair-haired', as one newspaper recorded, she had been sent to a finishing school in Paris. The school was owned and run by the Russian-born Princess Vera Kirillovna Mestcherskaïa (frequently Anglicised as Mestchersky) and taught, among other things, foreign languages, and in particular Russian. Dorothy's initial wilful refusals to submit to the in-house discipline were quashed when the Princess made it clear that there was only one principal in this establishment. Once Dorothy had come to terms with her unfamiliar situation abroad she began to flourish, perhaps seeing in the Princess an acceptable mother substitute. Her father was said to have been scarcely able to believe his eyes when he received a report that his daughter was 'proving herself an exemplary student'.

Now Dorothy was sending the Princess the money to buy a building in Sainte-Geneviève-des-Bois on the outskirts of Paris, to enable her to open a home for elderly refugees from the Russian Revolution, after which more than a million Russians had fled the country. '*Je viens d'avoir 21 ans,*' wrote Dorothy: '*Je voudrais que le premier chèque que je signe soit destiné à aider vos compatriotes.*' Residents of 'La Maison Russe', the Russian Home, had to have been officers in the Imperial Russian services, and the first was buried in a nearby local cemetery in 1927. From then on a large part of the cemetery became the Russian cemetery, and a beautiful Russian church was built there. Part of the building is still run as a retirement home under the control of the state health authorities, while the main part now houses a Centre for Russian Studies. One summary of Dorothy's contribution to the home suggests, in a quaint English translation, that:

One day she came across the ocean and on Bastille Day decided to
please Russian oldies. On trucks, with great risk to their fragile health,
she drove all – 250 people – to watch the fireworks in Paris on the
Seine. In the capital Miss Paget bought champagne and treated all.
She wanted to give to the impoverished Russian aristocrats at least for
one day, the illusion of their former rich life.

Dorothy's determination to remain a key contributor to the costs of running the Home is reflected in the home's accounts, which show that in its first six months, of its 890,810 francs income, 834,135 francs, or nearly £7,000, came from her. In the next three months she handed over a further 435,700 francs. She continued to support the Home until the Germans occupied Paris during the Second World War. To this day, touchingly, Dorothy is commemorated nearby by a street named Rue Miss Paget.

The Princess's sister, Madame Orloff, also became a confidante, companion and friend, and when Dorothy decided on a visit to America to inform the trustees of her forthcoming fortune that she needed monies with which to sustain the Russian Home, it was she who went with her.

Dorothy's involvement with the Russian Home may have been prompted by the need for a building project of some kind to compete with her sister, who had recently decided that a castle was just what *she* needed. Olive was also a seriously wealthy woman now: their mother had left a total estate of about $5 million in property.

Leeds Castle, set on an island in Kent, and described by the historian Lord Conway as 'the loveliest castle in the whole world', had been a Norman stronghold, the private property of six of England's medieval queens, a palace used by Henry VIII and his first wife, Catherine of

Aragon, a Jacobean country house, a Georgian mansion, and an elegant early 20th-century country retreat for the influential and famous. Olive had recently remarried, to Arthur Wilson-Filmer, an independently wealthy film buff, big-game hunter and collector of tapestries (while the newly-weds had been renting Bawdsey Manor in Suffolk, Olive's pet monkey had allegedly caused £2,000 worth of damage to carpets); now, in 1926 still only 26 herself, and seeking a country retreat in Kent, she purchased Leeds for a reported £180,000.

As work instigated by the Wilson-Filmers progressed, Olive, her two daughters by her first marriage and their aunt, Dorothy, would pay weekend visits to the castle to inspect progress. Olive installed unheard-of luxuries like underfloor heating, onyx en suite bathrooms, a swimming pool complete with wave machine, and an ebony dance floor. There were tennis and squash courts, croquet, riding and boating facilities, and zebras in the grounds. Dorothy was allocated Leeds Castle's Turret Room by her sister, where she would stay whenever she was in residence, which was frequently.

Having now embarked on her own second marriage, Olive also, according to Quintin Gilbey, 'turned her attentions to solving Dorothy's problems', and 'did all in her power to arrange a marriage'. It would prove a fruitless undertaking. Dorothy had shown little interest in the young bucks being pointed in her direction by parents well aware of the financial attractions of a liaison with Paget junior. She had attended parties, dances and balls, but been known to simply disengage herself from her partner without comment and walk off the floor.

In 1931 Olive divorced Arthur, and within months was married again to Maxwell Baillie, becoming Lady Baillie, in 1934 giving birth to her third child, Gawaine George Hope Baillie. Although he was Dorothy's nephew (and subsequently creator of one of the world's finest, most valuable stamp collections), he later confessed to the *Racing Post*'s David Ashforth 'that he had met his aunt only twice, and gave the impression that twice was sufficient'.

By now Leeds Castle was 'the most stimulating salon in Britain', as Olive attracted the great and the good of the day, with film stars, politicians and royalty mingling shoulder-to-shoulder, cheek-to-cheek, and who knows what other body parts may have made close contact during the party season. Those who came included the Prince of Wales with Mrs Simpson; Prince George, later Duke of Kent, who married Princess Marina of Greece and other members of international royal families; politicians like Winston Churchill and the Foreign Secretary Anthony Eden; even Nazi Germany's Ambassador to Britain, Joachim von Ribbentrop, put in an appearance. Stars of the stage and silver screen included Charlie Chaplin, Noel Coward, Douglas Fairbanks (senior and junior), Errol Flynn, Gertrude Lawrence, David Niven, James Stewart and Robert Taylor. 'Above all,' said the socialite Pamela Harriman, whose three husbands included Winston Churchill's son Randolph, of Olive as a hostess, 'she was discreet, which many were not. She did not need to seduce rich men; her special aphrodisiac was power.' Pamela Harriman's own biographer writes, nevertheless, that a 'good deal of bed-hopping' went on after dark at Olive's weekend parties.

The papers were also, however, preoccupied, like her sister, by Dorothy's marital status. What would she have made of the description of her by one of the popular newspaper gossip columns in 1927 as a 'bachelor'? In 1930 the *Daily Mail* called her 'the richest unmarried girl in England', while four years later the *Eastern Daily Press* pondered, after describing Dorothy's 'really attractive singing voice': 'We accept incurable bachelors of the male sex, why should we not accept incurable bachelors of the female sex?' It was around this time, though, that Dorothy did, in her way, answer the media's questions by forming what would become one of the most important relationships of her life.

Olili de Mumm was born Olga Nadine Mumm on 14 June 1910 in Paris, to Olga de Struve, subsequently Madame de Mumm, the sister of

Princess Mestchersky, Dorothy's finishing school principal and founder of the Russian Home, and the Prussian national Peter Mumm von Schwarzenstein. Olili's brother was the manager of the Mumm family vineyards. Dorothy would sometimes join Olili in Germany, while Olili would also come to England and take up residence with her for long periods. We know very little about Olili as a person, to the extent that no photographs of her appear to have survived, but this would be a relationship that would endure for the rest of Dorothy's life, with some observers implying a closer, possibly sexual, dimension.

Dorothy herself, meanwhile, also kept a place in Bryanston Square in Mayfair, close to Berkeley Square, and was now renting a house close to Leeds Castle in Maidstone called The Mote, which looked out over the town's Mote Park. Here she installed a tennis coach to improve her already decent game, and bought herself four hunters that, rumour had it, cost her the princely sum of £500 apiece.

Dorothy had been taught to ride by the famed royal riding master, Horace Smith, who instructed many society figures of the day at his school in London's Cadogan Place. Later he taught the young princesses Elizabeth and Margaret. She made up into a perfectly respectable rider, and now became interested, intrigued, and eventually deeply involved in the equestrian pursuits of showjumping, eventing, hunting and point-to-pointing. In 1929 her cousin, Jock Whitney, meanwhile, won the Cheltenham Gold Cup with his Easter Hero, following up with another victory the following year, and it seems reasonable to speculate that this might have stimulated Dorothy's competitive instincts and hastened her move into racing.

She began hunting with the Mid-Kent Staghounds, riding side-saddle with, according to Gregory Blaxland, 'bowler hat crammed down on her bobbed head'. According to Veronica Beeny, it was the Master of the Mid-Kent Hunt, Edwyn Sandys Dawes, her grandfather, who found Golden Miller. Jean Rountree, whose family was involved with the Hunt in those days, remembers Dorothy arranging a hunt one day, for which everyone duly arrived on time: 'The horses and riders were there. The stags were there. They were waiting for "Madam", but she wasn't up and about yet. She kept them waiting and waiting until they were livid. But that was the way she was. She was spoilt.' Jean's father, William Lancelot Dawes, was an Olympic yachtsman and a talented rider who rode Dorothy's horses on occasion: 'My father, known by everyone as "Slotty", rode point-to-pointers and chasers for Dorothy. He was on one of hers which broke down in a race, so he pulled the horse up and led it off the course – she went ballistic at him, insisting he should have finished the race. Father lost his temper, flung the reins towards her and told her, "At least you've still got a horse because of my actions," and walked off.'

Dorothy began riding in point-to-points herself, taking third place in the ladies' race at the Mid-Kent's Sutton Valence meeting a few miles from Maidstone, and by 1934 was going out regularly with other hunts too, like the Pytchley Hunt in Leicestershire, one of whose events she had first attended years previously. 'Her inclination was to go to the top of every good hunt,' says Clive Graham, but the social set in Leicestershire had rather less appeal to her: 'She was unpopular with the local gentry and their wives who came to call and deposit the engraved visiting cards, formal etiquette for such occasions,' regarding all this as 'stuff and nonsense' and instructing her then butler, Carter, to return the cards with the message, 'Miss Paget regrets to inform you that she has plenty of friends of her own choosing and does not want for any new ones.'

The former trainer Michael Pope told a story of Dorothy's 'quandary' when, on the day of a Cheltenham meeting where she had fancied runners, 'hounds were due to hunt her favourite stretch of the Pytchley country.' Dorothy decided to do both. A private plane would be chartered 'for herself and her companion' (possibly Olili or her riding friend Mrs Walker), 'both already dressed in their hunting gear, to land them

in the park at Greatham Hall where the hounds were due to meet at
11 a.m.' Her two best hunters were lined up ready to be mounted.

Off they went, Dorothy riding side-saddle 'kicking on like a woman
possessed, and when a formidable-looking double oxer loomed up she
rode at the fence, shouting "Tally ho!" as if it wasn't there.' Eventually
the 'exhausted old Reynard' took refuge in an oak tree and was allowed
to live to flee another day, and Dorothy and friend rushed to the plane.

The pair changed clothes during the flight, Dorothy into her soon-
to-become famous 'Speckled Hen' overcoat and beret, her companion
into a new two-piece tweed suit with matching hat – at which Dorothy
'took one horrified look and snorted, "You stupid woman. There's
green on that collar and on the hat. Green is unlucky. The minute
we touch down you get Fred [her chauffeur who was at the course to
drive them home] to take you into town. Buy a new outfit and burn
that one."'

Companion duly did, all three of Dorothy's runners won, after which,
recalled Pope, she turned to her companion and said, 'There you are, my
dear, what did I tell you? Don't let me see you wearing anything green
again – even your bloomers!'

Dorothy also enjoyed riding in London, notably in Hyde Park's Rotten
Row, where on one occasion at least she ordered her horse to be saddled
and waiting at her door at three o'clock, only for the groom to be kept
waiting there until she finally consented to appear at eight.

Maidstone Council had vetoed Dorothy's hopes of buying land on
which to build stables for breeding horses near her home at the Mote,
having earmarked it for what became the Shepway housing estate, so
for a time her horses were stabled at Leeds Castle, with Golden Miller
reportedly amongst them. During the war, when the castle was taken
over by the Royal Army Medical Corps and busy with patients from both
sides in the Battle of Britain, a medical staff office was set up in one of the
looseboxes previously occupied by Dorothy's racehorses.

Through a friend of her brother-in-law Arthur, Dick Briscoe, Dorothy was invited to dinner at the Savoy Hotel, where she and Dick were joined by his younger brother, Basil, an up-and-coming trainer, as well as Dick's sister, Mollie, who later recalled Dorothy as a 'slight, plainly clad girl' with 'straight, bobbed hair…and a pale face unadorned by any make-up, which was a rarity. It was not a very pretty face but there was a certain delicate charm about her, made the more appealing by contrast with her intensity.' Dorothy and Briscoe discussed racing, but when she did make a move into the sport she would initially look elsewhere for a trainer, opting for Alec Law, whose stables were near Findon in Sussex. However, Dorothy Paget and Basil Briscoe would team up soon enough, and go on to make racing history together.

She sent Law her hunter Bridget to train, after the horse had run away with her in the Ladies' Race at the Ashford Valley point-to-point in Kent, when Dorothy had been riding her side-saddle. Clive Graham takes up the story.

The going was slightly wet, but probably not as damp as Dorothy's forehead under her bowler hat, which was held in place by an elastic chin-strap. The fourth obstacle was a 'drop-fence' where the take-off was considerably higher than the marshy landing point.

Bridget approached with her ears cocked, saw the reeds on the far side below her, weighed up the difficulties involved – and slithered abruptly to a halt. Miss Paget went straight ahead, described a curve in the air, and landed on her back on the far side of the obstacle.

In April 1930, Dorothy purchased a horse from Alec Law, a five-year-old called Dunshaughlin, and that June it became her first winner on the turf, taking the Kelham Hurdle, worth £58, at Southwell. Dorothy must have looked back fondly at this landmark when some years later she named another of her horses Dunshaughlin. In October Dorothy had her first Flat winner, Eileandonan, at Catterick, over one and a half miles, at odds of 5/2, in a race worth £167.

A letter dated the same month from Dorothy's father to his daughter suggests their relationship was by this time returning to more of an even keel. Mind you, he seemed to have a good reason to hope so: 'Darling,' he wrote by hand, before adding in type, 'I will call you up in the morning to see if you would care to discuss the acquisition of some of these horses.' There were eleven named on the attached list. Clearly, father was keen to help daughter acquire some horseflesh – or to get rid of some dead-beat plodders of his own! He signed off, 'Devotedly, father.'

At this stage in her life she was certainly not a reclusive young lady moping around at home and shutting out the world. She was going to lavish fancy dress balls in London – sadly, we do not know as who – and mixing with genuine princes, dukes, duchesses, ambassadors and count-esses galore, and attending other functions at prestigious high-society venues like Grosvenor House in Park Lane, Café Anglais and the Savoy. That she was not averse to showing off in gladrags and expensive jewel-lery is evident from the insurance valuation of her jewellery and furs she had not long after the Café Anglais outing: a cool £60,000.

Some time in 1930 – the precise date is not recorded – Dorothy hosted a party of friends and an artist/caricaturist was on hand to record the gathering, which consisted of herself, a female friend and three gen-tlemen guests. (see plate page 2); the dark-haired Dorothy is wearing a black dress with a plunging neckline, while her blonde female friend, whose name signed on the picture appears to be Gwendoline Foster, the married name of Dorothy's good friend Gwennie Brogden, is wearing a light-blue dress.

Even allowing for the artist wanting his work to be purchased, and thus possibly emphasising his subjects' more appealing features, Dorothy looks not unattractive, a smile on her face and completely at ease. And why shouldn't she? At this point she is enjoying an interesting, varied social life – for at the same time as she was saddling up to gallop into the heady, charismatic Sport of Kings, she had also recently accelerated into the glamorous, high-speed world of motor racing, and would become as close as she would ever get to a man who was neither a relative nor an employee.

Four

REVVING UP

Dorothy gets up close and personal with ace racing driver Tim Birkin, prior to a race at Brooklands.

Dorothy Paget loved speed, whether on a horse, or via motorised horse-power, and during her lifetime she came to own many expensive, very fast cars, and received many inexpensive – to her – fines thanks to her love of driving faster than the speed limit.

The 21st birthday gift of a Rolls-Royce from her father sparked a lifelong interest in the marque. The Rolls-Royce expert Graeme Calvert-Thomson has identified this first model as a New Phantom (later known as Phantom 1), fitted with a Barker open touring body. Dorothy later christened it 'Hilda', and kept it for many years, latterly unused, presumably for sentimental reasons. Around 1929 she bought her second 'Roller', registration 31HC, the 'first and last supercharged' Rolls-Royce, according to its first owner, Jack Kruse, who had had it souped up by the technical wizard Charles Amherst Villiers to become the ultimate grand touring vehicle. It was apparently always a handful to drive. In the Rolls-Royce Enthusiasts' Club magazine Isobel Haes records that Dorothy appears to have acquired a third Rolls in 1930, and a fourth in 1931, a Phantom II Continental Sports Saloon, and that the varied collection of motor cars she went on to own included a V12 Lagonda,

a Mercedes-Benz, several Rovers and a Bugatti, while she also had a fond-
ness for Jaguar cars – her XK120 was affectionately named 'the Tiddler'
and her Mark VII 'Balloon'. Her love of motors, competition and betting
just may have combined to result in the actual love of her life.

Sir Henry 'Tim' Birkin (he acquired the title on his father's death in
1931) was a dashing, high-profile racing driver in his early thirties with a
touch of James Hunt or Graham Hill about him, and the most famous of
his day in England. A slight, dapper man, he was one of a renowned, patriotic group of racers known as the 'Bentley Boys', who all raced that famous
make of vehicle and competed ferociously at the banked racing circuit at
Brooklands down at Weybridge in Surrey. 'These guys lived life in the fast
lane,' says Richard Charlesworth, the head of the Bentley Heritage Collection. 'They raced hard and partied hard. There was a corner in Grosvenor
Square known as "Bentley Corner" where they all had their London apart-
ments. It was said the police used to turn a blind eye to the parties there.
They used to drive their cars to Le Mans…stop off at Leeds Castle for
a black tie dinner, then drive on to the race, and drive back again.'

Birkin became aware that Dorothy Paget owned this fabulous supercharged 'Roller': '31HC was the car that brought most of the leading
players in the Blower Bentley story together,' writes Paul Kenny, the
biographer of Charles Amherst Villiers. Soon Birkin was manhandling
31HC around Brooklands' banking at speeds in excess of 100 mph.

In no time Dorothy became part of the racetrack scene. 'Racing
drivers – then and now – have a huge appeal to women,' says the motor
racing historian Doug Nye,

> and, as a very dashing English hero, Birkin would have had his
> pick of the many women drawn to the sport. Dorothy may not have
> been the most attractive-looking of those who hung around the paddock
> at the various European circuits where he raced, but her wealth, and
> her ability to spend it, made her a completely different proposition.

While Birkin was well able to turn on the charm, adds Nye, he may well have been pushing an open door, because Dorothy was very receptive to his persuasive skills. 'It would appear that she was quite captivated by sport in general and motor racing and horse racing in particular. It would also appear she was captivated by Tim Birkin.'

Birkin had already clashed with W. O. Bentley, the leader of the Bentley Boys and proprietor of the marque, over wanting to 'supercharge' his own 4½-litre model, which W. O. felt 'corrupted the original design'. Birkin was adamant that such innovation would add the best part of 20 mph to their top speed, and was the only way to compete with Mercedes at Le Mans, even though he personally could not afford the necessary investment.

What happened next Birkin himself explained, a little floridly, in his 1932 autobiography *Full Throttle*:

> At the beginning of the new year [1930] it was announced that
> a fairy godmother in the earthly guise of the Hon. Dorothy Paget,
> had come to the Cinderella of the British motor industry. She bought,
> in March, my three Bentleys, among them the track single-seater which
> was begun at the end of 1929, and increased them to four. Hers was
> a most sporting action, prompted by a genuine sympathy with a cause
> in which she herself was well-versed; it gave a new lease of life to
> the motor racing world in England.

Birkin, in other words, suggested to Dorothy that she bankroll his team of Blower Bentleys. He had already been 'giving high-performance driving lessons' to her and, writes Paul Kenny, as she 'respected Birkin as a racing driver of the highest quality and had experienced Amherst's supercharging wizardry in person after buying Jack Kruse's Phantom', she therefore 'decided to broaden her sporting ambitions beyond horse racing, and to sponsor Birkin's team.' Richard Charlesworth of Bentley Motors believes rather that Birkin 'was very focused on getting sponsor-

ship for the team, and preyed upon Dorothy's patriotic streak' to persuade her to stump up. 'She knew her own mind, and took her time
before deciding what to do.' 'On the face of it she had little in common
with Birkin,' writes Nicholas Foulkes in *The Bentley Era*, 'and yet these
two great characters of the Jazz Age formed one of the most unlikely
alliances of the day.'

The figure of £40,000 is often quoted as the amount she invested in
1930 in Birkin's team, the equivalent of nearly £2.2 million today. It's also
possible Dorothy's younger relative Whitney Straight, who would himself
start racing at venues like Shelsley Walsh and Brooklands in the early thirties, encouraged his cousin to get involved with Birkin, from whom he
would soon purchase a Maserati that had been raced by him at Brooklands.
'The cars were, of course, her property,' continues Birkin in *Full Throttle*,
'but I was to run them for her under the famous green colours.'

This is puzzling, given Dorothy's well-known aversion to green. Is it
remotely possible that, when they met, the recently-divorced Birkin immediately went into full dashing, good-looking, playboy heart-throb mode –
despite being nine years older – and Dorothy simply fell for him? 'Miss P.,
it is said, rather took to the "young blade"', wrote Timothy Houlding in
a 1983 article, suggesting they may have met at Birkin's favourite dining
place, 'Louis Corber' at the Berkeley Hotel in Mayfair, very much Dorothy's
stamping ground in those days. The feature film of *Full Throttle* portrays
Birkin (Rowan Atkinson) at their first meeting as mistaking Dorothy's more
conventionally attractive companion for her, and expressing a desire to get
to know her better, only to have to be corrected by his chum that it is the
plainer of the two who is the wealthy heiress.

The new Birkin-Paget operation initially purchased three 4½-litre production cars from W. O. Bentley and rented adjacent factories at 19 and
21 Broadwater Road in Welwyn Garden City, where they set about the
supercharging modifications to turn them into 'blown' Bentleys. Birkin
hoped to have them ready for the 1929 Le Mans race but, although

entered by Dorothy, they were not deemed ready in time. Nonetheless, Birkin and his co-driver Woolf Barnato still won the race in car number 1, the 'Speed Six' Bentley 6.6 Litre 16, leading home three other Bentleys as they dominated with the first four cars to finish.

The first Brooklands Meeting of 1930 saw Birkin drive Dorothy's Bentley to a one-second victory in the four-lap Kent Long Handicap at an average speed of 119.13 mph, setting a fastest lap at 126.73 mph – the first race victory ever achieved by a 'Blower' Bentley. On 21 April he beat Kaye Don's Brooklands lap record, clocking an average 135.33 mph over the distance in 1 minute 13.3 seconds. He also won the Bedford Handicap (6.5 miles) from scratch, at 117.81 mph. The caption to a photograph of Dorothy alongside Birkin in the car reads: 'The Hon. Dorothy Paget, who owns the car with which the record was broken, and who made the trip as mechanic.'

In the 1930 Le Mans in June, Birkin was taking on the hot favourite Rudolf Caracciola, who was driving his supercharged Mercedes-Benz SSK. According to Richard Charlesworth of Bentley Motors, who still drives one of the Birkin Bentleys and in 2016 took it to Leeds Castle, 'You can still see the oil stains from when the Birkin Bentleys stayed there en route to Le Mans.'

But it was the Bentley company chairman, Woolf Barnato, driving a Speed Six, who stormed to victory. W. O.'s contention that supercharging would make the Bentley engine too 'fragile' for 24 hours of racing seemed to be borne out as Birkin, driving with Jean Chassagne in a Dorothy-entered Blower Bentley, clocked the fastest lap, but eventually failed to finish, the other Dorothy-entered Blower, with Dr Dudley Benjafield and Giulio Ramponi on board, not going the distance either.

In July, Dorothy attended the Irish Grand Prix, 'driven in a fast car from the mail boat at Kingstown to the Phoenix Park. She arrived there about 6.30 a.m.,' reported the *Irish Times*. This was not a time of day when Dorothy was normally likely to be out and about. Birkin took

Dorothy out on 'some fast laps' around the circuit before, wrapped in a heavy fur coat, she joined Captain Malcolm Campbell, who'd set the World Land Speed Record in *Blue Bird* in 1927, for more circuits of the track in his Mercedes, appearing to 'like the speed and the course'. A breathless Harold Pemberton, the *Express*'s motoring correspondent, made Dorothy's spin with Birkin sound a ravishing experience:

> *Young 'Tim' Birkin, who has been 'lying low' in practice, showed a bit of his hand this morning. He created uneasiness in the Mercedes camp by putting in a lap at 88.7 miles per hour. Perhaps it was because he had with him, as a passenger, the Hon. Dorothy Paget, who owns the British team of Bentley cars. Few women would care to be driven at the speed at which Birkin travelled this morning. His cornering was dazzling, but Miss Paget thoroughly enjoyed herself. 'It was just exhilarating,' she said as she jumped out of the mechanic's seat and lit a cigarette. 'I must do more of it.'*

Maynard Greville, the *Mail*'s motoring correspondent, added that Dorothy 'has issued a "Win at all costs" message' to her team. Birkin took fourth place, just ahead of Campbell in fifth.

Meanwhile, Dorothy was becoming a racing driver in her own right. In July 1930 she entered four hill-climb races at Shelsley Walsh under the pseudonym 'Miss Wyndham'. There were four runners in her class, all in supercharged Mercedes-Benz SS variants, and each car had a team of two drivers. The Grand Prix works driver Rudolf Caracciola had by far the most powerful car, and won the class by quite a margin, his time of 46.4 seconds a new record. Dorothy, or 'Miss Wyndham', was paired with the experienced Brooklands and Le Mans driver Jack Dunfee, who drove the course in 50.2 seconds. She managed 54.3, but was beaten to the Ladies' Cup that day by Mrs Elsie Wisdom in her supercharged 1500cc Frazer Nash in a time of 53.0 secs.

The August edition of *Motorsport* carried details of her debut: 'The Hon. Dorothy Paget, driving a Mercedes, was the first to the starting line, but did not make a very good start, and gave place to Mrs Hall, who brought her 4½-litre Bentley up in good style, while the Hon. Dorothy Paget climbed later on, but was not very fast.' The editor of the *Sporting Life*, Ben Clements, was rather more obsequious: 'Her face attractively framed in a fur-lined helmet, a dashing "Miss Wyndham" was found to be figuring in four-wheel fiestas. She drove a monstrous Mercedes with aplomb – and skill, too. Birkin, a sound judge, pronounced her one of the best women drivers he had ever known' – a pronouncement designed to keep his benefactor sweet, or because he fancied her? The motoring journalist John Bolster, however, wrote that Dorothy 'nearly caused a massacre by giving her Mercedes-Benz full boost on the start line at Shelsley – in reverse!' Certainly she only actually raced in one of the hill-climbs, non-starting on the others. Few other details of Dorothy's short-lived racing career appear to exist, and the anonymous *Daily Telegraph* correspondent who declared her 'one of the finest woman drivers of fast cars with whom I have ever come in contact' may just have been damning with faint praise.

Dorothy would be a frequent visitor to the Bentley works on Broadwater Road in Welwyn Garden City, often coming to wish the team luck, and after a race partaking of tea and cakes with everyone. However, as early as the July, the *Daily Telegraph* was reporting her as considering whether to withdraw from motor sport. Paul Kenny backs this up, suggesting that 'the amount of oil thrown out by all three Blowers' at the Irish Grand Prix – in which only Birkin, of her three drivers, finished, taking fourth place – 'left Dorothy so disillusioned that she concluded it was time to focus solely on horse racing'.

At Brooklands' August Bank Holiday meeting a further mishap saw the fuel tank split on Birkin's single-seater Bentley, forcing him to retire. But in September, Birkin was still representing Dorothy when he contested the French Grand Prix at Pau in the south west of the country. Birkin's secretary, Bill Lambert, had written to Dorothy a fortnight before the race to tell her that his long-time co-driver Jean Chassagne 'is of the opinion that your car stands a very good chance in this race, as he is personally acquainted with all the Bugattis entered, and he does not think that they are likely to last the course. Your car will be completely stripped and will carry no weight, and you, therefore, can look forward to seeing some very fast times.'

The letter wasn't far wrong. In an eventful race Birkin somehow managed to drive round rather than over a fellow driver who had been flung out of his machine as the result of a crash which left him lying face down and bleeding in the middle of the track – Birkin's right-hand wheels were reportedly blood stained as he squeezed past. He then charged through the field to take second place.

On 29 October 1930, however, the *Daily Mail* proclaimed, SPEED QUEEN QUITS. The failure of the Bentley team to win any races in the season was enough for Dorothy to cut off her funding. The London *Evening Standard*, however, put Dorothy's decision to bail out down to the fact that she had clashed with Woolf Barnato. Birkin himself summarised the situation through slightly gritted teeth in *Full Throttle*:

> *Miss Paget had hinted that she would not extend her patronage to a second season; for a year she has played the fairy godmother with patriotism and generosity, and that year was shortly to be revealed as a seven days' wonder.*
>
> *At the end of 1929 motor experts had prayed for a miracle, and behold! Dorothy Paget. She had thrown the lifebelt to the sinking sport, and for a few more strokes it had kept its head above water. But when the lifebelt was withdrawn, what could stop it drowning under the risen floods of foreign competition?*

The Broadwater Road Bentley works were closed down at the end of 1931, after just two years, and never again would the whine of Birkin's blown Bentleys be heard or seen roaring up and down Broadwater Road. W. O. Bentley himself was certainly unsurprised but, perhaps embittered by the collapse of his own company, commented: 'The supercharged 4½ never won a race, suffered a never-ending series of mechanical failures, brought the marque Bentley disrepute and incidentally cost Dorothy Paget a large sum.' In June 2012, however, one of the supercharged Bentley Blowers came up for sale at Bonhams, and the auction catalogue's footnotes corrected W. O.: 'The car offered here is the exception, and it would not only become a multiple Brooklands race winner, but also holder of the Outer Circuit lap record there…and while Sir Henry, car owner the Hon. Dorothy Paget and their supporters were delighted, W. O. Bentley had perhaps mixed feelings' observed the Bonham Footnotes.

Nevertheless, in retrospect these 'blown' Bentleys were a technological dead end, an attempt at mere modification which masked the deeper unwillingness of British car manufacturers to come up with new designs of racing car that could be truly competitive with the Europeans.

There may have been another factor behind both Dorothy's move into motor racing, and her peremptory decision to pull out. A photograph of the Brooklands paddock shows the presence of bookmaker 'Long Tom' and a number of other layers, displaying their odds for imminent races. Whether Dorothy indulged her gambling instincts while she was funding the Birkin team is unclear, but given her frenzied flutters on the horses it seems unlikely that she would not have wanted to take a financial interest in the outcome of races her team were contesting. But perhaps she was put off by not being able to get large enough wagers on? In a 1925 article in *Motorsport* 'Long Tom' himself, F.T. Harris, explained why Brooklands' bookies were circumspect about the size of bets they took and who they took them from:

No one outside of a few of the sharps who have had their stopwatches
at work during a few days before the meeting knows who has an
outstanding chance – and these particular gentlemen make very
few mistakes…the volume of business in comparison with horserace
meetings is very small indeed…the biggest [bets] I have laid at
Brooklands that I recollect have been £150.

That would have been small beer indeed to Dorothy.

According to the Bonhams catalogue, 'The Hon. Dorothy Paget loved being involved with competition, but only if she was on the winning side.'

But this was not the full story. Even though Dorothy withdrew financial backing for Birkin's team, their personal relationship endured, and she continued to support him in the red single-seater track car, the original Blower No. 1, nicknamed 'the Brooklands Battleship'.

September therefore saw him in Pau in France, records *Motorsport* magazine, where he drove the single-seater Bentley, finishing second in the French Grand Prix and, possibly uniquely during a Grand Prix, using his horn to warn rival cars out of his way! At the Brooklands 500-mile race in October the car's front tyre burst at speed during practice, with car and driver surviving despite 'some astonishing gyrations'. In the race itself Birkin came ninth. In three out of five races that year he failed to finish.

The year 1931 was a traumatic time for Birkin, becoming Sir Henry Birkin 3rd, Baronet, on the death of his father, surviving an emergency landing of his Imperial Airways plane in a field in Kent, and, a couple of days before the Brooklands 500, in an incident apparently typical of his career, sustaining burns to his hands when the petrol tank caught fire. Dorothy, meanwhile, was still involved in motor racing, from the evidence of a *Daily Herald* report at the end of 1931 that she was to send a team of Bentleys to Buenos Aires under Captain Alastair Miller to contest world championship races, including not Birkin but drivers like Jack Dunfee.

In 1932 Birkin was back at Brooklands in Dorothy's red Blower, breaking the Outer Circuit lap record with a time of 137.96 mph, and four days later, on Easter Monday, driving through 50-mph winds at up to 145 mph, the gusts lifting his car off the ground for three or four seconds before depositing him back on the track, only for him to veer off and narrowly miss some railings.

On the August Bank Holiday Monday, Birkin faced his great rival John Cobb in a three-lap invitation event, for a wager of 100 sovereigns – which must have alerted Dorothy's gambling instinct – Birkin in the 'Brooklands Battleship' Bentley, Cobb once holder of the land speed record, in the V12 Delage. It was to be the last great motor racing showdown for Birkin.

The French car was the faster starter, leading by 3.8 seconds at the end of the first lap. But on lap two, Birkin flashed round at 135.70 mph and was just 1.2 seconds off Cobb's tail. 'The crowd was on its toes,' writes the motor racing historian Bill Boddy. 'And round they came, the Bentley gaining, yard by yard, on the Delage. In a supreme effort, Birkin caught Cobb and drew ahead, winning one of Brooklands' most intense races by a mere one-fifth of a second, or about 25 yards. He averaged 125.14 mph, and that glorious last lap was run at 137.58 mph (0.28 mph below the record).' The duel was subsequently commemorated by the artist Terence Cuneo in the painting, *The Spirit of Brooklands*.

In March 1933 Birkin's workshop was put up for auction by the liquidators. His final race was the 1933 Tripoli Grand Prix in May, in which he finished third. Shortly after the end of the race he burnt his hand on a hot exhaust pipe as, according to some reports, he reached for one of the cigarettes he smoked almost constantly. He died on 22 June, either because the burn wound turned septic, or from malaria contracted during his First World War service in Palestine. He was 36 years old.

The impact of Birkin's death on Dorothy has been debated ever since. She refused to part with the red single-seater Bentley for some years.

'Sir Henry had said it was an extremely difficult car to drive fast so perhaps there were no takers,' pondered *Motorsport*. Much more likely that she had no appetite for allowing anyone else to own it. Later, the car was driven by Ian Fleming's famous character in the first James Bond novel, *Casino Royale*.

But the wife of one of Dorothy's racehorse trainers, Fulke Walwyn, puts her finger on something much more profound. 'When she was young she rode well and was quite thin,' reflected Cath Walwyn, 'but something changed and she just got fatter and fatter.' Just nine months after Birkin's death, when Golden Miller won the Grand National in March 1934 and Dorothy led him in from the racecourse, press photographs clearly show her as already far from thin. In 1993, the Sir Henry Birkin Memorial Rally was held to mark the sixtieth anniversary of his death, and David Ward, the Chairman of the Fellowship of the Motor Industry, summed up the legend: 'It is said that when Birkin died, [Dorothy] Paget was so overwrought she couldn't stop eating through her grief, and eventually died of overeating herself.' Pondering the onset of Dorothy's obesity, and without prompting, another trainer's wife, Mercy Rimell, widow of the late Fred, who rode but never trained for Dorothy, concluded, 'Maybe she had a tragic love affair.'

Dorothy was clearly not unaware of her own body image, and in a later handwritten note to her doctor she asks him about the 'apparent illness' affecting one of her secretaries. 'I want you to use this chance to really frighten her about her size. Everyone has tried here, but she does not seem to care. She may listen to a doctor, and you can say that being that size and being an enormous eater she is much more likely to pick up germs. Anyway, frighten her about this because it is only for her own good.' She adds: 'If she mentions that Miss Williams [one of the senior members of DP's staff] and Miss Paget are overweight, you must say that as we are made of sterner stuff it does not apply to us.' Is it possible Dorothy was using the secretary's illness in order to voice concerns about her own obesity?

Was Tim Birkin, then, really the one man Dorothy Paget believed she loved? A photograph of them sitting companionably together in one of the cars at Brooklands hardly suggests she could not bear to have a male in close proximity. Nor does it suggest that Dorothy had any aversion to orange peel – Birkin apparently loved to suck on oranges whilst driving, and the vehicle would end up littered with the peel.

Does W. O. Bentley offer another clue when he writes that Birkin brought Dorothy to Brooklands 'and then showed her the cars lined up at the pits at the unsuitable hour of 7.30 a.m.' That would, indeed, have been an unlikely hour to see Dorothy out and about, raising the possibility that they could have spent the night together prior to heading to the track?

An alternative verdict, however, is given by the man who ghost-wrote Birkin's *Full Throttle* autobiography, the *Times* correspondent, poet and playwright, Michael Burn. 'I don't think [Birkin] liked Dorothy Paget,' he said in an interview published in *Motorsport* magazine in 2004, when the 'ghost' was 92 years old: 'He was vaguely related to her. She was generous, and eccentric, but I think it very unlikely that they had an affair – she was a lesbian.'

Burn's contention that the two were 'vaguely related' does, however, turn out to be almost correct. There was an indirect family link through Sir Stewart Menzies, who became the Chief of MI6 from 1939 to 1952: his second marriage was to Pamela Beckett, the daughter of Dorothy's second cousin, and his third would be to Audrey Chaplin, whose previous husbands included, in 1921, Tim Birkin. It is unclear just when the two actually met, but not unlikely that they moved in the same circles and knew of each other before they met up.

They remained on very good terms into 1932, not only at the motor racing track, but also socially, attending the glamorous opening night of *The Cat and the Fiddle* at London's Palace Theatre, suggesting they were happy to be seen out on the town as a couple. And a dramatic indication that she did indeed retain very strong feelings towards Birkin emerged only after her death.

Dorothy left no will. However, Donald Seaman, a respected *Daily Express* journalist, reported just a week after her death:

> *Dorothy Paget made a will, but tore it up nearly 30 years ago. A second*
> *will, disposing of her fortune, was drafted, but for some reason that*
> *may never be known, she did not sign it. In the will she did sign,*
> *Miss Paget mentioned the great Sir Henry 'Tim' Birkin, who was for*
> *a while the manager of her Bentley racing team. But she tore it up after*
> *Tim Birkin, himself the son of a millionaire, died in 1933.*

Only a few close friends and Miss Paget's legal advisers know what was in the will she did *not* sign.

Five

NOW SHE'S RACING ALONG

It began as a close relationship – Dorothy and Golden Miller's trainer Basil Briscoe.

During the relationship with Tim Birkin Dorothy's horse racing career had been developing rapidly, and on 27 March 1931 she had her first big race runner, when her recent purchase Solanum, who had been trained by Basil Briscoe but was subsequently moved to Alec Law's stables, started in the Grand National, unfancied at 50/1. The National was very much the biggest deal in National Hunt horse racing, one of the biggest sports events of any kind at that time, and from an early stage clearly the race Dorothy was most determined to win – all the more so, perhaps, since she was aware how close her cousin Jock Whitney had already come. His Easter Hero started favourite in the 1929 running and eventually finished second, and the following year his Sir Lindsay was third. But in the 1931 race Solanum not only fell but badly hampered her cousin's well-fancied Easter Hero in the process. Whitney would never achieve his ambition of winning the National.

Solanum suffered no ill effects from the fall and came back quickly, winning the £1,725 Lancashire Chase at Manchester on Easter Monday – the first significant win for the woman the *Mail* was now talking of as 'a recent addition to the ranks of enthusiastic patrons of the turf'. Solanum's triumph gave Dorothy an early success over her cousin. Meyrick Good, the racing reporter of the *Sporting Life*, had originally acquired the horse himself, he told readers, specifically with the intention of selling him to Jock Whitney, 'but the American was abroad. I then gave Alec Law the chance to buy him, telling him that I thought the horse was certain to win the big Manchester Chase, which he eventually did, much to the delight of his new owner, Miss Dorothy Paget.'

By now, Dorothy was also creating a stir by betting big on her horses: 'Miss Paget's horses threw the betting market into chaos at many a Kentish point-to-point,' observed Golden Miller's biographer, Gregory Blaxland, 'often bringing great bounty to the backers of what should have been the favourite.' He was obviously referring to her own hefty wagers on horses with no realistic chance of winning, which would force bookies to lengthen their odds for the genuine contenders to even out their liabilities.

It shouldn't be forgotten that this was a time of intense financial insecurity for the country. The Great Depression, also known as the Great Slump, had its origins in the Great Crash of the American stock market late in 1929, and was Britain's largest and most profound economic depression of the 20th century. Between 1929 and 1933 Britain's trade with the rest of the world fell by half, the output of heavy industry fell by a third, and profits plunged in nearly all sectors of the economy. At the depths of the Depression in the summer of 1932, registered unemployed numbered 3.5 million. A further consequence for horse racing was, as the *Sporting Life* put it, that 'Abominable Snowmen were easier to locate than bloodstock buyers'.

But Dorothy's affluence was unchecked. At the start of 1931 she had laid on a party for 200, mostly children, with a hired cinema, Charlie Chaplin films, and a Hungarian with six performing monkeys, the children applauding so loudly that one monkey got over-excited and ran around the stage refusing to do his tricks – and presents for every child.

And by the end of the year the *Daily Express* was reporting that, despite many owners cutting back, Miss Dorothy Paget 'proposes to race on a more extensive scale in the future.' At the 1931 Doncaster Sales she had made her intentions clear to the racing world, shelling out a hefty 6,600 guineas for the yearling Spion, a half-brother to the St Leger winner Sandwich, and Derby-winner Manna, who would go on to be named Tuppence and go down in infamy as the subject of one of the biggest and most misguided of Derby gambles. She was already finding out about the downside of owning horses, however: her Eileandonan was one of several horses killed on racecourses in 1932.

Within the Paget family, meanwhile, a feud was about to break out. On 8 January 1932, Dorothy's step-mother Edith sued for legal separation from Almeric Paget, citing cruelty, and, despite an annual income of $250,000, also charged him with non-support. An American newspaper in San Antonio, the *Light*, claimed that 'after a few years' of marriage, Almeric had refused to be seen in his wife's company, and 'went so far as to forbid the use of his name and title when she sent out invitations.'

The newspaper also made a point of referring to the couple's three daughters, perhaps laying bare the truth behind the break-up of the relationship. Lord Queenborough already had two daughters from his first marriage, Olive and Dorothy – but was still without a son and heir. That seems to have been his 'one aim in life', wrote *The Times*' racing correspondent Alan Lee, and he 'apparently did not take kindly to failure in this department. Some of his sourness transmitted itself to his daughters, and Dorothy, despite inheriting vast family wealth, evidently found little fulfilment in life, outside the self-satisfaction of backing her own horses with quite ruthless courage.'

The final straw which broke the back of their marriage occurred, claimed Edith, when Almeric suggested to his wife one day that she take herself and her three young children off for a 'nice, long walk'. He would remain at home.

When the four pedestrians returned to their big London town house, Lady Queenborough wondered why her key no longer would work the lock in the front door. She rang the bell and rapped on the door, but could get no response from her husband or any of his fifteen servants. Edith even visited the tradesmen's entrance, to no avail, and was about to go and call the police when Almeric, who had had the locks changed in her absence, appeared at a window, and, related the *San Antonio Light*, 'simply shook his head and motioned to her to go away.'

This was the story Edith Miller related in the New York Supreme Court.

Lord Queenborough, she claimed, 'seemed not to want to breathe the same air' as her, or their children. Lord Queenborough made no denial or explanation of the incident, but had allegedly described his wife as 'an impediment and obstacle to his political preferment'. (During the thirties a number of articles written by Almeric prompted suggestions that he was pro-fascist.) The Texas paper further alleged that Almeric had told Edith that his first wife Pauline 'made him sick', though, confronted with this allegation, he had explained that what he really said was that 'she had been the cause of an illness that he had suffered.'

Bizarrely, Edith and Queenborough seem never to have officially divorced, and in January 1933 Edith died suddenly in Paris following an operation.

Dorothy's racing career, meanwhile, had entered a new and, it would turn out, historic era. Back in 1930 she had been tipped off by Captain Sandys Dawes, the Master of the Mid-Kent Staghounds, that the trainer Basil Briscoe might have a decent horse or two for sale. Dorothy hadn't hung about. 'Miss Dorothy Paget telephoned me at Longstowe [his training yard],' Briscoe himself recalled, 'and asked me if I knew of some good chasers and hurdlers. For the only time in my life I was able to tell an owner that I knew of the best steeplechase horse in the world and also the best hurdle racer in the country.'

Six

THE MILLER

Racing's greatest partnership? Dorothy and Golden Miller rewrote the sport's record books. Their Cheltenham Gold Cup achievements may never be equalled, let alone surpassed.

Golden Miller was born in April 1927, when his eventual owner and partner in one of the all-time great racing stories of the 20th century was only just 22.

The Miller's dam, Miller's Pride, had been brought to Pelletstown in County Meath by a moneylender called Julius Solomon in 1914, and left in the care of a small-holding farmer by the name of Laurence Geraghty, who also kept a few brood mares, without any provision for her keep and welfare. Solomon returned to Dublin and was never seen again. Today the Pelletstown Riding Centre is still run from the homestead by Laurence's grandson Tucker and his wife Bea, and their son, Barry, has become one of the most successful National Hunt jockeys of all time. The sire – for a five-guinea fee – was called Goldcourt, who came from an illustrious line of male racehorses including the dual Ascot Gold Cup winner Isonomy, and sired two Triple Crown winners in Common and Isinglass.

In the wee hours of Saturday, 30 April 1927, Miller's Pride went into labour, and daylight revealed a dark bay colt foal with large intelligent eyes either side of a white star on his forehead. The Geraghtys were delighted with the result. Today the Miller's birth is commemorated on a plaque outside the foaling barn. As Laurence had had Miller's Pride for twelve years, fed and looked after her, arranged her matings and borne the costs involved, he was now recognised by the editors of the *Stud Book*, Weatherbys, as the de facto owner.

Golden Miller, albeit unnamed at the time, was sold at Goffs' Sales in Dublin for 100 guineas, a massive sum then, to a man called Paddy Quinn from Tipperary, who had bred Goldcourt. However, Solomon now reappeared, and successfully applied to have his name inserted in the *Stud Book* in place of Laurence Geraghty. The new owner recognised that the Miller's physique suggested a chaser in the making, so he had him castrated as a yearling. He thrived and grew to a height of just over 16 hands. Then, although there is no record of the sale, the horse changed hands again – it is believed between £350 and £500 was paid – and was acquired by a neighbour of the Geraghtys, Nat Galway-Greer.

Captain Dick Farmer was a partner in a big Northamptonshire horse dealing business who knew Galway-Greer, and liked what he saw in the Miller's Pride gelding, especially when Galway-Greer told him he could send it to England straight away. In March 1930 Farmer sent a telegram to Basil Briscoe asking if he'd be interested in this 'really good-looking three-year-old out of Miller's Pride'. The response came by return: 'Will buy horse, forwarding cheque.'

Briscoe had registered his own racing colours in 1926. Those cherry and gold halved silks became very well known, and in October 1929 he sent out his first winner as a trainer, the appropriately named Longstowe, from stables he'd built on land given to him by his father.

A week later the horse arrived. 'My goodness,' recalled Briscoe,

> I had a shock. Never had I thought that I had thrown away £500 so easily. He stood in his box with his head low to the ground, his wet bear-like coat sticking up in places like a porcupine and plastered in

mud from head to tail. This unbroken three-year-old did not look worth
a tenth of what I had paid for him.

Briscoe now had to name the horse. Following the tradition of com-
bining elements of the names of his sire and dam, he chose Golden
Miller. His head lad Stan Tidey's response became part of the lore of
racing: 'What a good name for a bad horse.'

The Miller was readied for his first race. Briscoe felt the horse was
'fit enough', but in a Southwell hurdle against another 16 hopefuls,
the 25/1 Golden Miller was a disappointing also-ran. Briscoe was now
approached by Philip Carr, an owner with horses at Briscoe's yard,
who agreed to buy him for £1,000. Ten days later the Miller changed
hands again and next time out he finished third in a 20-runner maiden
hurdle, the jockey Bob Lyall saying the horse had jumped superbly
throughout, never putting a foot wrong.

The horse continued to gain experience and improve, but in August
1931 Philip Carr passed away after a short illness. Before he died, Carr
asked Briscoe to sell Golden Miller for him. The trainer put the word out
that the horse was for sale, and shortly afterwards received a phone call
from Dorothy Paget asking if he knew of any good chasers and hurdlers
she could buy.

Whether Dorothy had heard on the grapevine that both Golden Miller
and Carr's hurdling starlet Insurance were for sale, or her query was
merely a lucky coincidence, we may never know. In any event, Briscoe
told Dorothy he had the best steeplechase horse in the world and also
the best hurdle racer in the country. 'I should be an exceedingly lucky
man if I could ever make that remark with confidence again,' Briscoe
reflected, 'but it was so true.' Briscoe could not but have been impressed
by the amount of money Dorothy was prepared to lavish on horseflesh:
according to him the new owner paid a total of £12,000 for the two
horses, though Stan Tidey claimed there was a third horse involved in a

total transaction of £21,000. However much and however many horses were involved, the Sport of Kings was about to get a new, eccentric and very unconventional Queen.

When Dorothy had bought Solanum from Philip Carr and transferred him from Briscoe's yard to be trained by Alec Law at Findon, he had done very well and won a number of big races. But now she decided to send the seven horses she had with Law back to Longstowe. Basil Briscoe was yet to discover the full extent of the demands his new owner would make on him and his staff.

On 20 January 1931 – the same date on which, 31 years later, another candidate for the accolade of 'greatest chaser ever', Arkle, won for the first time at Navan – in a maiden hurdle at Leicester, Golden Miller won his first race. As the New Year approached, he was winning Newbury's Reading Chase and grabbing the attention of the *Sporting Life* in a story headlined GOLDEN MILLER BEST YOUNG CHASER IN TRAINING. After a couple more decent displays and a wide-margin win, Dorothy and her trainer started plotting a tilt at the Cheltenham Gold Cup, whilst aiming Insurance at the Champion Hurdle. These were important races at the time, albeit relatively newly-established – the Gold Cup had first been run in 1924, the Champion Hurdle in 1927 – but they weren't universally perceived as the premier contests they are nowadays.

In 1929 and 1930 Easter Hero, owned by Dorothy's American cousin Jock Whitney, had landed the Gold Cup with 20-length wins, with a couple of Grand National near-misses thrown in for good measure, and was the first horse since the First World War with that touch of charisma that makes a horse a real draw for the public. But in the run-up to the 1932 Gold Cup money came in heavily for the previous year's Grand National winner Grakle.

Insurance kicked off the opening day of the two-day meeting with a resounding 12-length win in the Champion Hurdle. Dorothy and Briscoe were elated. They presented a bizarre sight in the parade ring, the ever-elegant and coutured Briscoe contrasting greatly with the million-airess in the drab ankle-length 'Speckled Hen' coat and beret that would become her racecourse apparel for the rest of her life. The pair certainly stood out from the crowd.

On Gold Cup day the ground at Cheltenham came up rock hard, and both Briscoe and the Miller's jockey Ted Leader were of the opinion that he should be withdrawn. Dorothy put her foot down; the horse would run. Owner and trainer fretted nervously as the field was led into the ring. Grakle was the people's choice as market leader at 11–10. There were five other runners. The distance was three miles, three furlongs; there were a total of 21 fences to be negotiated.

At the first two fences Dorothy's horse was very uneasy, and Ted Leader held on for dear life. Dorothy and Briscoe, watching through bin-oculars from the stands, drew breath sharply when, having produced fine jumps at the water and the open ditch on the back straight, the Miller clattered the next fence. Leader managed to stay aboard, and found his horse responding willingly when asked for effort. Then Golden Miller drew clear, jumping the final three fences in an unspectacular but safe fashion, to stroll home the four-length winner.

'He's won it – he's won it – he's won it!' yelled Briscoe.

A majority of racing writers seem to have felt that the Miller's first Gold Cup was at worst flukey and at best highly fortunate. Dorothy and Briscoe felt what they had on their hands was, as the trainer claimed, 'a champion of champions'. At season's end, Dorothy penned a letter to Stan Tidey:

Tidy [sic],

We have had a wonderful and unique Jumping Season and been very lucky in having such exceptionally High Class Horses which makes all the difference – But they have always been well trained and beautifully turned out – Well done and Thank You.

Dorothy Paget

In April 1932, Briscoe expanded his training operation, moving from Longstowe to new premises at Beechwood House Stables in Exning. By the time the move was completed there would be over eighty inmates at his new base.

The Miller's 1932/33 season began with something of an upset for the team when, dispirited by Dorothy's constant meddling and her refusal to accept the advice of the professionals who were supposed to be the experts, Ted Leader fell out with her. Billy Stott, the champion jockey for the previous five seasons, took over. After four convincing wins, now came the first defence of the Miller's Gold Cup title.

This year the going at Cheltenham was heavy. Once again Insurance won the Champion Hurdle to kick the day off well for Dorothy and Briscoe, but it was a hard-fought victory in more ways than one. While the horses were waiting at the start for the tapes to go up, Song of Essex took a fancy to Billy Stott's arm and bit him savagely, causing a nasty wound. Stott had his wound properly attended to, and the Miller was sent off the 4/7 favourite against six opponents. This time he defended his title from Thomond II, Dorothy's cousin Jock's horse, by a comfortable ten lengths, and a second Gold Cup victory forced many observers to reconsider their opinion that this was an ordinary horse.

The Miller's season was not over and, as Dorothy had asserted after the Gold Cup, he was indeed headed for Aintree just seventeen days later, where both owner and trainer dreamed of success in the biggest challenge of all: the Grand National. Undoubtedly alerted by newspaper reports about the 'stable money' being on the Miller, the public had taken note, and minutes after Dorothy announced him as a confirmed runner he was made ante-post favourite.

The handicapper allotted him a weight of 12st 2lbs. Many felt this was a very big weight for a six-year-old to haul around the daunting Liverpool venue; many more – owner and trainer included – felt he was well up to it. Only two horses were asked to carry more, and only one of them, Gregalach, allotted 12st 7lbs, ran.

On the Monday after Cheltenham an announcement was made that Ted Leader would ride the Miller at Aintree. Leader had won the race on Sprig in 1927, and Dorothy and Briscoe were now anxious their star turn should have the most capable man on board for the National. The news was actually made public by Billy Stott, who claimed he had requested the change on the basis that he felt he would not have the length of leg necessary to keep the Miller straight over the Aintree fences. The racing public did not quite see it that way, though, and both Dorothy and Briscoe were pilloried for their shabby treatment of the popular Stott. As ever, Dorothy did not feel the need to explain her actions. The whiff of cordite followed her around like a perfume – even when she was not behaving badly at all.

The Miller, 9/1 favourite, was quite tentative over the initial fences of the National, as Leader eased him into the race, but he settled down and did not disgrace himself at either Becher's or Valentine's. His troubles started at The Chair, when he was blindsided by a loose horse and only just made it across the gaping chasm of the ditch in front of the fence, landing more or less on top of the obstacle. Then the Miller started jumping to his right and began to look novicey. Leader had to give him a crack of the whip to prevent him refusing at the first open ditch, and the pair were very nearly sundered on the second circuit when he hit Becher's Brook hard and reportedly made as big a hole in the fence as had ever been seen. His demise finally came at the Canal Turn when, although he cleared the fence, he slipped badly on landing and tipped Leader out of the saddle, standing on the jockey to add injury to insult. Kellsboro Jack won the race after fighting off Pelorus Jack and Billy Stott, who fell at the last. Dorothy did not take too kindly to Leader's view, expressed to Briscoe after the race, that Golden Miller would 'never make an Aintree horse'. She demanded that a new jockey be retained to ride her horse the following season.

Dorothy's other side, showing her to be a demanding, inconsiderate, hard-to-please termagant, was coming to the fore, and for Briscoe that meant a lot of heartache and, in some cases, humiliation. 'Training Dorothy Paget's horses is child's play,' he was once quoted as saying, 'but it is a hell of a job trying to train Dorothy Paget.' He was not exaggerating. Aside from the regular late night/early morning phone calls when Dorothy demanded lengthy and comprehensive reports on her many charges, she also made irregular trips to Exning to see her horses. And because by now she had turned night into day, these visits were the cause of much grief to the trainer and his staff. When she announced she was going to make such a visit, Briscoe had to implore her to come to Exning in time for evening stables at 6 p.m. so she would not disturb the daily routine of the yard.

Sometimes Dorothy came up by train from London and stayed overnight in a special carriage in a siding at Newmarket station, nourished by a battery of hampers which travelled in another carriage, but more often than not she came by car and blithely ignored Briscoe's request for her to come early. Usually it was between 9 and 10 p.m. at night when her Rolls-Royce pulled into the yard, and Briscoe had to have all her horses and their stable-hands at the ready so she could inspect each and every one of them. These visits could sometimes last until midnight, and while Dorothy was always polite and apologetic to the staff – as well as doling out cash to them for having kept them at work so late – she was far from civil to the trainer. Briscoe himself would usually smile and try and fade into the background to allow Tidey to do what Dorothy had requested of him, but it must have been galling for the trainer to be treated in such an offhand and mean-spirited manner. Such, he knew, was the price of having such a wilful – and rich – owner, and he accepted it as part of the deal, even if he did not like such treatment one little bit. Supping with the she-devil that was Dorothy would prove destructive and dangerous for Briscoe.

Seven

EQUINE IMMORTAL

Golden Miller leads the way in the 1934 Grand National.

The pre-war era was indeed a great one for racing, and horses like Golden Miller and Brown Jack – the great Flat gelding who won the Champion Hurdle in 1928, and then the longest race in the Flat calendar, the Queen Alexandra Stakes, for six successive years from 1929 to 1934 – caught the imagination of a public which adored its sporting heroes, both two- and four-legged. Part of their appeal was their longevity and familiarity, allowing racegoers to get to know and support them and their connections for years on end, taking public ownership of them in the process. People turned out in vast numbers to race meetings to see their idols in action.

The late Sir Peter O'Sullevan was a very young man back then, but he recalled the times with characteristic clarity.

I remember the Golden Miller era and the public love of the horse. An analogy of that era would have been the popularity of Brown Jack, because he evoked a similar sort of hysteria to Golden Miller, with ladies plucking hairs from his tail and that sort of thing.

There were enormous crowds, because there were no real alternative attractions. You'd get hundreds of thousands at Aintree, because it was a punctuation point in the sporting calendar. The Manchester November Handicap and the Leger at Doncaster were two meetings that were populated by miners – look at any pictures of those meetings and you will just see rows and rows of flat caps. Apart from football, there were few other attractions for people to go to, and most of the footballers were miners anyway. There was no suggestion of women having any say in anything – it just wasn't the way of it back then.

In the run-up to the 1933/34 season there was no doubting the Miller's growing popularity, but for his trainer the focus was on getting the horse to Aintree and getting him to win there. Dorothy had left Briscoe in no doubt that this was the primary aim; if Gold Cups and other successes came along, all well and good, but the real goal was to win the Grand National.

Having prepared the horse throughout the summer months, Briscoe set the Lingfield Open Steeplechase at Lingfield Park on 25 November 1933 as the race in which his charge would open his season. The man chosen for the ride was Gerry Wilson, the champion jockey from the 1932/33 season. A superb horseman as well as a tough and uncompromising jockey, Wilson had ridden the Miller in his first steeplechase, finishing second to Rolie at Newbury in February 1931. Wilson was a hard man in the saddle, but to the outside world he presented a positive and jovial demeanour. Dorothy was said to be disarmed by his general breeziness, her overwhelming shyness moderated by the jockey's overt personality and his disinclination, unlike many others, to bow and scrape in her presence.

The renewed partnership lined up at Lingfield, facing a very strong field which included old rivals Thomond II and Kellsboro Jack. It was very unusual for the reigning Gold Cup and National winners to be pitched in against each other so early in the season, but there were few complaints from the huge crowd which turned up to see them going head-to-head. Thomond II had already had two outings that season, winning both, while Kellsboro Jack also had a run under his belt. Briscoe was confident of a good run, and his horse duly started as 8/11 favourite for the three-mile contest on good ground.

As probably the fittest of the five runners, Thomond II made the initial running. But coming to the fourth last Kellsboro Jack and the Miller eased past Jock Whitney's horse and entered into a gruelling duel to the line. Wilson felt his horse jink to the right at the third last as both he and the National winner winged the fence, and his mount soon found out that the jockey was not amused by such behaviour. As they approached the second last Wilson got his whip out and hit the Miller down the cheek. The Miller got another smack in the face as he veered right at the last, but he cleared the fence easily and came home six lengths clear in a course record of 5 minutes 56 seconds, beating Thomond II, who ran on well.

The Miller now suffered a couple of setbacks, beaten into second at Kempton on the day after Boxing Day, before finishing third as Southern Hero won with Persian Sun second at Hurst Park three weeks later. Neither of these races were amongst the horse's main targets for the season, yet after the second defeat, the *Sporting Life* declared, 'It can be questioned now whether he is entitled to be styled champion.' 'He was trying to do the impossible, as Southern Hero was a really useful horse and Persian Sun won his next race by six lengths,' felt Briscoe, maintaining that while the Miller's many backers grumbled when he got beaten, 'possibly at Hurst Park he put up one of the greatest performances of his career, as time eventually proved.'

With the horse's fitness in mind, after the Hurst Park failure Briscoe hired the cultured Flat jockey Harry Beasley to ride the Miller in his gallops and to make him settle into his work and exorcise his sometimes headstrong habits when working out on the Newmarket Heath. After one such gallop Beasley reported – appropriately for an owner who drove

such vehicles herself – that the horse was 'a real Rolls-Royce'. Briscoe was
able to tell Dorothy that the Miller was shaping up fine for his forthcoming tilt at a third Gold Cup, and he could certainly not advise her
against taking a plunge on the outcome. She took his advice and duly
waded in, and undoubtedly her investments had a marked effect on the
horse's starting price when he lined up at Prestbury Park in early March.

This time around, the Miller's trip to the Cotswolds would be made
alone, as his good friend Insurance was unable to accompany him. His
forelegs had proven unable to withstand the work necessary to get him
fit, and he would not be able to defend his Champion Hurdle title.
The Miller, 6/5 favourite, lined up in a strong seven-runner field which
included several familiar faces and a few new ones too. Newspaper reports
recounted a dull, dreary and wet morning ahead of racing, dampening
the spirits of the massive crowd, but much pleasing the Miller's connections, who felt their horse was crying out for a bit of give in the ground.

As the field came into view from the old Gold Cup start behind the
stands, a massive roar arose from the crowd. Gerry Wilson was getting
such a good feel from the Miller, whose jumping was pitch-perfect,
that at the water jump he moved him alongside the front-running
Delaneige, taking the lead after a big leap. The Miller remained at the
head of affairs as the run to the post got serious. Danny Morgan, aboard
Kellsboro Jack, briefly took the lead at the third last, but the Miller had
plenty left and lengthened his stride to crush Morgan's hopes, easing
back into a lead he would not relinquish, running on up the final climb
for a six-length win.

Dorothy and Briscoe were overjoyed as their horse landed a true hat-
trick of Gold Cup wins, passing the record of her cousin's legendary Easter
Hero in the process. Dorothy, whose fleetness of foot had often been
remarked upon, largely because now it belied her increasing size, dashed
from her vantage point in the main stand down to the chute to lead her
horse into the unsaddling enclosure and a rapturous reception. Ironically,

in the moment of one of her greatest racing successes thus far, she appeared stony-faced, perhaps alarmed by the size and noise of the huge throng.

Press reaction to the victory was somewhat curious; it was as if the daily newspapers still did not know what to make of the distinctly unconventional 'Miss Paget'. Their stories painted a picture of a fantastically wealthy dilettante willing to squander money whimsically on horses and cars, even if she did display some element of social conscience by entertaining the lags in Wormwood Scrubs. There was very definitely a sense of societal jealousy seeping in – something perhaps no different today.

Seventeen days. It might not seem a lot of time to rest a horse after a big race and prepare him for a bigger one, but that was how long Briscoe was given between the 1934 Gold Cup and the Grand National. The only two 'modern' Gold Cup winners to attempt to win both races in the same season have been Alverton in 1979 and Synchronised in 2012, the former ridden by Jonjo O'Neill and the latter trained by the same man. Alverton had a 16-day gap between the two races and Synchronised 28. Sadly, both efforts ended fatally.

Back in 1934, Briscoe was quite happy he had enough time to 'give the Miller some finishing touches in his training' before sending him to Aintree.

'After a few days' rest, I gradually and slowly sharpened him up. He was the most sober of characters and nothing ever upset him. He reserved all his energy for the finish of a race.' The Miller relished the work he was given against the smart hurdler Trapper and the Derby failure Tuppence. What little condition was left on him was slowly worked off as he became slimmer but more muscular, reportedly scoffing 21lbs of oats every day, washed down with several pails of milk. 'And so to Liverpool he went on Wednesday, 21 March 1934 for the race two days later.'

The Miller was sent to Liverpool by train from Newmarket, accompanied by his lad Mick Boston. The two slept together in their allotted horse box. Dorothy took the trip to Aintree from London in her private railway carriage. She was entertaining a party of 12 on race day, and some of them travelled up with her in splendid style and with considerable confidence that her horse would do the business. Owner and trainer were so confident of the Miller's chances that both are reported to have had considerable amounts of money riding on the outcome. Golden Miller had been given a weight of 12st 2lbs.

Aintree was bracing itself for the biggest crowd it had ever seen, before or since. AIR AND RAIL DASH TO BIG RACE, blazoned the front page of the *Mirror*: RECORD CROWD TO WATCH TODAY'S GRAND NATIONAL. Predicting that £1 million would be spent by racegoers in the city, the *Mirror* also said a feature of the race that year would be the increased number of people arriving by air from London, Cardiff and Portsmouth. The railway companies were providing 50 special trains from Edinburgh, Glasgow, Newcastle, Swansea and many other towns and cities. Even transatlantic passengers leaving Liverpool for America were being accommodated, their sailing time scheduled for two hours after the race to enable them to get to Aintree if they wished. Some 250,000 people from every corner of the British Isles were said to have descended on the track, packing the stands and enclosures, bars and restaurants.

On the morning of the race Briscoe gave his charge a 'sharp canter', then got the horse back to his box to keep him 'as quiet as possible for the rest of the morning and early afternoon'. A mist which had shrouded the course from early morning had blown over by the start time, and the 30-runner field massed evenly waiting for the tapes to go up, with Golden Miller starting as second favourite at 8/1. At 3.16 p.m., a minute late, they were sent on their way, accompanied by a deafening roar.

There was carnage at the first, with Billy Stott and Pelorus Jack the first to hit the deck. Sorley Boy was also down, while other casualties included Southern Hero, who refused, Flambent and Fortnum. The hot pace continued as they headed out into the country, but there was only one further casualty before Becher's Brook, where Delaneige led, followed by Remus, Egremont, Trocadero, Golden Miller, Thomond II and Really True. Wilson was wide on the outside of the course, allowing the Miller to see the monstrous fences clearly. Even so, there was a moment at Becher's when the horse got too close to the fence, brushed through the tightly-packed spruce branches and sprawled slightly on landing, taking a couple of strides before fully righting himself and regaining momentum.

The Miller jumped beautifully at the next four fences, including the Canal Turn and Valentine's. He made something of a mistake at the fence before the water jump, but a massive leap at that obstacle restored equilibrium, and the field headed out for the second circuit with Forbra taking up the running with Delaneige and the Miller bowling along comfortably.

Approaching Becher's again, Delaneige suddenly veered right, bumping Golden Miller as the two horses took off and, although they did not collide with any great violence, it was enough to unsettle him and he landed very awkwardly. Wilson recounted that the horse was 'on his nose on landing' and it took several nerve-shredding seconds to get him back into his stride. A massive leap from the Miller at the Canal Turn regained some of the ground lost to Forbra and Delaneige. After a slow start the favourite Really True loomed into the picture alongside the leading trio, and looked to be going best of the lot, only to come down shortly after.

Wilson, along with Jack Moloney on Delaneige, was now at the head of affairs. A roar went up as the two horses crossed the Melling Road, the crowd watching closely as Delaneige skipped over the second last while the Miller fiddled it. A hush descended as the transfixed throng anticipated the leaders' jumps at the last.

'Just for a second the vast crowd held its breath while the pair were in the air,' recalled the *Mirror*. 'It was the tensest moment of the race, and you heard a sigh of relief, followed by a terrific roar, as both landed safely. Golden Miller, on the outside, made the better jump and it took him into the lead.'

Briscoe was watching from the press box and in a state of near-apoplexy, roaring his horse on. It was a very fraught time for the 'extremely nervous' trainer, who had asked one well-known reporter next to him to dictate the race to him as he watched through his own binoculars.

The jump at the last was as close as it got, and the Miller then surged clear for a five-length victory, crossing the line roared on by Briscoe in the press box: 'What a horse! What a horse! What a bloody horse!' Watching from the stands, Dorothy was said to be 'so overwrought as to be deathly pale', but as she got up to lead in her winner the journalist George Quest saw her 'doing little jumps of joy'.

The crowd, remembered Briscoe, went mad. 'There has never been such a scene on the Aintree racecourse. Policemen gathered round the Miller to protect him from the crowd, hats went into the air, and women were shrieking with joy. The police could not prevent women from rushing the cordon and picking hairs out of his tail for mementos.'

Dorothy ran from her private box down to the winner's enclosure with her usual surprising alacrity and, Quintin Gilbey later recalled: 'No other woman owner would have been able to fight her way through that dense, cheering, dancing throng and seize Golden Miller's rein and lead him in ... Dorothy Paget was in the limelight she has ever since detested.' The victory was, he stated categorically, 'the greatest moment in Dorothy's life, made all the more wonderful by the disappointments which had preceded it.' 'If Miss Dorothy Paget ever wins the Grand National again,' reported the *Daily Mirror*, 'she will come prepared with a bodyguard to save her from her friends!' 'Never have I seen a woman receive such a good-natured buffeting as she underwent before she escaped to the shelter of the grandstand,' recalled the paper's special correspondent breathlessly. 'Her back was thumped by innumerable fists, her right hand was almost wrenched off as entire strangers made a grab at it – she had to fight her way through a surging, shouting mass of well-wishers.'

The cheering hordes gathered around the winner's enclosure would find more to applaud when word went around that the Miller had not only won the race, but had also done so in a record time of 9 minutes 20.4 seconds, knocking almost 8 seconds off the time set the previous year by Kellsboro Jack. There was much to cheer for all concerned, although when the cry went up for 'Three cheers for Dorothy Paget', the recipient of this accolade was reported to have been appalled at such commonness, although she did give an awkward acknowledgement to the mob.

The bookies, meanwhile, were devastated, the leading layer James McLean calling the result 'disastrous' and claiming 75% of the betting public had backed the 8/1 second favourite. However, logically, plenty must also have been on the 7/1 favourite, Really True!

Dorothy made a little more effort appearance-wise for the after-race celebration at Liverpool's Adelphi Hotel organised by her father, turning up at 10 p.m. in a red velvet dress with her short hair parted in the middle. Photographs show her happily lifting the race trophy in the air and sitting convivially with the jockey and trainer either side of her. Subsequently she had large chocolate effigies of Golden Miller made for Basil Briscoe and Gerry Wilson to mark the historic occasion.

In the aftermath of this historic Grand National, Sidney Galtrey, the *Daily Telegraph*'s top racing writer, wrote a brilliant portrait of Dorothy and assessment of her significance to horse racing.

Fifteen years after the resumption of normal racing, who shall we say is foremost as a woman owner? Undoubtedly Miss Dorothy Paget. She ought every year to be mopping up at least one classic race in a large and varied bag, that is, if rewards are to be measured by wealth of patronage.

She is out to be the first woman to lead in the Derby winner at Epsom.
I cannot see that such a history-making triumph will be much longer
delayed. She has bought brood mares much sought after by others with
special pride in their own judgement. They have seen to it that what she
secured at auction was not exactly given away.

Such lavish buying had an inevitable result; she became one of the few
of whom it can truthfully be written that they are what someone must have
described them as ages ago – 'Pillars of the Turf'. I think we may concede
to her that she is the first woman in history of whom this has been said.

Miss Paget has shown singular impartiality in her patronage of Flat
racing and National Hunt racing. While one day she would buy the most
expensive yearlings at Doncaster, she would on another possess herself of the
presumed best steeplechaser of his day and the proved best hurdler.

When Golden Miller made his triumphal return through the rushing,
excited crowds in the paddock [at Aintree], he had for escort his owner upon
whom many were looking for the first time. They looked at her with a mix-
ture of envy, admiration, and wonderment – envy of the marvellous part she
was filling, admiration of the determination she had shown to reach this part
of her ambition, and wonderment that a woman should be aided by great
wealth and be willing to use it in such a thrilling and spectacular cause.

She was not dressed as the people expected a rich woman to be. A thick
tweed coat with a beaver collar embraced quite tightly to her ample figure.
She wore a simple, close-fitting hat, low-heeled shoes, and stockings worn
strictly for utility. No face creams, no artificial tintings and no lipstick.
Her round, even features are somewhat pallid at all times. If she was paler
than ever now, who could wonder under the stress of such emotions as she
was experiencing? She did not quite suggest the outdoor woman.

The evening after the race, Galtrey was 'privileged' to be invited
to Dorothy's celebratory dinner at the Adelphi. Dorothy finally arrived:

She was dressed in a sort of crimson red, with a cape in velvet which was adjusted high both back and front. My descriptive powers of these feminine details are sadly limited, but such is my vague recollection of Golden Miller's owner on the night of the victory. Her hair she wore in a bob, parted down the centre and innocent of such a thing as a wave. Again, I noted the entire absence of any facial scheme of decoration.

Her father introduced her to those of her guests who had been bidden to the feast and to whom she had been hitherto unknown.

Anyone less likely to have a circle of friends on the racecourse I cannot imagine. She is naturally shy and reserved. Some people may misinterpret it, but I have no doubt it is the lady's natural manner and in no way assumed. She was a gracious hostess.

Her cousin, Mr Jock Whitney, with a second and two thirds in Grand Nationals as his limited gifts from Fortune and, therefore, with great ambition still unfulfilled, proposed the lady's health. And the lady acknowledged it – all in the space of sixty seconds or so, a little more than a ninth of the time Golden Miller had taken to set up a new and wonderful record for the Grand National course.

Our hostess remained until after midnight and then, rather than go to her rooms via the crowded dance floor, she preferred making a covert exit with the friendly aid of a baggage lift. It was so typical of her utter lack of ostentation and determination to shun publicity.

Another eyewitness account of the celebrations described Dorothy's

reserved place in the centre of a horseshoe-shaped table on a stage overlooking the band and the ballroom…Miss Paget's 50 or so guests gyrated with increasing uncertainty around the temporary bar, as 9 o'clock and 9.30 passed by – Joe Orlando, baton poised, waited anxiously for his boys to give out with a version of 'Here Comes the Bride' on the appearance of the millionaire hostess.

Clive Graham of the *Express* and Bill Curling of the *Telegraph* recalled
Dorothy arriving at the reception

> *almost unnoticed, by a side curtain, clutching to the arm of her father*
> *(who, it had earlier been reported, had won £1,000 on the race).*
> *Without ado, her plain, plump, face semi-circled by lank strands*
> *of hair, dressed in a heavyweight, crumpled, maroon-coloured ankle-*
> *length gown which fitted where it might, the 28-year-old millionairess*
> *wasted no time on ceremony before seating herself.*
>
> *Sometime after midnight, Lord Queenborough [whom the writers*
> *have earlier described as Dorothy's 'frail old' father] arose to propose his*
> *self-appointed toast: 'My daughter, her horse Golden Miller – and the*
> *British Empire.' Few present, alive or dead, could have given you next day*
> *a verbatim report of that sleep-inducing oration.*
>
> *It served a purpose which none of us guessed. Close at hand, behind*
> *a screen, Miss Paget's secretaries were peeling off £5 notes from a thick*
> *pile – one for every member of the Adelphi Hotel staff – pageboys, lift*
> *attendants, chambermaids, commis waiters and all.*

Only Joe Orlando was left musing that it was a 'funny thing' he and his
boys were left out.

Dorothy returned to London on the Sunday evening, two days after
the race, and was spotted on the train by a *Daily Mail* reporter opening
sheaves of congratulatory telegrams, smiling at the contents, and also, for
once – another indication that the received image of Dorothy refusing
to mix with or acknowledge the 'lower orders' may not be entirely accu-
rate – smiling as passengers peered inquisitively into her compartment.
'She had dinner in the train, which must be rare, as the hour was only
7.30 p.m. – for she usually dines at midnight.' The cameo also shows
how the media focus on her would now step up a gear: she had become
a genuinely national figure.

An interesting footnote to the Miller's 1934 Grand National victory is the amount of money Dorothy and Briscoe took from the bookies' satchels that famous day. After Aintree, Briscoe showed his bank book to another of his owners, Major Philip Gribble: he was £35,000 in credit. ('Finally, of course,' noted Gribble, 'he lost the lot.') Dorothy, meanwhile, according to the usually reliable chronicler of the betting ring, Geoffrey Hamlyn of the *Sporting Life*, was reported to have staked £10,000 on the Miller for the Gold Cup at 5/4, £10,000 on him for the National at 8/1, and 'multiplied odds for the double'. This suggests a profit of £12,500 on the Gold Cup, £80,000 more from the National and, assuming the same £10,000 stake for the double, a profit of £192,500 – and from the three bets combined, a total profit of an absurd £285,000, or the equivalent of £18 million in 2017.

Eight

END OF A LEGEND

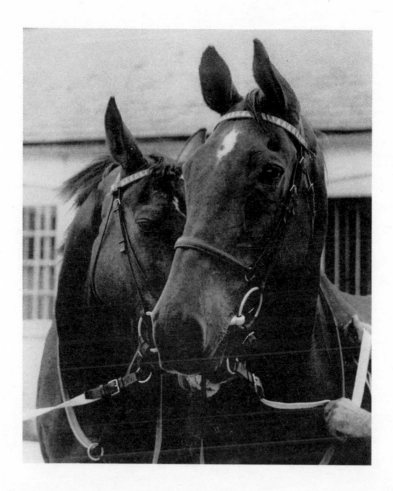

Best of friends – quintuple Gold Cup-winner Golden Miller (right) with retirement pal and dual Champion Hurdler Insurance, in 1950.

On top of feeling he was not getting a fair crack of the whip from the media, Basil Briscoe now also had to deal with an increasingly contrary Dorothy, whose eccentricities and excesses were becoming more and more marked. Shortly after the National win she disappeared completely from England and was of no particular mind to tell anyone, and particularly a minion like her trainer, where she was. The late night/early morning phone calls continued unabated, however, and while Briscoe always knew when Dorothy was on the other end of the line, he would initially have no idea where she was.

That she was in Germany with Olili would eventually become clear, but the mercurial owner had felt no need to inform Briscoe or anyone else in advance where she was or what she was doing. Inevitably during this period there were many rumours as to her whereabouts, some as fanciful as they were funny, especially the one whispered around racing circles that she had secretly got married and was living on a desert island.

An incident related by Clive Graham of the *Daily Express* from February 1934 demonstrated just what Dorothy's trainers, and Basil Briscoe in particular, had to put up with. 'I was staying with Briscoe when Miss Paget was expected to look over her string of horses,' related Graham. As Miss Paget would be expecting to stay, Briscoe warned Graham he would have to 'turn you out after lunch and ask you to stay the night in a hotel. Dorothy is nervous of strangers, keeps fantastic hours and might possibly stay up talking all night.'

Anticipating a 5 p.m. arrival, Briscoe was pacing up and down waiting, all of the Paget horses out in the yard, as 6 p.m., then 7 p.m., came and went.

'Shortly before half-past seven,' Briscoe later told Graham, 'a big Mercedes, headlights blazing, came swooping up the drive.' Out stepped Dorothy Paget from behind the steering wheel, 'puffing at a Turkish cigarette and demanding without ceremony, "I want to see them. Where are they?"'

'They're here, all twenty of them,' said Briscoe, gesturing to the yard.

'Fool!' she snapped at him. 'Don't you know I'm only interested in Golden Miller and Insurance?'

She looked at them 'for no more than a few seconds, then returned to her car.'

Asked to join Briscoe for a glass of wine and something to eat, he was ignored as 'two secretaries were removing a vast picnic basket from the boot. Miss Paget handed over a teapot. "Get this filled up with boiling water", she ordered, tearing off a wing from the cold roast capon which had been laid before her on the back seat of the Mercedes.'

An hour later after eating and drinking, 'she switched on the headlights and the engine and tore off into the night, hoping, she said, to top the 110 miles per hour she had achieved on the outward journey', and leaving Old Etonian Briscoe to bemoan the fact that there had been 'Not a word of thanks for anyone, not even a pound note for [head lad] Stan Tidey.

"What a right one she is, to be sure!"

Another visit to Briscoe saw the dinner gong sounded at 7.45 p.m. – but no sign of Dorothy. At 8 the butler announced dinner; she was still absent. Briscoe waited five minutes for her before leading the other guests into the dining room.

At 9 p.m. Dorothy finally made her entrance, strolling in 'clad in a maroon pyjama suit'. When the port made its first round of the table, Mrs Briscoe and the ladies – other than Dorothy – withdrew. 'The gentlemen then finished the port at one end of the table while Miss Paget had her dinner at the other.'

Signs of wear and tear on Briscoe were beginning to show. Privately he had long believed that the Miller hated Aintree, and confided to Dorothy's friend Gwennie Brogden that he hoped the Miller would be spared another crack at the National. His feelings on the matter would, though, be ignored.

In Dorothy's absence Briscoe had to arrange all the horse's races and training programme while keeping in touch with her as often as possible. 'She rang me up many times from Germany,' he wrote in 1939, 'and I told her as much as I possibly could about the horse's progress; I also told her that barring an accident he was certain to win the Grand National again.'

Before his next tilt at the Gold Cup the Miller had four 'prep' races. He won chases by eight lengths at Wolverhampton on Boxing Day, 1934, and by fifteen at Leicester twelve days later, followed by a facile win at Derby a fortnight afterwards. With his fitness coming along, the Miller contested a chase for the first time at Sandown Park's uniquely designed track, but cruised to victory over some decent opponents.

The trainer did not expect much of a challenge to his horse at Prestbury Park three and a half weeks later, but nonetheless felt he needed to give his stable star a couple of tough training sessions. Indeed, the horse was not his main concern at all – the jockey was. Gerry Wilson had wrenched his shoulder muscles in a fall at Gatwick and was struggling for fitness.

On the opening day of the three-day 1935 Cheltenham Festival, Wilson won the Champion Hurdle on Lion Courage, but in the next race he exacerbated his injury. So bad was he that he cancelled all his rides the following day, Wednesday, when Jock Whitney's Rod and Gun won the National Hunt Chase, and told the press he was travelling to London for treatment and Golden Miller would be his only remaining ride at the Festival.

At midday, 24 hours before the Gold Cup, Thomond II's trainer Jack Anthony approached Bob Wigney, the manager of Cheltenham race-course, asking how much it would be worth to the course for him to run Thomond II. Wigney is said to have laughed and replied, 'About a monkey [£500], I suppose.' Anthony then handed him a telegram and said, 'Read that.' It was from Jock Whitney to Jack Anthony, instructing him to declare Thomond II as a runner in the Gold Cup as the owner would definitely be present for the race.

Briscoe made it clear to Whitney 'quite honestly' that he regarded the decision as a great mistake; 'I told him it was bound to be a great race between these great 'chasers and that their chances of winning the Grand National in a fortnight's time would be much imperilled.' The media didn't agree: on the morning of the Gold Cup the *Daily Express* looked forward to 'a clash of the champions – owned by millionaire cousins – after all'.

Dorothy was Cheltenham-bound from Germany after her nine-month sabbatical, as ever leaving everything to the last minute before flying to Croydon in a private plane, arriving so late another aircraft had to be chartered and, with the permission of the Royal Air Force, land at Staverton just outside Cheltenham. Her temper was not light-ened when she learned that Thomond II was set to face her horse and that her cousin was being accused by some in the Miller's camp of duplicity and worse.

Perhaps this had something to do with the well-attested story that she had fallen out with her American cousins: supposedly Jock Whitney's family had barred her from going to Saratoga during the August race meeting, and she in turn had once locked his chauffeur in a coal cellar!

This might also explain why Dorothy went virtually unmentioned in E. J. Kahn's excellent biography of Jock. At least now Dorothy would have had an opportunity for revenge.

Wilson came into the weighing room about an hour before the big race and to his fellow jockeys looked deathly pale. The mere act of trying to remove his shirt was a nightmare. Briscoe summoned medical attention to get Wilson through the race, and half an hour before the off a doctor administered a pain-killing injection.

The official attendance on the day was 16,367 – small by comparison with the modern era, for sure, but massive for the time – and in any case is probably way short of the actual number because several fences around the course gave way under the pressure of the crowd and plenty of opportunistic punters gained free access. Lined up against Golden Miller and Thomond II were just three other runners, but it was to be a contest Briscoe would later describe as 'probably the greatest race that had ever been witnessed by followers of steeplechasing.'

Over the third last and Thomond II and the Miller were as if conjoined. The crowd was on its feet roaring approval. Coming to the last, the Miller's renowned stride seemed to be winning the race for him as he was half a length in front, but Billy Speck drove Thomond II into the final obstacle and conjured a massive leap out of his horse and they once more landed upsides. At this point Dorothy was observed 'furiously hitting Charlie Rogers as the two horses battled together', demanding, 'Why didn't you buy me the other horse, too!'

Up the final lung-busting hill Thomond II could get no nearer to his great rival, and as they passed the post the Miller was in front by three parts of a length, having completed the course in another record-breaking time.

Now there was just a 15-day break before the other great chase in the National Hunt calendar. Briscoe knew the horse was ready, and backed up that judgement with a bet which would net him £10,000 if the Miller triumphed again in the National. Dorothy, he revealed, had invested enough to win her 'a great deal more than this'. Briscoe had a call the weekend before the race from the respected bookmaker Ted Heathorn, who told him that there was so much money riding on the Miller that a no-expense-spared effort was being made to stop him winning at Aintree.

Briscoe took this advice very seriously; amazingly, one of those upon whom suspicion fell was the jockey, Gerry Wilson. As a precaution, the Miller was sent to Liverpool on the Wednesday before the race in the company of two private detectives. The detectives kept an eye on the Miller at night, and his lad slept in the box with him. In the parade ring the horse was adorned with added protective clothing, designed by Dorothy, to guard against any villain squirting acid at him, lending the proceedings an ugly and fearful feel. But still the money contin-ued to pour onto him, and just before the off his price hit 2/1. It had always been felt that the odds were at least 3/1 against any horse getting round Aintree successfully. Dorothy told Briscoe before the race that she did not approve of the punishing gallops he had given the horse in the run-up to the race.

Many modern jockeys will tell you that fence number 11 on the Grand National course is one of those obstacles which, because it has no particular name, has never gained any notoriety, and yet is known to be a tricky and difficult jump. Early on in the race Golden Miller was in the vanguard of the 27-runner field, but as he and Wilson approached the 11th the horse looked as though he was going to refuse. Wilson kicked him in the belly: on the British Pathé newsreel you can clearly see the horse baulking before the fence, then clearing it with an astonishing leap, before pitching Wilson out of the saddle and into infamy. Reynoldstown went on to win the race by three lengths from Blue Prince, with the gallant but exhausted Thomond II in third eight lengths back.

Wilson told a shocked Dorothy and Briscoe that the Miller appeared to fall lame as the pair approached the 11th fence, made a floundering

attempt to jump it and pitched the rider into the turf. Dorothy immediately concluded that her earlier suspicions about the harshness of
the training routine having blunted her horse were correct. She asked
Briscoe to accompany her back to her box, where she unloaded both
barrels in her own uniquely venomous style, telling him in no uncer-
tain terms that he had soured the horse, and that his training of the
Miller in the run-up to the race had been nothing short of disgraceful.
Briscoe shouted back, accused Wilson of lying about what had happened and – worse – alleged the jockey had fallen off the horse deliberately. If it were true that Wilson had been the cause of the incident
and Briscoe suspected he would do something like this, Dorothy spat
back, why he had not done something about it? Briscoe snapped. He
grabbed his gold cigarette case and flung it against the door of the box,
and roared at her that if she felt that way about the whole thing, then
she should 'Take your bloody horse away.'

For once Dorothy and her companions in the box were stunned into
silence. It was at this point that an element of sanity entered the proceedings. As a gesture of reconciliation Dorothy agreed that the Miller should
be examined by the available vets and, if passed fit, he would run in the
Champion Chase the following day.

The Miller was duly sent out to run in the 2-mile-7½-furlong
Champion Chase. He unseated Wilson at the first.

'Miss Paget unfortunately blamed me for the incidents and considered her horse had not been properly trained,' reflected Briscoe, and
before he left Aintree he wrote a letter to Dorothy telling her – and the
press – that her horses would have to be removed from his yard by the
end of the week.

Dorothy had initially been unwilling to be drawn into a public
debate, but realised she needed to issue some form of statement on this
public relations debacle. This was done on 1 April and was obviously
written by Dorothy herself:

Miss Paget asked her trainer after Saturday's race what work
he had given Golden Miller in the interim between Cheltenham
and Liverpool.

The day before, Mr Briscoe had definitely been dissatisfied and mystified
with the way Golden Miller had run.

The jockey had said the horse was never going like his usual self, he felt
[to Gerry Wilson] sore etc. Mr Briscoe would not hear of such a thing.
Miss Paget disagreed with his severe criticism of the jockey and naturally
put up the old successful partnership.

When the disastrous performance was repeated, Miss Paget naturally
felt justified in criticising her trainer, who had the previous day so seriously
criticised and disagreed with her jockey. It is a terrible thing for an owner
when a trainer and jockey disagree. One feels one would like to be loyal to
both. Unfortunately, Miss Paget's trainer has taken the matter entirely into
his own hands by his public statement.

Miss Paget is much upset by the whole matter. As is well known, she
never gives press interviews, but she feels in this case that she has to make
an exception to explain it from her point of view.

Miss Paget is more than grateful to Mr Briscoe for all the wonderful
successes and joy he has brought her through Golden Miller, and wishes
him the best of luck.

As regards Golden Miller's future, nothing has yet been contemplated,
as the whole thing came as such a colossal shock and surprise. He will
probably move into temporary quarters.

In the pubs and clubs of the working classes who had backed the horse,
Wilson's name was muck, amid the commonly-held belief that he was in
the pay of bookies.

Suspicions and gossip remained forever unsubstantiated. Briscoe felt
there was enough evidence to support the theory that Wilson had, in
racing argot, 'stepped off'. Wilson himself conceded to reporters that

film of the race looked damning against him, but later gave his name-
sake, the racing journalist and broadcaster Julian Wilson, his version of
what happened during the National: 'I'm convinced that the Miller was
frightened by what seemed like a mirror glinting in his face. As he came
to the fence something startled him – I was conscious of it myself. He
seemed to freeze, and he never forgot that experience.' The jockey, wrote
Julian Wilson, believed the 'mirror' was in fact 'a flare put down by a
newsreel company to prevent a pirate camera crew from operating on the
far side of the course.'

Stablemen were now sent from Donald Snow's yard to collect seven
horses, including the Miller, from Beechwood House Stables, to be
transferred, albeit temporarily, to Dorothy's cousin-in-law's yard at East-
bury in Berkshire.

For Briscoe, although he could not know it at the time, it was the beginning of the end of his sparkling training career. His heavy gambling certainly did not help, and in 1940 he was declared bankrupt. He died in
1951 following a fall and was buried in a grave alongside that of his young
wife Yvonne in the tiny churchyard at Longstowe.

Dorothy, meanwhile, set about finding a new trainer. There wasn't a
lengthy queue: she herself was one of the primary reasons why.

Walter Nightingall took nearly all of her Flat-racing team and a couple
of National Hunt horses. On Snow's recommendation it was the experienced Owen Anthony to whom the Miller was sent that September – the
brother of established trainers Ivor and Jack Anthony.

A large, jolly bachelor, Welshman Anthony had had his own successes,
winning the Grand National in 1922 with Music Hall and the Gold Cup
in 1927 with Thrown In. Very much a trainer of the old school, he only
plunged in on his horses when he felt the odds were well and truly in his
favour. His new owner very much liked this sort of attitude.

The Miller's first outing from his new headquarters saw him finish
third in a Sandown National Hunt Flat race. In the parade ring, Basil

Briscoe was a clearly still-interested, if saddened, onlooker. The day before New Year's Eve the horse won a chase at Newbury, but in February unseated Wilson five from home at the same course, and was pushed out to 10/1 for the National.

Wilson now realised that his association with the Miller was adversely affecting his reputation, and it was announced that he was to step down as the horse's jockey and be replaced by Evan Williams, a 23-year-old Welshman.

In March 1936, then, the Miller set off at 21/20 in a six-runner field, in heavy going, in his attempt to win a fifth consecutive Cheltenham Gold Cup. The race was uneventful, and Golden Miller duly created more racing history. Dorothy decided not to lead her horse in, instead waiting in the winner's enclosure for him to return to a rapturous welcome. In retrospect this moment of racing history, unlikely to be bettered, becomes ever more incredible.

Now the Miller was prepared for another National bid.

Yet again, though, for the Miller's connections and supporters the Grand National was to be a massive disappointment. Having started off on the outer of a field of 35 in order to allow the horse to see each fence properly, the pair never got past the first. A 100/1 outsider called Oeil de Boeuf crumpled on landing and brought the Miller down, putting him on the ground for the first and only time in his racing life. He reappeared almost three weeks later in the Welsh Grand National at Cardiff, finishing third to round off his season.

For the 1936/37 National Hunt season there was a change of emphasis.

Fulke Walwyn, recently retired from the Army, where he had been an officer, and now making his way in the ranks of professional jockeys, became the 13th jockey to ride the horse. The Miller opened his campaign with a bloodless win at Wincanton in mid-October, then was second in Aintree's Becher Chase.

Evan Williams now regained the ride after Fulke Walwyn broke his arm. The reunited pair won easily at Wincanton on Boxing Day, then dead-heated at Gatwick. 'I have never lost faith in him as an Aintree performer,' pronounced Owen Anthony, adding ominously, 'He will be entered again for the National in March.'

The cancellation of the Gold Cup because of bad weather prevented the horse from winning for the sixth straight year, and meant he was now going to Aintree whether he, or anyone else, liked it or not, and with yet another new jockey, the Irishman and Grand National specialist Danny Morgan.

A late flurry of support saw the Miller go off the 8/1 favourite as King George VI and Queen Elizabeth watched the race from the grand-stand. Morgan steered his mount to the outside of the course as the field approached fence 11 – as far away as possible from the inner line Gerry Wilson had followed. He had also deliberately gone stride for stride with one of the other runners as they approached the ditch, hoping it would give the Miller a lead into the obstacle.

But the jockey's wily planning came to naught. As they approached the fence Morgan could feel his mount's previously relentless stride shorten and falter. He kicked and cursed him, but was essentially pow-erless as the Miller swerved to the left and, rather than jumping over the ditch, jumped into it and, as nimble as you like, jumped out of it, with the stunned jockey still in the plate. As Morgan later recalled, 'He jumped down instead of up.'

The Miller's refusal to take the fence on caused him to baulk at least two other runners, but did not cause outright chaos. Morgan, mad as hell, rode him back from the fence, turned, and had another go. It was no good. The Miller had made his mind up, and refused once again. The great horse's Aintree adventures were over once and for all, and in truth his racing endeavours were from now on moving towards an inevitable conclusion.

But Dorothy's opinion – and Owen Anthony's – was that the horse was in fine fettle and full of enthusiasm, and another tilt at a sixth Gold Cup was a reasonable target.

The summer of 1937 proved unproductive for Dorothy's ambitions on the Flat. In June she lost Ormstead, who had cost her £5,000 as a yearling and never won a race, and in a bizarre incident at Lewes, Blandonette, running in a three-year-old handicap, fell 200 yards from the finish and, attempting to get up, was bumped by another of Dorothy's horses, Malay Lady, pushed into the running rail, broke a shoulder and had to be put down.

The Miller's first big test of the 1937/38 season came in the Prince's Handicap at Sandown in mid-January. Going off at even money in desperate conditions, with hail and sleet dousing the track, he put on a performance which led writer Cyril Luckman to proclaim him to be 'as great as ever and perhaps the greatest ever' after he overhauled Thomond II on the run-in.

The Miller's final prep race for Cheltenham came at Birmingham, where he cruised to a 25-length victory over moderate opposition.

At the Prestbury Park turnstiles on Gold Cup day, 10 March 1938, a record crowd of nearly 20,000 handed their money in – back in 1932 just 5,500 punters had paid to see his first Gold Cup win. The weather was dull but dry, the going good. The Miller opened in the ring at 6/4, finally going off the 7/4 favourite.

With Frenchie Nicholson on board, the horse closed on the leaders at the second last. Airgead Sios made a terrible blunder and Macaulay swerved violently. Both lost critical momentum, and the race was left between the Miller and Morse Code, with the latter closing in. Nicholson produced his whip to encourage his mount for a final effort, while Morgan was not yet persuaded that he needed to summon a similar response from Morse Code, who had moved marginally ahead. Both horses jumped the last cleanly, but Morse Code retained a slender advantage and, despite the deafening urgings of the mighty crowd, the Miller simply could not get back on terms. Two lengths separated the pair as they crossed the line. The stands fell, if not completely silent, then muted in the extreme.

Back at the unsaddling enclosure, someone in the crowd shouted, 'Good old Miller', prompting a roar of approval from the masses. It was a very emotional scene. He was cheered and cheered again as he came for the first and only time at Cheltenham into the second horse's stall. In the aftermath of her beloved horse's defeat Dorothy had nothing to say to the press. Perhaps that should have been enough for the Miller, clearly now a shadow of his former self.

It was not until 1939 was well under way, with most racegoers assuming they'd seen the last of him, that on 23 February Golden Miller finally reappeared, neither looking nor running at his best, finishing seventh of 13 at Newbury. The writing was on the wall.

But it was just two days before the 1939 Gold Cup that Owen Anthony confirmed the Miller would not be running, blaming a lack of fitness. Even then, it took until 15 July 1939 for an announcement that Golden Miller had retired, and that he would be sent to Dorothy's Elsenham Stud Farm in Essex, which she had acquired in 1936. Typically, though, Dorothy drew upon herself a large dollop of public opprobrium when she was asked by a charity to donate a set of the Miller's racing shoes to be auctioned to raise money and refused point blank. Privately she donated a large sum of money to the charity – yet this was never made public, and that was the way she liked it. It was as though she needed to feel alienated from the outside world, and went out of her way to make that happen, even while privately proving herself to be a thoughtful, charitable, caring person.

Awaiting the Miller at their retirement home was his former stablemate, the dual Champion Hurdle winner Insurance, retired several years previously despite being the same age as the Miller. The pair spent most of their time in a large meadow with a stream running through it. A large shed was built for them to allow them to take shelter. The two became great friends, and a third buddy was added to the paddock when Dorothy, in one of her moments of impetuosity, purchased an Anglo-Arabian donkey called Agapanthus – Aggie, for short – who had huge ears and a big personality. Occasional visitors came to visit the Miller – Dorothy often paid a typically nocturnal visit and doled out carrots to her beloved retirees.

Despite the passing years, interest in the Miller never waned, as evidenced by a short British Pathé News film from 1945 showing the Miller and Insurance being led out of their specially-built accommodation for a gallop around the Elsenham paddocks.

Golden Miller was three months shy of 30 when his time finally ran out. By then Dorothy had purchased Ballymacoll Stud in Ireland, and the majority of her broodmares and stallions had been transferred there. Golden Miller, Insurance and the remaining residents at Elsenham were tended to by Percy Purcell and his sons Leslie and Mick. On the morning of 11 January 1957, Mick Purcell entered the Miller's box to find him lying on his side and barely able to raise his head. In a memo to Dorothy from one of her numerous secretaries, the news was broken:

Miss Paget,

Mr Wakely the Vet. telephoned to say he has put Golden Miller down. He has kept his forelock – which Purcell has – but there were no shoes on his feet as Mr. Wakely had ordered them to be taken off recently, he thought it might help his walking as the ground was very soft.

The memo contained stark details of the horse's ultimate decline.

It was only by virtue of her ownership of this hugely loved and wonderfully talented horse that Dorothy emerged unwillingly into the spotlight. Certainly as an unbelievably wealthy young woman whose ability to spend money became legendary she was a great story in her own right, but there were plenty of other such people around in those days who were far more glamorous and equally interesting. But it is often those who don't conform to the accepted norms who attract the most attention. For the public at large she become a curiosity because she was the wildly eccentric and unpredictable owner of Golden Miller. She became an integral part of the horse's story in her own right.

She herself was not remotely concerned about what the public thought of her, reasoning with some justification that as she owned the horse and incurred whatever cost that entailed, she was entitled to make whatever decisions she deemed necessary about anything to do with Golden Miller.

The other aspect of the story – the greatness of the Miller by comparison with other champion jumpers since like Arkle and Kauto Star – has been debated for years, and of course there will never be a resolution. Was Dorothy, who clearly loved the horse, just too hard on him during his career, asking him too many hard questions during his racing life, despite his ability more often than not to come up with the right answer? 'I think Golden Miller was considered by the public to be more important than her,' reflected Sir Peter O'Sullevan, 'but then isn't that always the way, and rightly so? People made allowances for her eccentricities, but many people felt she could have been – as the French say – more *sympathique* with the horse.'

The three-time champion jump jockey and four-time Grand National trainer Fred Rimell had no doubt. Analysing the 1935 failure at Aintree, Rimell said it was not until later in life he realised what was surely only too obvious: that a top horse remains at his real peak for no more than three seasons. 'This,' he maintained, 'is particularly so when he had had a lot of hard races, and that one at Cheltenham [the 1935 Gold Cup] must have taken much more out of Golden Miller than anyone could possibly imagine. From that day he was steadily deteriorating.'

Insurance survived the Miller by about three months, but was one day found collapsed by a brook where he had been drinking water. He was buried alongside the Miller at Elsenham, where headstones still mark the graves. There are fourteen other headstones on either side of these under which were buried the hearts of more of Dorothy's favourites, Red Rufus, Solanum and the mare Bridget among them.

Nine

PONY RACING BREAKS
THE DERBY DUCK

Dorothy and Pat Donoghue, trainer of her ponies at Northolt, discuss the condition of her Double Rose II in the parade ring.

The Pony Turf Club was a body regulating the racing of horses of under 15 hands in the UK from its foundation in 1923 until the early 1950s. It was officially recognised by the Jockey Club in 1924. In 1929, a dedicated racetrack was opened in Northolt in Middlesex, and during the 1930s pony races also took place throughout the south-west of England, as well as at courses in places like Worthing, Chelmsford and Sketty Park near Swansea. The oval-shaped course at Northolt Park covered an area of almost 150 acres and gave racegoers in every enclosure an uninterrupted view of the races from start to finish, as well as comfortable refreshment rooms and bars in every stand and enclosure.

Throughout the thirties there was racing at Northolt Park every Saturday and Monday from mid-March until November, with evening racing on summer Wednesdays. In 1937 a record 236,000 racegoers visited Northolt Park, and the £496,000 gambled via Tote bets was also a course record. 'It was without a doubt the best-appointed track for its size that this country has ever known,' declared Geoffrey Hamlyn, who covered racing and betting there for the *Sporting Life*. Much though

Dorothy Paget wanted to win *the* Derby, it would be at Northolt that she would finally win a Classic of that name.

Having already taken a great interest in hunting and racing, it was no surprise that once Dorothy became aware of pony racing she wanted to be involved. 'Every owner with a large string has a number of under-sized animals,' notes Quintin Gilbey, 'and Dorothy Paget was no exception.' When Pat Donoghue, son of the ten-times champion jockey and six-times Derby winner Steve Donoghue, retired from riding and began training ponies at Sandown Lodge in Epsom, Dorothy asked him to take on her runners, becoming his major owner. In order to accommodate her large number of ponies he moved to Woodruffe stables in Ashtead, near Epsom. She also took on the jockey Tommy Carey to ride them for her.

Dorothy was one of the biggest supporters of pony racing at Northolt, and in 1937 she began farming its biggest events, when her Double Rose II was too good for the other 20 runners in the Harrow Cup, run over five furlongs and worth £300. This 'quality pony' won several races there, and Dorothy sent her to one of her own good sires, Wyndham, via whom she produced a very useful thoroughbred, Daily Mail, who would finish second in Newmarket's Free Handicap.

The following year, Dorothy's Donoghue-trained Scottish Rifle, a son of Epsom Derby winner Cameronian, won the six-furlong Champion Two Years Old Plate at the course, worth 500 sovereigns at 1/8 (the prohibitive odds no doubt reflecting Dorothy's enormous wager) against nine opponents. When her Crumb won a race at Alexandra Park in April, the *Guardian* pointed out that 'the filly was intended for Northolt but won her race in a style so convincing that it is apparent she would have a bright future under the senior code.' This shows that the sport at Northolt was of a decent standard. The year ended with Dorothy as the top owner at Northolt, with winning prize money of £1,900, despite her Night March failing to win what was claimed to be, at 44 inches high, the largest-ever racing trophy, the British Empire Cup. But with spectator numbers and Tote turnover both dropping significantly at the course, Northolt was experiencing financial problems that forced it to bring in a receiver and threatened its future.

Someone else experiencing financial problems not of their own making was the artist Dorothy had commissioned to produce a portrait of Golden Miller. Thomas Percy Earl had duly painted her equine hero in oils, having previously done likewise for Insurance, her Champion Hurdle winner. But this time, it appears, there may have been a little friction between artist and patron.

'I took pretty good care that the likeness of Golden Miller should be all that I could make it', noted Earl – working in the open air with the horse standing in a paddock at Exning until he was confident the result would please Dorothy. He showed it off first: 'I am quite satisfied with the picture, and so are my friends who have seen it and know the horse well.'

But it seems Dorothy wasn't satisfied at all, to the point that she had overlooked payment for his work. So Mr Earl turned up, unannounced, at Dorothy's Balfour Place residence in London to discuss the matter. Having made no leeway he resorted to writing to her – again – on 21 June 1939, pointing out that 'no notice' had been taken 'of my letters concerning the picture'. Eventually he learned from one of Dorothy's secretaries, Mme Fregosi, the reason why he had not received a cheque. Earl wasn't going to accept this: 'My reputation as a portrait painter of animals is at stake and as that is my livelihood I cannot submit to what I consider unfair judgement', especially as Mme Fregosi had indicated to him that Dorothy would like him to have another go. 'Certainly I will paint another,' he replied, 'if you will pay for this one.' The eventual resolution is unclear, but in 2012 the painting was sold at auction for $9,808 US dollars.

Also in June 1939 Scottish Rifle went off at 1/2 favourite in the Northolt Derby, and saw off his five rivals under Tommy Carey, who, together with trainer Donoghue, had now won the same race four times in the previous five years. A delighted Dorothy accompanied her Derby winner back to the winner's enclosure after a victory which saw William Hill's runner, Win Over, dead-heating for second place. The Derby win pushed Dorothy towards becoming the leading owner of 1939 at the course too, with 19 victories.

Many high-profile bookies 'stood' at Northolt Park, and Dorothy's secretaries, remembered Geoffrey Hamlyn, whose job it was to report on the betting rings there, 'would arrive on the rails and give a £5,000 bet to Ernie Hunter Simmonds, William Hill and Billy Chandler.' Once she moved into betting action at the course, 'it was often impossible for a layer to quote a realistic price about her runners, so lopsided a book would he have.' Hamlyn estimated that every £1,000 Dorothy staked back in the 1930s was the equivalent of a £32,000 stake at the time his book appeared in 1994. When Scottish Rifle landed the 1939 Metropolitan Plate over one mile, worth 500 sovereigns as a three-year-old, it was at odds of 1/10, largely down to Dorothy placing the biggest bet ever recorded at the course, of £10,000 to £1,000 (the equivalent of £600,000 today).

William Hill bet on the rails at Northolt between 1933 and 1939 as he began to create a name for himself in the bookmaking world. At Northolt he began to take regular business from Dorothy, and soon their relationship was sparking rumours. These were eventually given voice by the racing writer Richard Baerlein, who opined that at the course William 'had a lot of help, as he was in close contact with Tommy Carey, the leading rider, who was retained by Miss Dorothy Paget, the leading owner.' Indeed, according to the racing journalist Ivor Herbert, 'William Hill never bet on a racecourse proper until the Second World War in 1940. He amassed some capital betting on pony races at Northolt, Middlesex, before the war, where he found the jockeys particularly co-operative. This was especially true of the leading rider, Tommy Carey.' The respected trainer Barry Hills spells it out more categorically: 'It has been suggested that William's system at Northolt Park in the early days was quite simple: he laid heavy gambler Dorothy Paget on her horses, then ridden by her jockey Tommy Carey, who was retained – but the good news [for William] was that he [Carey] was stopping them for him – but not so good for Miss P., as she was called. Everyone started somewhere.'

John Hislop, who was champion amateur jockey on the Flat for 13 consecutive seasons, started riding for Dorothy after the war, and told a cracking story about 'the greatest bookmaker of my time', William Hill, and Tommy Carey:

> I was standing near the rails one day at Newmarket when the late Tommy Carey came up to him and said, 'What's mine, Bill?'
> '6/1.'
> 'I'll have 6,000/1.'
> 'Right. 6,000/1 [naming the horse] for T. Carey.'
> Hill then immediately called out '7/1', knocking the horse out a point, somewhat to Carey's consternation and embarrassment.
> The horse lost.

Dorothy's long-running support for Tommy Carey has always been difficult for racing historians to understand. Born in 1905, he had been apprenticed to Stanley Wootton as a teenager and initially rode over jumps, but at 16 had turned to the Flat. His career stalled due to a lack of support from owners. Changing course, in tandem with Pat Donoghue, he took the pony racing scene by storm.

But Carey also had a reputation as 'one of the most professional villains' in the racing game, in the words of Chris McNamee, who worked for him in later years. Carey 'did a lot of punting', and wasn't averse to misleading his owners, and once managed to sell a filly for an enhanced price after staging a trial over five furlongs with two other horses, but managing to bring the filly in after three furlongs so she was fresher and more impressive than her opponents.

McNamee said that when working for Carey he soon learned

to keep my mouth shut or I'd be sacked. The strokes he got up to were
unbelievable. He was a pretty hard man to take to. The bottom line
with Carey was that he made a lot of money, fell out with most of those
he worked with, treated his wife like dirt, and died penniless. I'll always
remember him pulling off one of his strokes and coming back with
jodhpurs full of bank notes.

A rather extraordinary story from this time that involves both Dorothy
and William Hill comes from *Racing Post* reader Bruce Atkinson:

My father's family were mid-Sussex farmers, and in 1939 took
delivery of a brand new horsebox, having recently started a horse
transport business. As a young boy, nicknamed Curly, father was
introduced to Dorothy Paget who employed him to carry some
of her horses to the races.
Dorothy loved cock-fighting, although illegal, and she asked Curly
to bring some roosters to Cheltenham races. Dorothy usually got her own
way, so Curly was well paid to procure a bunch of cocks and put them
in a sectioned-off part of the horsebox above the cab. Dorothy had booked
the top two floors of the Queens Hotel, Cheltenham, for her private party,
using the staircase as the cock-fighting arena. I think Billy Hill was there
to take her bets.

Though war in Europe would only be a few weeks away, in July 1939
Dorothy entered four horses for a race meeting in Munich at which the
principal prize was the 'Brown Ribbon of Germany' – perhaps to tie in
with seeing Olili in Germany, though whether owner or horses actually travelled is unclear. An Australian newspaper didn't pull its punches,
headlining the story NAZI RACING.

But Dorothy was worried by the threat of war, and had been considering whether to move out of her London house at Balfour Place, presumably in fear of the capital being bombed. Her staff began negotiations for her to lease a property in Chalfont St Giles in Buckinghamshire.

Hermits Wood had been bought in 1928 by Lady Mabel Blair, the wife of Sir Reginald Blair, a former Conservative MP who had become the first chairman of the Racehorse Betting Control Board, later 'the Tote'. The appropriateness of the name of Dorothy's new abode to her lifestyle has often been remarked on, but it seems the consonance was entirely coincidental, as it already bore that name when she became the owner – indeed, had been called the Hermitage when Lady Blair acquired it. It was a large property with four reception rooms, eight principal and four staff bedrooms, three bathrooms, central heating, garaging for three cars, a lodge and cottage each with its own bathroom, well-maintained gardens with lawns, fruit and vegetable kitchen gardens, a paddock and woodland, and altogether over 40 acres of land.

The negotiations were hardly smooth: Mme Fregosi's valuation of the annual rent at £4,000, 'if as much', received a rude shock with Sir Reginald's request for £12,000: Mme Fregosi managed to get it down to £10,000, but 'I still consider it excessive.' It's unclear how long Dorothy leased the property for before she bought it outright. The embattled secretary was further vexed when Sir Reginald

calmly informed me that the Chauffeur's Cottage – which is needed for me to sleep in – would not be furnished. His agent, after I had protested that I had taken a furnished place and not an unfurnished one, suggested that he would reduce the rent – by £20 per annum! I was furious and told the agent I must insist upon the cottage being furnished. This is being done. I find Sir Reginald very Scotch!

War was declared on 3 September 1939, and by November the future of pony racing at Northolt was under severe threat. Pat Donoghue, according to his father's biographer, advised Dorothy to 'get rid of all your ponies. It is now a dead loss. Pony racing will certainly not be resumed after the war.' That month she sold Scottish Rifle for £180, and went on to sell all but four of her ponies.

'Thus Pat had an almost empty yard.' It was a terrible setback for Donoghue, who depended almost exclusively on Dorothy Paget's ponies for his livelihood, and he was left virtually unemployed and having to make a brief comeback in the saddle. But it proved to be an opportunity for his father, Steve, who had previously ridden for Dorothy, and now moved into the yard to launch his own training career. Scottish Rifle was eventually exported to Malaya during the war to be trained by the Englishman Michael Silley – both trainer and horse were captured by the Japanese in 1941.

Northolt Park closed in June 1940, when the land was taken over for a prisoner-of-war camp. It never re-opened. Dorothy now applied to the Jockey Club for a licence for Tommy Carey to ride her Flat horses. It was granted in 1941, and so began his hugely successful second career as a Flat jockey. It would also see him play his part in Dorothy's greatest wartime triumph in racing.

Ten

WARTIME DERBY

Horse racing's ultimate prize is the Derby. Not only owning, but also breeding Straight Deal to win the accepted major Classic race, the Blue Riband event, effectively placed Dorothy amongst the sport's immortal figures forever more.

Dorothy found herself abroad when war broke out, in Aix, almost certainly with Olili. Back in England, however, things were changing fast. Mme Fregosi discovered that Dorothy's London residence in Balfour Place was being virtually requisitioned by the government: 'I was told that five adults and fifteen children were being sent here,' she wrote to her employer. 'More would have been sent had I not assured them that you were returning from France.' So she had decided to take action on her own initiative. 'I thought you would by far rather your own staff should be here than when you returned, a host of strangers.'

But when Dorothy found out that a member of her staff had ensconced herself at Balfour Place – indeed, had brought another colleague, Mme Djakelly, with her – she was not best pleased, and instructed another member of staff, Mme Orloff, to tell Mme Fregosi as much.

'You do not realise what it was like in England at the outbreak of war,' responded a wounded Mme Fregosi.

The government asked everybody to leave London, and inhabitants were installed everywhere they could be put.

If you wish me to leave your house I will, of course, do so at once.
I will have to leave before dark, as it is quite impossible to find one's way
about after dark. I wrote you on September 1 that I was moving down
to Northaw [in Hertfordshire] with the rest of your staff,

she continued indignantly, 'and I cannot think why I have not heard, only today, in a letter written four weeks after war had been declared.

But out in the south of France Dorothy appears to have been rather distracted, by, of all things, a fishing trip. 'I went this morning at 8 a.m. to see the fisherman,' writes her anonymous correspondent, presumably some kind of ghillie:

the man will be waiting for us between 12 and 1. The baits are: small
fish, worms, paste, and the spoon.

Following my conversation, he advised me to let you know that because
of the bad weather he did not go fishing yesterday, so he has no small fish,
but would get them if we could postpone our trip till tomorrow.

The best place for fishing is Hautecombe and that is where he would
like to take us. It would take 30 to 45 minutes to get there.

This morning the mist was very heavy on the lake but was lifting.
The air was very cold and damp.

Five days later, Mme Fregosi was writing to Dorothy again from Balfour Place.

I am expecting an official to call one of these days in regard to billeting
some soldiers here.

If this war is going to continue (which I personally do not think)
it would be just as well to give this place up if you have no intention
of staying here, as it seems a pity to keep it on for nothing.

But I would not advise giving it up until you have seen Hermits Wood.

Negotiations were finally concluded on the new property in Chalfont St Giles, and it was going to be available to move into from late September. Mme Fregosi wrote again on the 26th in a somewhat admonitory tone:

I have just returned from Hermits Wood with Carter. We both liked it better. Although we agree it is not the type of house you are used to, but it is wartime, and things may never be the same again. You will find things very different when you return, everything will be rationed...

Despite there being a war on, and all the ructions between them, Mme Fregosi still managed to send Dorothy by telegram the information so vital for her to decide where to bet her money:

Nightingall reports Isleham Plate, Apple King, very fair. Chesterfield Ann very fair. Taquinette very small chance. Cambridgeshire: Fairfax only sporting chance; Clare Plate, Heskett not a betting chance; Beaufort Plate, Racla very good chance, STOP; Thursday, Fairyfriend no, will improve; Anarchist has chance; Anthony fancies Ard Macha a little each-way; Butters says Bandinelli well but no chance.

While she was in Aix Dorothy paid a visit to the Château de Garibondy in Le Cannet, near Cannes, which had been in the family for years, acquired by Dorothy's English grandparents back in the late 19th century, and here she met a young Russian girl, in her early teens.

In 2016 Tatiana Chomcheff was 89 years old, but still remembered what a glamorous figure Dorothy seemed to her, with her chauffeur and her secretary.

She used to be around during the school holidays, and would have
parties at the château with friends. My little brother, then about five,
was often invited by the governess to come and play at the château and
occasionally stayed the night. I used to go to pick him up and Miss Paget
was very friendly to me. She allowed me to walk round the gardens,
and I often went to the market with the governess and chauffeur to help
with the shopping – I was even given a drawing of Dorothy at that time
which I still have.

Much later, in the mid-1970s, Tatiana became involved with the work
of the 'Russian cemetery' in Paris, eventually becoming president of the
association which looks after it. Coincidentally it was the very same
cemetery where the elderly Russian émigrés from the retirement home
Dorothy had funded for Princess Mestchersky were buried. When the
Germans swept into France and Paris was taken in June 1940, however,
a distraught Dorothy found herself unable to stay in contact with the
Russian Home; she would be further distressed to find that the money
she had endowed it with to last the war had by 1941 run out. This setback
would be another blow to her already fragile equanimity.

Once Dorothy had decided to return home, of course, wartime travel
restrictions made getting back far from easy, and she had to plan to have
her cars and luggage shipped back from Bordeaux. But she made it back,
and took up residence at Hermits Wood.

All horse racing in Britain had been cancelled when war broke out,
though it had resumed in October at Newmarket. Dorothy Paget's
racing empire, however, hardly missed a beat – in fact, although the
glorious Golden Miller era was over, it was expanding at an incredible rate, in both Flat and National Hunt codes. At the start of the
war she had an estimated hundred racehorses in training. In the early
war years, according to the racing writer Bob Harman, some saw
Dorothy's numerically dominant presence in many races – for the 1940

Cheltenham Festival she had entered no fewer than 48 horses, then seven in the Derby, nine in the St Leger and nineteen for four 'Royal' Ascot races – as somehow 'unpatriotic'. A number of other owners had been declining to run their horses, fearing racing was 'detrimental' to the war effort. Dorothy, however, says Quintin Gilbey, 'explained her obsession away by claiming that racing is essential for preserving the morale of the country.' Sir Peter O'Sullevan valued her contribution far more highly. 'It would be fair to say that British racing does owe Dorothy Paget something,' he said. 'During the war years she almost singlehandedly kept racing going in this country through her blood-stock purchases and the fact she retained so many trainers.' Many more successes were to come.

Dorothy would sometimes travel to the races by rail, generally booking a whole carriage to herself and making sure she wasn't troubled while dining in the restaurant car by block-booking whole tables – sometimes eating most of the meals served, too. When she arrived at the course she would disappear into her private box to watch the races. After the last she would lock herself in the lavatory, the door of which would be guarded by a phalanx of secretaries until almost all the other racegoers had departed, when she would emerge and sit down to eat a huge meal, attended by one or more of her trainers.

Caroline Ramsden, whose father was chairman of Manchester race-course, recalled Dorothy racing on successive days at Manchester and asking for food and drink to be laid on for her and her trainer after the last race. Caroline's father ensured that Miss P. and her party were being looked after before heading home to Stockport – only to be telephoned some hours later by the racecourse caretaker, who wanted to leave for the day but informed him that Miss Paget and her party were still occupying the club room. She didn't finally depart until gone 10 p.m.

There was a further Gold Cup triumph in 1940 with Roman Hackle, the even-money favourite, completing another memorable double after

Solford, from the Owen Anthony stable and also favourite, won the Champion Hurdle by a length and a half, despite losing his protective boots en route. In Ireland Dorothy provided a cup for the first hurdle race to be held at Phoenix Park for 35 years, which the course named the Dorothy Paget Cup. Fifteen winners, worth £1,325 in prize money, made her the most prolific owner of the 1940/41 National Hunt season.

From September 1940 the capital faced up to the onslaught of the Blitz, as the Luftwaffe launched air raids on 57 consecutive nights, killing some 20,000 and destroying or damaging around one million houses. 'In case of an air raid,' the racecard for Plumpton's February 1941 meeting warned racegoers, 'the public is requested to act promptly, on the instructions of the police. The presence of enemy aircraft in the vicinity will be notified to the public by short blasts on police whistles.'

Dorothy needed somewhere safe to store her two valuable Rolls-Royces, and the National Hunt and Flat trainer Cliff Beechener offered Top Barn at his farm in Denton in Northamptonshire. 'The cars were put up on blocks to preserve the tyres,' remembered his daughter Angela Macintosh,

> the rotor arms removed and put into the bank for safekeeping, and the mascots detached and left on our mantelpiece for the duration. One foggy Sunday afternoon, a stray German bomb was dropped within yards of Top Barn and the resulting crater became a pond, but the cars were luckily undamaged. Immediately after the war, the chauffeur arrived with the rotor arms; on refitting, both cars started first time!

The sport of racing had political support from the Prime Minister, Winston Churchill, and his cabinet colleagues, who were aware that the British people needed some small distraction from the privations and sacrifice demanded by a total war, but by 1942 National Hunt racing was so severely curtailed by the war that during the whole season there were only eighteen days of racing, and virtually confined to Cheltenham in the south and Wetherby in the north. Early in the season Dorothy's Champion Hurdler Solford, trained at Epsom by Bill Payne after Owen Anthony's death, fell at Worcester and broke his back. Then on 10 September a notice appeared in the *Racing Calendar* which brought National Hunt racing to a juddering halt: 'The Stewards of the National Hunt Committee have received notification from His Majesty's Government that they are unable to sanction National Hunt Racing during the season 1942/43.'

Dorothy therefore took advantage of a lifting of the ban by the Stewards of the Irish National Hunt Committee on horses who had not been in Ireland before 15 June 1941, and duly sent Roman Hackle and several other horses over to be trained there by Charlie Rogers. In 1943 Roman Hackle was slated to run in the Irish Grand National at Fairyhouse on Easter Monday; he didn't, but Dorothy won it anyway with Golden Jack, like Golden Miller a son of Goldcourt. The victory of the 5/2 second favourite, unplaced last time out, resulted in a stewards' inquiry, following which Charlie Rogers was 'severely censured' and 'warned as to his future conduct'.

At the same time Dorothy had brought almost two dozen yearlings over from Ireland to Walter Nightingall's stables, a decision that, in these times of stringent rationing, resulted in a question being asked in the House of Commons.

Nightingall had been training for Dorothy since 1936, and they had gained their first winner together that year with Wheatley, in a hurdle race at Gatwick. He had trained 55 winners in his first season as a trainer, and won his first Classic in 1930 with Rock Star in the Irish Derby. From the outset Dorothy required weekly written reports from him on every one of the horses he trained for her. It was a chore he came to hate.

Dorothy's wartime activities, however, were by no means limited to horse racing. She threw herself into helping the Women's Voluntary Service through their branch in Rickmansworth, and had an ambulance custom-built and fitted with a refrigerator, cots and other equipment to evacuate babies from London to safer homes in the country. Indeed, *Racing Review* magazine suggested she presented the WVS, who played a key part in the evacuation of civilians from urban areas, and are credited with helping to move 1.5 million people (the majority of them children) out of cities in the early days of the war, with a whole fleet of ambulances. She further donated £1,000 to the Red Cross and the St John's Fund for Sick and Wounded in War, and £750 in September 1940 to the Lord Mayor's Air Raid Distress Fund.

The following month she presented a mobile canteen to the WVS at Rickmansworth for the use of civil defence services and troops. In 1942 she funded 'toddlers' parties' near Hermits Wood, and the WVS opened a 'gift clothing depot' with its fittings given by Dorothy. At the end of the year she sounded out the WVS about supplying money for school Christmas parties, but was advised her money would be better spent with them on 'destitute and poor families, and old people in hospitals.' She gave a cheque for £75. She donated again in 1943 as the WVS supplied items to a local Troop Welfare camp, paid for four chairs for 'a neighbouring searchlight station', gave the Red Cross £500 more, then provided 2,500 cigarettes for troops of the 8th Army attending local film shows, which were 'very much appreciated'.

Olili, meanwhile, much to Dorothy's distress, spent most, if not all, of the period, it seems, in Germany, and having a somewhat more eventful war than her English friend. In August 1942, according to the White Russian émigré Marie Vassiltchikov's 1987 book *The Berlin Diaries 1940–45*, the Schloss Johannisberg, next door to where Olili lived, was hit during an air raid. 'The Mumms…had seen the flames and hurried over. Olili Mumm, with a steel helmet poised rakishly at an angle of 45 degrees, jumped onto chairs, and cut some of the pictures out of their frames with scissors. They managed to save quite a lot of things but everything upstairs perished.'

Having now been living at Hermits Wood for some three years, Dorothy added to her portfolio the nearby Pollardswood (also known as Pollards Wood) Grange, a large cottage-style house with a thatched gate-house and no fewer than eleven bedrooms and four bathrooms, set in six acres of wooded grounds. But within a few months it was requisitioned by the Government for the Special Operations Executive (SOE), the organisation established by Hugh Dalton in 1940 to conduct espionage, sabotage and reconnaissance operations in occupied Europe. Later in the war the Grange was used by Polish air crews, and according to Bernard O'Connor's book *RAF Tempsford* 'all the ground staff, kitchen staff and other personnel were said to speak Polish.'

With jump racing in Britain suspended – it would not resume until January 1945 – Dorothy now concentrated on the Flat, and by 1943 its season had also been restricted, to meetings on just 39 days. Southern meetings – at Windsor, Ascot and Salisbury – were open only to horses trained south of the Trent, northern meetings at Pontefract and Stockton only to those trained north of it. Other than for the Classics run there, only Newmarket-trained horses were eligible to race at Newmarket.

Dorothy persisted with Tommy Carey as her principal jockey, though just why remains difficult to fathom. Nonetheless, she appeared to have no qualms about his loyalty and integrity. She even supported him, says Chris McNamee, when he lost his licence for a particular misdemeanour, apparently for ensuring he didn't carry as much weight on horses as he should have done, and 'refused to run her horses if he wasn't given his licence back.' She once fell out with trainer Fred Darling when she told him she wanted Carey to replace Gordon Richards on one of her horses. Darling immediately told her that if she persisted with the idea she could remove her horses from his stable there and then. This time she did back down.

On 17 April Dorothy decided to go to Salisbury races, in a hire car, ending up in trouble with the law for going more than 75 miles from where it was normally kept, and was duly fined £25 with ten guineas costs. The case was delayed by nine days because she had failed to turn up for the original hearing, claiming to be 'indisposed', and she found herself 'strongly advised' by the magistrate not to appear in front of him again on similar charges.

The 1943 Derby came round on Saturday, 19 June, moved from Epsom to Newmarket during the war and run over its Suffolk Stakes course. A hefty percentage of the crowd was in uniform, and military police were prowling around checking identities. Given the difficulties of travelling in wartime – there were just 177 cars in the car park but several thousand bicycles – the official attendance of 9,755 represented a decent effort. Afterwards, the London trains were besieged with home-going crowds, carriages crammed tight with dozens standing in nearly every compartment.

Dorothy's horse in the field of 22 was Straight Deal, a medium-sized bay colt foaled at Elsenham in 1940. Sired by the Ascot Gold Cup winner Solario, he was one of only three foals produced by his dam, Good Deal, who although from an undistinguished family had scored seven wins on the track, netting a total of £4,000 in prize money. Carrying number 17 and partnered by Tommy Carey, he went off at a starting price of 100/6.

Straight Deal had been brought carefully to peak form by Walter Nightingall, and in a driving finish the horse won by a head, in a time of 2 minutes 30⅖th seconds. As well as having listened to her trainer and had a decent investment in her runner, Dorothy had now emulated her grandfather and bettered her father! Planes flying overhead added to the excitement, and on Pathé News footage a delighted Dorothy can be seen patting the horse in the paddock, smiling and shaking hands with Nightingall.

There is always another contest coming along in the racing world, and after the Derby along came the Coventry Stakes, one of the principal two-year-old races of the season. It was won by Orestes – also owned by Dorothy. 'Not a bad half hour for Miss Paget!' noted *Racing Review*. 'When one of her horses is running she can hardly keep her glasses sufficiently steady to make out the colours, so great is her excitement.'

Perhaps because Dorothy was his owner, some racing figures sought to play down her achievement in not only winning the great race but also breeding Straight Deal.

'Not a very good racehorse,' wrote Derby historian Vincent Orchard; 'Second class Derby,' sneered the *Sporting Life*'s Les Scott.

Since Straight Deal was not being transported back to Epsom until the following day, Dorothy invited the Nightingalls to meet her at his stable for 'a little celebration' – but when the others arrived she merely gave the horse a congratulatory pat, pulled a hip flask of brandy from her voluminous blue-and-yellow racing handbag, took a swig and passed it round.

Straight Deal went on to start 100/30 favourite for the St Leger, but could only manage third place and was retired to stud, eventually going off to stand at Dorothy's Ballymacoll Stud. Disappointing as the defeat was, Dorothy could nevertheless look back on what had been a stunted, but very successful campaign and she ended up as the 1943 season's leading Flat owner – the only year she achieved this feat. Her total prize money of £13,445, from 26 races won by 16 of her horses, was well ahead of Lord Derby on £7,045, the Aga Khan on £5,596 and Lord Rosebery on £4,585. 'Since the days of Caroline, Duchess of Montrose,' gushed the *Guardian*, 'no woman has been so prominent in racing.' Even turf traditionalists like Rosebery were warming to Dorothy: 'She is certainly a greater asset to racing than the Aga (Khan),' he wrote in a private letter to Lord Derby, 'and it was with feelings of great relief that I saw her animal emerging to beat the Aga's pair.' Rosebery's *schadenfreude* can only have been intensified the following season when Dorothy entered no fewer than 40 horses for the 1944 Classics, while the Aga Khan had to make do with a mere 25! On top of all this Walter Nightingall had comfortably won the 1943 trainers' championship, while Tommy Carey finished second in the jockeys' championship.

Not long before the June 1944 Normandy landings, Dorothy learned that one of her horses had suffered a fatal accident during a race in Ireland. Unable to discover any more information, she instructed one of her secretaries to contact the well-known racing correspondent for the *Daily Sketch*, Norman Pegg, to see whether he could assist. Pegg wrote subsequently of 'a personal experience which revealed the true nature of a woman who was admired by the racing world, yet puzzled it.

> *As part of the cloud of secrecy which descended on this country, all contact, telegraphic and telephonic, with Ireland was virtually cut off. To get through a call you had to obtain the consent of a military high-up, and consent was next door to impossible.*
>
> *A secretary phoned me to say that Miss P. had read somewhere in a newspaper that a steeplechaser of hers had met with a fatal accident at the Curragh. Could I find out for certain what had happened, or, indeed, if the report was true? The secretary explained that Miss P. was particularly fond of the chaser in question.*
>
> *I went to no end of trouble to try to obtain the official OK for a phone call, but was turned down, and it was not till weeks later that Miss Paget learned the report was true.*
>
> *The story was of the real Miss Paget. The Miss Paget so many reporters found taciturn was really a shy woman, and at times a spoiled woman. She just liked to remain in the background, and enjoy her racing unmolested.*

Eleven

A BREED APART

Dorothy purchased the Ballymacoll Stud in Ireland – but never actually saw for herself the scene captured above, as she did not ever pay the Stud a personal visit.

During the war, Dorothy had controversially maintained her racecourse presence by supporting the sport wherever possible, believing that Flat racing was the key to the bloodstock industry, and that unless the sires and dams of tomorrow were tested on the racecourse, breeders would have no means of establishing which horses are best fitted to pass down their bloodlines. Shortly after Straight Deal had won the Derby, the *Guardian* had paid her dedication the highest compliment: 'Miss Paget is not only our largest owner but our largest breeder, her stud farm being at Elsenham, in Essex, where the late Sir Walter Gilbey bred heavy horses and hackneys.' 'Miss Paget did not breed for sale,' confirmed Olili de Mumm shortly after her death, 'and therefore not for quick returns, her intention being to breed horses which stayed one and a half miles. The offspring of this policy will, therefore benefit British bloodstock for many years to come.'

Dorothy had started buying mares in 1933 with a view to breeding her own racehorses, as a way of cutting back on the need to spend big at the sales, and then in 1936 had bought the stud at Elsenham. Having to send many of her horses to Ireland during the war, however, must have influenced her decision to expand her breeding interests by acquiring an Irish stud to add to her English one.

In April 1946, therefore, she acquired the Ballymacoll Estate in County Meath. Founded by Henry Hamilton, it had remained in the Hamilton family's hands until 1911, when it was sold to Lord Nugent. Other owners and tenants followed, and during the Second World War it had been taken over by the Irish Army. She didn't visit it before purchase. What she paid is not known, but when Lord Sobell bought it in 1960 after her death, he paid £250,000 for the 300 acres and 130 horses.

There is, nevertheless, an element of Irish blarney about how Dorothy actually came to own Ballymacoll. When the war ended, the Irish Army decided Ballymacoll was now surplus to requirements and Tom Carr, who was managing the property, was told to arrange its sale. A local Post Office linesman, Paddy Kennedy, was instructed to take out the telephone lines to the stud. Starting work, he overheard a phone conversation between the trainer Charlie Rogers and his brother George, in which Charlie said he needed accommodation in a hurry for 41 horses being sent to him from Dorothy Paget in England.

Sniffing a chance to 'broker' a favour for his friends, from which he might benefit personally, Kennedy quickly contacted George, and within a matter of hours Charlie had contacted Dorothy and persuaded her that acquiring the stud would be an ideal solution: not only would it provide a suitable base for her immediate Irish racing interests, but it could also have a long-term future as part of her ambitious breeding plans. Soon she was the owner of the stud farm – and the phone lines never had to be removed. Charlie Rogers was appointed stud manager, a position he would retain until his death in July 1971, and set about bringing in stallions and brood mares to make Ballymacoll a true breeding establishment. One of his early successes was persuading Dorothy to send her Derby winner Straight Deal to stand at the stud.

'Charlie Rogers was the man who put this place on the map,' confirms Peter Reynolds, who took over from him as stud manager, running the place successfully for over 40 years for the Sobell and Weinstock families who purchased it on Dorothy's passing: Rogers was the man who populated the stud with the stock that would eventually bring Ballymacoll to prominence as the breeder of 29 individual Group 1 winners of over 50 Group 1 races, including Troy, Pilsudski, Islington, Sun Princess, North Light, Conduit and, more recently, Fiorente, the 2013 Melbourne Cup winner.

Effectively it was Charlie Rogers' own fiefdom. Given that she trusted him so much he pretty much did what he liked here. He was able to tap into a bottomless pit of money, and there were probably too many horses here. Dorothy was in the same league then as someone like Sheikh Mohammed is now.

Straight Deal was not a good enough sire to have been important in the development of Ballymacoll. He was a good sire, but the thing about him was that it was Charlie's idea to have him here as a Derby winner. It would have been good for Ballymacoll because he would have been an attractive stallion for local people to bring their mares to.

Ballymacoll still turns out produce from the same bloodlines Dorothy established several generations ago. I am not sure she knew a lot about breeding, but if you employ the right people and get the right advice then you'll get the job done. We have eighteen mares at the moment, sixteen descended from the same mares that were here when Michael Sobell took over.

If you go back and look at, say, 1951, where we had a mare called Jamaica, and if you come right through the line from her you will find horses like Conduit, a King George winner, or Sun Princess, who was an Oaks winner, and they are all from the same family – one of our main families. Also back in 1951 would be Coventry Belle. Go down her line

*and you'll find Islington, winner of four Group One races including two
Breeders' Cups for Sir Michael Stoute.*

*Desert Bloom bred the Melbourne Cup winner Fiorente. These are
the families we inherited from Dorothy. Any decent success we have had
has come from these families.*

According to Quintin Gilbey, Dorothy may have been rather too
trusting of those she tasked with supplying her with horses. 'Dorothy
Paget was God's gift to breeders and, in giving what amounted to a blank
cheque to her agents, she was playing into the hands of the unscrupu-
lous…it is a big temptation for a breeder to get a friend to "run up"
his horse in the knowledge that this bid would be capped.' But despite
Dorothy's wealth, Peter Reynolds is firm in his belief that Charlie Rogers
was not a reckless spender of her money, and that many of her horses
were purchased quite cheaply. 'Some of them, like Coventry Belle, if
you look them up and check their racing ability, they were not fantastic
racehorses. A lot of them came from National Hunt stock and were not
in any way precocious, yet they turned out to be tough and they bred
tough horses too.' Thus it has to be concluded that, in an era in which
she was taking on a lot of major English breeders, Dorothy was very
successful at it. 'It was very competitive then,' says Peter Reynolds, 'but
when Dorothy came into the breeding business she had no experience of
it and she had to compete with people who had been doing it for years.
And she proved to be very good at it.'

Brendan Lynch, now in his eighties, worked for Charlie Rogers for
23 years from 1949. His assessment of the relationship between Dorothy
and Rogers, whom he remembers as a no-nonsense man with quite
a short temper, was that it was based on implicit trust.

*Dorothy trusted his judgement completely. There was no one like him,
as far as she was concerned. A lot of trainers fell out with her because*

she interfered with things, but Charlie never gave a damn what she did. He let her do what she wanted, and I suppose that was because he knew she was the one paying the piper. She had a reputation as a very mulish woman who treated men very badly, but she was different with Charlie for whatever reason.

It was funny that she was so loyal to Charlie, considering the way she went through trainers. They got on famously. Dorothy used to call Charlie 'Romeo', and she was on the phone an awful lot to him. But he was an awful man, and he used to tell her all sorts of things about how he'd been watching the horses on the gallops – and he'd have never been near the gallops. He used to butter her up no end. Danny Daly was the head man at the stud, and when any of Dorothy's pals would be coming over the whole place would be gone over, to ensure things were spick and span at all times.

In many ways Ballymacoll, when Charlie was running it for Dorothy, was the Coolmore of its day. It was one of the biggest and busiest studs in these islands. Part of the reason was that Straight Deal was there. He was the main stallion at Ballymacoll. He was there for years and Charlie was given a present of him when she died.

There is one aspect of Dorothy's tenure at Ballymacoll that Peter Reynolds finds extraordinary: the fact the owner never actually visited. Breeding was always one of the driving forces of Dorothy's horse racing enthusiasm, and although she may not have seen Ballymacoll for herself, she found a way of staying in touch. She contented herself with photographs, detailed written reports on her horses, and hearing from others she sent on her behalf. 'She sent secretaries,' says Reynolds.

Charlie used to treat them royally when they came over, but he was a bit of a rogue and didn't always show them the things they wanted to see, because he might have had stuff of his own going on and didn't want that reported back to Dorothy.

Danny Daly told me a story once about how one of the visiting secre-
taries had asked to see a specific field, and on their way to see it Charlie
collapsed in front of her and put on a great show of being poorly. The visit
to the field she wanted to see was promptly cancelled.

Who knows what was in that field? It might have been his own stock,
or it might have been that it was not tended properly and was full of weeds
or something. All the fields he wanted her to see would have been beauti-
fully manicured.

One account of a visit to Ballymacoll by Olili de Mumm and Barbara
Allwright – her Hermits Wood favourites – on Dorothy's behalf in the
summer of 1955 seems to bear out Reynolds' reservations about Charlie
Rogers. Their tour of operations also included a visit to the Dublin
Horse Show and the Phoenix Park races, with instructions to deliver a
full telephone report back to Hermits Wood on the conclusion of their
inspection. The transcript of their report reads as follows:

Mrs. A. (Allwright): We have been round Ballymacoll this afternoon
and evening. It has been a perfect day and our hands were full
of lovely muzzles. It so happens that quite a few of the yearlings
are chestnuts and 'Romeo' thinks they are the best of the bunch.
We are going to inspect the mares tomorrow. Hang on, here's Olili.

Olili: I am adoring every moment. Everyone is missing Miss Paget:
she really should be here. I am sure she would enjoy it and it would be
wonderful to have her with us. I think 'Romeo' was rather hurt that
she did not come.

We had a wonderful flight. The horse show was wonderful and 'Romeo'
had everything laid on. He got us through all the locked doors by saying
'Miss Paget's people'. Afterwards he took us to a place called the Pocket
and all the people were so horsey they were like caricatures.

After the horse show we dashed off to Phoenix Park when we saw the
big two-year-old race and then dashed back to the horse show.

Today 'Romeo' came to lunch, and I need not tell you that it took
longer than it should have done, so we were rather late starting out
for Ballymacoll.

The Stud Farm is breathtakingly beautiful. First we saw a dozen mares
in two paddocks and then all the yearlings and of course we fell in love
with them all. Oh, I forgot, before doing that we inspected the house,
which is very comfortable. Later we saw dear, wonderful Straight Deal
and it didn't seem possible that he is fifteen years old. We thought he looked
much better than when we last saw him, despite the fact this has been
his busiest season for some time and 'Romeo' told us he's served nearly
forty mares.

Then we went to 'Romeo's place and Miss Rogers gave us a wonderful
tea. Barbara sat on 'Romeo's teacup and got it all over her dress. Thank you
for this wonderful trip.

Olili signed off with, 'Hope ankle and tummy are better. Miss P. better
start getting ready to come to Ireland for a long stay.'

Even in the year she acquired Ballymacoll, however, Dorothy had lost
none of her ability to frustrate others in the racing and breeding business. She entered 20 of her horses for Newmarket's December Bloodstock Sales – but then withdrew nine of them on the eve of the event,
leaving the auctioneer to have to tell potential purchasers lamely, 'I am
exceedingly sorry.'

In 1949, an outspoken article appeared in the *Essex Chronicle*, under the
byline of Leslie Purcell, billed as 'Miss Dorothy Paget's Assistant Manager
at the famous Elsenham Stud Farm, Essex.' The article was headlined
MANY OF OUR BEST HORSES HAVE TO LEAVE ENGLAND FOR A GOOD
SQUARE MEAL and, said the journalist introducing the feature, 'condemns
in forthright manner our present food rationing system for racehorses'. It

would have been impossible for an employee of Dorothy to write an article
of this nature without his boss's absolute permission and approval, so we
must take it as a very rare example of public comment by Dorothy:

*As the Flat season approaches, one naturally wonders how we shall fare
against our rivals from France, Belgium, Eire and Italy. For the past
three years we have definitely lost too many of our valuable races to
competitors from overseas.*

*Many attempts have been made to explain our defeats. We have been told
that our tendency is to breed horses for races of one and a half miles, which
is the distance of the Derby, the Blue Riband of the Turf in England. But
here again we have lost to the invaders. So obviously that is not the answer.*

*We have also been told that our blood is played out; that we must
import some of the staying blood from France. But really the French blood
goes back to the English blood. It really looks as if foreigners have done
better with English blood than we have!*

*Again, we have our blood coming over from Eire and picking up many
prizes. Why is this?*

*Frankly, I feel sure, after a lifetime in the business, that our trouble lies
in the way we bring up our young stock. The root of the trouble is poor
feeding. Our young stock, fed on the ration as issued today, are definitely
under-nourished. Horses may look well on grass, but they make a sorry picture when they have been put through the rigours of breaking and training.*

Before the war, our youngsters were fed as follows:
- *7 a.m. half a 3-gall pail of oats and chaffed hay. Exercise,
and on coming in at midday another feed.*
- *4.30 p.m. Each horse received a pail-full of mash, made from
best quality oats, bran and boiled linseed.*
- *Evening: Milk, in which was mixed sugar and lime water.
In addition they had plenty of sainfoin.*

Today, owing to the meagre ration allowed, this is their feeding:

- *Morning: Each horse receives one bowl of oats and chaffed hay.*
- *Midday: No meal.*
- *Afternoon: Half a pail of mash, made from oats and inferior bran, mixed with hot water.*

Some breeders are fortunate to grow enough oats to increase these feeds, but many are not.

The answer:

It is obvious that the horses of today cannot have the stamina of the horses of pre-war days. The answer to our problem is more feeding stuffs. Give us the food and we can produce the best horses in the world.

Far too many youngsters have to be sent to Eire to be reared. It is not much comfort to British breeders to produce youngsters that have to be sent out of the country to be fed. In fact, it is a big disappointment to us.

Perhaps this season our horses reared in Eire will hold the invaders!

In 1950 it looked as though Dorothy had come up with a horse to beat the best of the French: Aldborough, by Straight Deal out of a dam by another Derby winner, 1934's Windsor Lad. The UK's finest stayer of the year, Aldborough brilliantly won the Doncaster Cup and the Queen Alexandra Stakes, and the plan was to retire him at the end of the following year and send him to stud 'for the breeding of a new and strong English staying line,' wrote a London racing correspondent in a syndicated column, in 'an ambitious attempt to breed a new line of thoroughbreds to challenge the French superiority.' But in the October the five-year-old met a tragic and sudden death, and it appeared that his stud value of at least £30,000 had not been insured by Dorothy.

By 1953, according to George Quest of the *Express* in a profile of 'The Fabulous Dorothy Paget',

*nobody outside her own retinue knows precisely how many horses
she owns, but it must be nearly 600.*

*To keep 100 horses is estimated to cost £60,000 a year [£1.5m in 2017],
not including purchase prices, so you can see how greatly all branches of
breeding and racing have benefited by Dorothy Paget's enthusiasm – and
you can see why people don't lightly cross her.*

Dorothy Paget never wanted praise or garlands, or public acclaim for
what she did. She simply wanted to be left alone to do what she wanted
to do with her vast wealth, and in her breeding she did just that. During
1948, 31 horses bred by her were the winners of 62 races. All were
bred at Elsenham, and ten were the progeny of Straight Deal. A touching snapshot of what she had created at Elsenham comes down from
1952, when Dorothy sent her secretary Ruth Charlton to represent her
at the funeral of its stud manager. After the service Ruth went up to
Elsenham Hall.

*Everything, the ground, the paddocks, the grass etc. is in tip-
top order; hedges, ditches beautifully cut, not a weed anywhere.
My only complaint is that it must have a coat of paint. The stable
doors and all the paintwork is in a deplorable condition owing
to lack of paint.*

*I went round the kitchen gardens and was amazed at the work that
only two gardeners had done. I brought back tomatoes, cucumber, lettuces,
peonies, etc., and a sack of corn for the chickens.*

*Your wreath was lovely, which surprised me being a local one, a circle
of blue iris with a blob of yellow roses at the top.*

The following year Dorothy had Elsenham valued: the price put on it
was close to a million pounds.

Dorothy did not live to see the full fruits of the work Charlie Rogers did for her at Ballymacoll. But now, over half a century later, it is a testament to her unrecognised vision. 'In the past twenty years,' observed Olili after Dorothy's death, 'most of Miss Paget's horses were mated on her instructions. She had an extraordinary knowledge of pedigrees, though she would say humbly, "The experts know much more about it than I do."'

Twelve

SHOWING OFF

Pat Smythe, one of Britain's leading showjumpers, on Dorothy's fine horse, Scorchin', who competed in the Olympic Games.

At the 1950 International Horse Show, at London's White City stadium, Dorothy's equine superstars Golden Miller and Insurance made personal appearances, to the delight of the large crowd. 'It was the last time,' wrote Gregory Blaxland in his biography of the Miller, 'Miss P. saw them.' The conjunction of this end of an era in her horse racing career with this venue is perhaps no coincidence, because it was in this same year, according to the top British showjumper Pat Smythe, four times winning rider in the Ladies' European Championship, that Dorothy decided to turn some of her attention to showjumping.

Had Pat seen the front page of Gloucester's *Citizen* newspaper on Monday, 11 July 1949, she'd have picked up a hint as to the coming conversion – for in it was a photograph of the well-known showjumping personality and Olympic medallist Colonel Harry Llewellyn partnering Dorothy's horse Housewarmer, who had fallen and finished 6th and 4th in the last three runnings of the Grand National, at the Lydney Horse Show two days earlier.

Once she had decided to enter the world of showjumping, Dorothy sought advice on who to get to look after her horses, and asked Harry Llewellyn.

Llewellyn suggested Peggy 'Pug' Whitehead, herself an experienced showjumper, born Dorothy Mary Verity in October 1912, who had taken an early interest in horses after holding a milkman's nag while he went on his round, before helping out with his other horses at weekends and visiting local shows. She and husband Reginald had opened a riding school in Birmingham, before moving to Abergavenny where she had joined the Monmouthshire Hunt Club and established herself as one of the finest huntswomen of her time. *Horse & Hound* magazine described her as 'doing it a great deal better than most men'. After the war she turned her energies to showjumping, and was soon competing abroad, including at Ostend – where she also rode a winner on the Flat at the local racecourse.

Dorothy sent Pug Housewarmer, her top-class jumper. The horse didn't make a very successful transition to the new discipline, but it was still a more successful start than might have been anticipated, as, along with Housewarmer, Dorothy gave Pug two blank cheques and, perhaps hoping to repeat the Golden Miller/Insurance double purchase, told her to buy the two best showjumping horses in Britain. Pug bought Scorchin' and Eforegiot (pronounced 'E for Eejit'), and subsequently rode both in the British team, as well as another of Dorothy's horses, Tommy XIII, and a number of others.

Pug's obituary in the *Daily Telegraph* recalled that working for an eccentric such as Dorothy Paget was not without its moments. The horses, for example, were not allowed to leave a showground in the evening until Miss Paget had given them the order to. It was not uncommon for all the horses to be unloaded again in the near dark so that the great lady could spend a penny in the privacy of the horsebox.

By 1951, such was Dorothy's enthusiasm for showjumping that, desperate to acquire tickets for the 1952 Olympics in Helsinki to be able to watch the showjumping, at Easter she sent two members of her staff rushing off to Finland. They flew to Frankfurt, then to Malmo, then

This photograph, kindly supplied by Amber Baillie from her private collection, illustrates the close relationship at the time between the daughters, Olive and Dorothy (right) and their American mother, Pauline. The siblings would not always remain on such intimate terms with each other.

Above left: Out on the town with friends in the 1930s, Dorothy, second from left, caught the attention of caricaturist 'Poli'. Miss P, who even signed the original, bought it and ordered two copies. She seems at ease in the company of males here. (From Martin Pipe's archive)

Above right: Dorothy as she was never seen in public, contesting a race in which competitors had to jump several fences, then dismount, eat a bun, open a bottle of lemonade, drink it, put on pyjamas, light a cigarette which had to remain alight to the finish, open a sunshade, remount, and jump the same fences back.

Right: Giving the lie to the claim that she was never conventionally attractive, Dorothy as seen by top society photographer of the day, Bertram Park, in her debutante period. (From Martin Pipe archive)

Artist Terence Cuneo's painting, *The Spirit of Brooklands,* depicts the thrilling 100 sovereign showdown between Tim Birkin and his great rival John Cobb.

Smiling affectionately, Dorothy sits companionably alongside dashing racing driver Sir Henry 'Tim' Birkin in one of the Bentleys she bought and sponsored for him.

A sylph-like Dorothy (centre) preparing for a day's hunting, having arrived via another of her favourite forms of horsepower, with young niece Pauline (left) and companion.

Billy Stott on Golden Miller (left) keeps tabs on his 1933 Gold Cup rivals, before easing his mount to victory.

Top: Dorothy's cousin and racing rival, Jock Whitney.

Above left: Dorothy's father, Almeric, later Lord Queenborough, at one of the three weddings of daughter Olive, later Lady Baillie, owner of Leeds Castle.

Above right: Dorothy leads in dual Champion Hurdler, Insurance, ahead of trainer Basil Briscoe.

Right: Dorothy, left, with whip wielding friend Mrs Daisy Walker, probably at a point-to-point meeting. Copyright © Press Association

THE HON. DOROTHY PAGET

Above: A stark image of the Russian Home in Paris, adopted and sponsored by Dorothy for exiled White Russians.

Left: Clutching the Grand National trophy on the evening of 24 March 1934, at the post-race celebrations at Liverpool's Adelphi Hotel. A beaming smile, red gown and showy necklace complete a rarely seen public view of the then 29-year-old.

Below: Royal racing photographer, Bernard Parkin, also a talented cartoonist, created this image for the book – having fun with Dorothy's 1940 Gold Cup win and her 1930s/1940s public image 'in kissing mode', as a misandrist preferring horses to men as objects of affection.

"COME ON, PUT YOUR HACKLES DOWN AND LET HER GIVE YOU ONE OR YOU REALLY WILL BE FOR THE HIGH JUMP!"

Left: Dorothy leads in Golden Miller (Wilson up) – and her father – after the historic 1934 Grand National triumph, which made the Miller the first horse to complete a Gold Cup/ National double during the same season.

Below: Runner-up, Avenger, is still steaming from the effort as delighted Dorothy leads victorious Golden Miller, with jockey Gerry Wilson on board, into Cheltenham's winner's enclosure after his third Gold Cup in 1934. Mackintosh-clad trainer Basil Briscoe follows them in.

Above left: Dorothy whetted her appetite for the real thing by winning the Pony Derby at Northolt Park with her heavily backed Scottish Rifle in 1939. It wouldn't be long before she added the authentic thoroughbred version to her collection.

Above right: This poignant image of Dorothy was taken not long before she died. The light in her eyes is dimming ...

Above: A bookie looks out over the Aintree scene as the field jumps the iconic Becher's Brook obstacle in the 1935 Grand National, fearing financial meltdown if Golden Miller wins. But the 2/1 hottest-ever favourite unseated rider Gerry Wilson in one of the race's most controversial incidents. Winner, Reynoldstown, is here just touching down over the fence.

Stockholm, before eventually arriving in Helsinki having experienced some nerve-wracking flying conditions. Finally, trekking around the Helsinki streets, they found the ticket office, where a member of staff told them, 'The tickets will be printed soon. I cannot possibly sell you any. There will be an allocation sent to England.' When the Olympics did take place, the Great Britain team, including Dorothy's friend Harry Llewellyn, won gold in the Team Jumping event.

Also in 1951 Eforegiot, ridden for Dorothy by Curley Beard, won the jump-off at the Horse of the Year Show at Harringay Arena in October to become leading show jumper of the year. Afterwards, Beard, carrying the cup he had won, joined Dorothy at her table, where she was sitting with her secretaries. To his surprise he – and his trophy – were ignored, until she finally looked up to find him standing there.

'What do you want?' she asked him, Beard later told the racing writer Tim Fitzgeorge-Parker.

'Well, you might at least give me a drink.'

'Silly man! Go away. I'm exhausted – I've been jumping up and down all the time.'

'What the hell do you think I've been doing?' demanded Curley – but he still had to go elsewhere for his celebratory drink.

This may have been the incident which prompted Curley to plot revenge on Miss P. for humiliating him in public. The story goes that he, his brother and the renowned Kent-based point-to-point trainer E. J. 'Joss' Masters, 'the Wizard of Tenterden', decided to sell Dorothy a horse they knew to be a suspect jumper. They told her about the horse, talking up its ability, and carefully set up a trial jump to prove that the horse could clear it effortlessly. Beard himself, who was to ride it, did not like fixed fences, so they made up a flimsy post-and-rails jump which the horse duly negotiated safely, to Dorothy's satisfaction.

She agreed to the purchase – unaware that the plotters had sawed through the top bars of the jump to ensure they would give way easily at the slightest contact should the horse have even brushed through the top of them.

If Beard's experience is evidence of Dorothy's contrarian and difficult side, there is also a nice story that, after one particularly successful showjumping competition, Dorothy sent a note to those who had been looking after and travelling with the horses: 'Done very well. Can call at house with horsebox. Collect bottle of champagne.' They duly called at the house, and informed the secretary who came to the door that they'd been told by Miss Paget to ask for a *case* of champagne each.

They got it.

During the early 1950s the Horse of the Year Show was regularly held at Harringay, and in a letter to Olili, Ruth Charlton wrote that

> *Miss Paget has asked me to tell you about the Horse Show we went to at Harringay last Thursday.*
>
> *I went down to Hermits Wood at 3 p.m. Francis [Cassel, Dorothy's self-appointed 'racing manager'] arrived at 3.30. I thought we would be off at any minute, but no. At 7.10 we went off – Miss P. driving – Irene and I in the Bugatti.*
>
> *I was told to go to the AA and look out the route to the Stadium. I did – but I was a fool – so was the man – we took out a route to the Station!*
>
> *We did it together, but I blame myself, and Miss P. had every right to be furious with me – but she didn't say a word.*
>
> *Irene luckily went to Harringay the previous day and she found my mistake, so she made out the route beyond the Station.*
>
> *Francis followed in his Rolls and we arrived around 8.10 and were shown into ringside seats which were excellent – Fulke and Joe Butler were already there. We arrived in time to see the Lonsdale Stakes. Colonel Llewellyn won on Foxhunter.*
>
> *We had food in a room under the grandstand, which was fun – and left there 3.15!*

Ruth closed her note to Olili: 'All my love Darling. I adore you. Toots.'

Dorothy would not have been used to having waiters at an event 'literally coming to her table and saying "Boo"', however, 'or expressions to that effect!' which was the complaint later reported by Lillian Falk, one of her most senior staff members. Ms Falk was writing to Harringay's Wing-Commander Wilson, who had asked her to report back to him any unfortunate situations which might have emerged during their evenings at the arena. On their first night, a Wednesday, reported Ms Falk, 'the dinner was quite good although the service was terrifyingly awful – and when I say "terrifyingly", I mean it in precisely that sense.' Things didn't improve much. 'On Thursday the dinner was more than indifferent and the service appalling. On Saturday the dinner was inedible, but the services of a waiter named Bradshaw and the head waiter Bertelli made the evening tolerable.' Amazingly, Dorothy herself 'did not complain about the meals or service,' wrote Ms Falk, adding pointedly, 'although she had plenty of reason to.'

'We are very sorry that Miss Paget had such a bad experience,' responded the Wing-Commander. 'It was in the restaurant that chaos was complete. We had already called for an enquiry.' The only excuse he could offer was that events of this nature started with a meal for grooms at 7 a.m., 'and before the staff get home it is well past midnight.'

Dorothy and Curley Beard must have patched things up again, as in 1952 he was riding Eforegiot and Tommy for her at the High Wycombe District Show, dead-heating with himself to win the Open Jumping competition, where her horses filled the first three places. But by 1953 Beard was about to fall completely out of favour. It was soon confirmed that Ted Williams – 'one of the old-time, professional jumping men, who had been winning competitions all over the country for many years', according to *Racing Review* – had literally been handed the reins.

Soon Dorothy's horses were 'going well' for Williams, while Pug herself had piloted Tommy XIII to several victories. This horse would accompany Dorothy's Eforegiot, Scorchin' and Carnadoe to the 1953 Badminton Olympic Trials in April.

Pat Smythe, too, was asked by Dorothy to ride her horses for her. 'Once at the Richmond Royal Horse Show,' she remembered,

> *Dorothy Paget had suddenly told me that I would ride two of her horses in the ladies' jumping: Eforegiot ('a lovely bay horse') and Tommy. I already had my little French stallion, Djort, that I was riding. One didn't say 'No' to Miss Paget, as she confronted you, enveloped in an enormous, shabby, sack-like tweed coat, that had seen every racing and show venue for the past decade.*
>
> *So I jumped the three horses and, including two jump-offs, had three clear rounds on each, eventually tying first with all three horses.*

However, at this point Pat's own strong nature saw her insist on partnering her own Djort at a forthcoming major tournament. As a result, 'Miss Paget was displeased and I was only requested to ride Eforegiot three years later, competing at Lisbon, Madrid (in the 1954 Showjumping World Championships there). 'Egiot won a class at Lisbon with me.'

Eforegiot and Pat also won the Vichy Grand Prix, as the horse 'jumped two unbeatable rounds', but Pat suspected that Dorothy was still harbouring the grudge from a few years earlier against her, and that this win gave her an excuse to 'gain her revenge for my claim on the Richmond Cup three years earlier, by firmly keeping the silver salver trophy'. Even after Dorothy died, 'although she didn't take it with her on her death, her executors told me that I could only have the trophy as a souvenir of Eforegiot on payment of £25, an offer I had to decline.'

In 1956 Smythe finished third on Scorchin' at the Lucerne International Show, and called him 'a consistent and great horse'. She was a member of the Great Britain showjumping team that went to the 1956 Olympics (the actual games were in Melbourne, but for quarantine reasons the showjumping took place in Stockholm), but though Smythe won a bronze in the team competition it was not on Scorchin': Peter Robeson had the ride. 'I am writing to thank you most sincerely for all the help you gave us by allowing Peter Robeson to ride Scorchin' in the Olympic Games,' wrote the Chairman of the British Show Jumping Association, Lt Col M. P. Ansell CBE, DSO, to Dorothy in June:

> It was a great triumph winning a bronze medal.
>
> It was sad we did not manage to win silver, however we got our revenge on the Wednesday when we won the Nations Cup, and Scorchin' played a very big part by jumping a clear round.

Dorothy once attempted unsuccessfully to have the schedule for a showjumping competition changed so she could arrive in time to see Scorchin' compete.

The 'Egiot, meanwhile, had already been sold by Dorothy to Japan before the Stockholm Olympics. She had haggled about the price, demanding 'three thousand' for him, meaning guineas, the traditional currency of horse auctioneers. The Japanese offered 2,500, and even though Dorothy then came down to 2,700 they would not budge, and she had to settle for 2,500, only to suffer another indignity when she was actually sent £2,500, rather than 2,500 guineas. 'I fear his end was no happier than that of the great Miller,' mused Pat Smythe – a slightly barbed reference to Dorothy's multiple Gold Cup winner who, claimed Pat, a little unfairly, 'did not get his due desserts on retirement, finishing his days on a distant farm with a donkey and insufficient food.' Several months after Dorothy died, it was announced that Eforegiot, having been bought specifically for the purpose, would be taking part in the Olympic Games showjumping event in Rome – with a Japanese rider – and would also compete for the Japanese team at the Royal International Horse Show at White City.

Dorothy once told a secretary that she got the same thrill from seeing one of her showjumpers winning an event as she did from a successful banco bet on one of her racehorses. Amongst the extraordinary amount of Paget memorabilia now owned by Martin Pipe is a large blue scrapbook, absolutely packed with press cuttings about her horses' showjumping exploits, which has definitely seen plenty of use over the years. Clearly she stayed involved with showjumping up until the end of her life, with the *Daily Express* reporting as late as June 1959 that at the Richmond Royal Horse Show 'Miss Whitehead [Pug's daughter] is riding Calder Hall, a horse owned by Miss Dorothy Paget.'

Thirteen

TRAINERS AND JOCKEYS

Dave Dick, probably Dorothy's favourite jockey, partners her Shock Tactics (on the right) to victory in Windsor's Royal Lodge Chase.

Dorothy had notoriously employed more than her fair share of trainers over the years. But as she would go on to spend 'upwards of £5,000,000 on the purchase of racehorses', according to the racing writer John Welcome, it is little surprise that, no matter how harsh the criticism from her former trainers, there was still a queue to be the next one.

As a jockey Fulke Walwyn had won on Golden Miller at Wincanton in 1936 and then, in what many regard as his finest feat in the saddle, got him round to finish second in Liverpool's Becher Chase. He partnered the final winner of his riding career, Mansur, at Uttoxeter on 17 April 1939, two days later sustaining a fractured skull in a fall at Ludlow that resulted in his retirement some nine years after riding his first winner.

Basil Briscoe had been one of Dorothy's first trainers; then, towards the end of 1946, there were reports that Walwyn, not long returned from military duties during the war, was to take charge of some of her jumpers. From then until 1954 Walwyn would become one of Dorothy's more successful trainers, sending out some 365 winners for her from his Saxon House stables between Lambourn and Upper Lambourn, amongst them the 1952 Cheltenham Gold Cup winner and Grand National runner-up, Mont Tremblant.

Walwyn was more patient with Dorothy than some of the other people who looked after her horses, but even he lost it when she once complained that he and his jockey, Bryan Marshall, who had survived a sniper's bullet during the war, had 'somehow conspired to bring about the defeat' of one of her horses, Prince of Denmark. 'If that's what you think,' a furious Walwyn countered, 'you know where you can put your horses – all 35 of them – and I've no doubt there'll be plenty of room for them.' They stayed put. 'She would drive you bloody demented', he would declare later in exasperation.

When on the morning of 8 December 1949, Dorothy rang Walwyn to say she intended to visit Windsor racecourse *that* afternoon, so could he send Semeur, the first horse she had bought from France since the war, to run there as she hadn't seen it since its arrival in England, such short notice seemed like another of the eventual final straws. However, it turned out to be worthwhile. Dorothy's horse Endless was beaten in the second race on the card, but Semeur was heavily gambled on down to 15/8 favouritism in the 1.45 Juvenile Hurdle and, also ridden by Bryan Marshall, duly cruised to a four-length win.

Fulke Walwyn must have retained a soft spot for Dorothy, though, as he hung in his office a painting of the five runners he sent out to win five races in one meeting for her. It happened at Folkestone, on 29 September 1948, when Legal Joy won the opening event, followed by Langis Son. Jack Tatters won the third, Endless the fourth, and Loyal King the fifth. Loyal Monarch contested the final race, but was beaten half a length. There was a suggestion that Dorothy had endeavoured to buy the favourite in the last before they came under orders. Bryan Marshall rode all five winners, but Dorothy expressed her disappointment when he was beaten into second place on her sixth runner in the last. Some sources have described her reaction as a 'screaming fit'. Others believe, with some justification, that she was misunderstood. 'Fulke managed to get Miss Paget to talk to the press at the end of the day's racing,' wrote Bryony Fuller, who produced an illustrated book of tributes to Fulke Walwyn, 'and when asked what she thought, she replied, "I am very disappointed". What she in fact meant was that she was very disappointed that Loyal Monarch hadn't given her the sixth winner.'

The relationship between Bryan Marshall and Dorothy could also be somewhat turbulent. 'I have been going to write to you all this week,' went a letter from him in 1951,

> because I wanted to tell you how very distressed I was to hear that you had heard a lot of rumours associated with me.
>
> I hope you will not believe any of them, as there is no word of truth in them at all.
>
> I want you to believe this.

Such rumours were at their height when Marshall was caught napping when clear on the run-in and managed to lose on Dorothy's favourite horse since Golden Miller, Lanveoc Poulmic. It seems clear, however, this was just complacency rather than skulduggery.

It is doubtful, though, that Fulke Walwyn was aware around this time that the notoriously demanding Dorothy was also monitoring his love life! A memo to her from her close friend Francis Cassel, dated 19 April 1952, discussed 'the fiancée – Cath', and reported to Miss P. that she had

> arrived just after me at Lambourn – she had borrowed the Duke of Norfolk's car, a Bentley, maroon, covered in crests, which she drove firmly into the wattle hedge, so straightaway, panic, to wait for the morning and see the damage.
>
> The first night I must confess to doubts. She and Fulke both smoked little cigars. She wanted to have a cocktail cabinet in the new car, (which

*I rather gather somebody is giving them for a wedding present) and I saw
Fulke eyeing her once or twice, rather wonderingly, but she has plenty of
S.A. [Sex Appeal?] and he always falls hook, line and sinker for her again.*

*I kept having doubts, but next day, she was really awfully sweet and was
always bringing one cushions and chairs and being generally rather kind.*

*Fulke was going to a dance with her and felt tired and did not want to
go. He wanted her to go alone, but she did not want to go if he did not,
which I thought was rather nice of her, because some girls badger like mad.*

*I think they have quite a good chance of being really happy. My hunch is,
a real good chance. You can put £2,800 to win that it will be a success.*

The couple married in June 1952, had one child, Jane, and stayed
married until Fulke died in 1991. When Cath Walwyn was shown the
memo in 2016 she roared with laughter, albeit claiming not to remember
ever borrowing the Duke of Norfolk's car, or having 'smoked little cigars'!

Characteristically, Dorothy only visited Walwyn's stables once, 'arriving at 11 at night and wanting to see everything', recalled Cath.

*She came with three secretaries, including Ruth Charlton and Francis
Cassel. We still had lads out in the yard at one in the morning.*

*She finally went upstairs, and then came down to dinner at two and
spotted a whole pressed tongue on the table which I'd got from Fortnum &
Mason – she said, 'That's wonderful, no one else is to have any – how clever
of you to get that'. She ate the lot of it, and then sat in the dining room
until around four o'clock.*

*She talked about her father and my father [a former Jockey Club Senior
Steward]. She eventually left in a convoy of Rolls-Royces, after saying, 'I
really enjoyed myself, we must come again soon.' But she never returned.*

Cath Walwyn is adamant that the press were always keen to disparage
Dorothy, and takes her side too on the Folkestone five-winners question.

Despite many articles over the years suggesting that Dorothy's reaction showed her sour, ungrateful side, Cath maintains that when she had condescended to speak the press on this occasion she was very nervous, and by saying she was 'disappointed' she had merely meant, at the fates which had prevented her going through the card.

> *I'd got on very well with her, but the press were very unfair, very unkind to her. She did a huge amount for racing. They never gave her enough credit. They often surrounded her trying to get a quote from her, but she was very nervous when talking, really she was hopeless with the press, which was probably why she was so keen to avoid them.*

One of Cath's favourite memories is of a fancy dress party she and Fulke went to, when he dressed up as Dorothy – 'He looked exactly like her. It was hysterical.'

Cath also remembers Dorothy going through a phase of being convinced people were listening in to phone calls to and from her house, then backing the horses they heard being talked about.

> *She and Fulke hatched up a scheme whereby he would say horses were fancied when they weren't, and vice versa. But both of them only succeeded in getting completely muddled up, and she ended up betting on things that weren't fancied, so they had to give up that idea. She still loved a coup against the bookies, and would often want two or three in a race – she loved that.*
>
> *I wouldn't say she was a bad loser as the money she'd lose didn't really matter, but she used to get really annoyed if one of her fancied horses was beaten.*
>
> *She smoked endless cigarettes, but would only drink the odd glass of champagne. One day at Alexandra Park she had four winners and she became frightfully excited – 'Come on, we must celebrate, bring champagne!*

We all sat around a table, glasses were brought and the champagne poured –
by the time the waiter got to me the bottle was empty.
  'I've been left out,' I told her, but she said, 'That's just bad luck,'
and refused to order another bottle.

Unbeknown to Dorothy, one of her secretaries, Annette Williams, 'a wonderful secretary, with a wooden leg – thoroughly English', remembered Cath, came to stay at the Walwyns' for a holiday.

She was absolutely wonderful, but had no family; she'd stay with
us when she was on holiday from Dorothy, who was never happy
when Miss Williams was away, and used to ring and complain to us,
'She'll never tell me where she's gone – how tiresome'. I didn't dare tell
Dorothy that Miss Williams was sitting in the next room listening
to the telephone call. But she did like working for her.

Eventually Dorothy and Fulke Walwyn did part company. Pug Whitehead was fond of telling a story from when relations between them had become particularly strained. Dorothy was sitting in one room, Walwyn in another. Pug was acting as go-between. Having given Pug her final instructions to pass on to Walwyn, Dorothy added, 'And kick him in the balls if you've got the guts.' Pug's grandson, the jockey-turned-journalist Marcus Armytage, has a slightly different take on the tale, suggesting it happened when Dorothy 'sat in her box at the races and sent grandmother increasingly rude messages for Walwyn, whom she refused to speak to in person.'

'I was not sacked,' declared Walwyn afterwards. 'I had had enough' – meaning, enough of Dorothy. Cath may well have agreed, having once had to bring meals to Fulke as he sat with the telephone receiver in his hand all day long, from 10 a.m. to 6 p.m., while he spoke and listened to Dorothy for the best part of eight hours.

Cath Walwyn herself had no long-term hard feelings.

It eventually all came to an end. Fulke said he wanted there to be no
fuss, no drama. By now she wouldn't buy anything, everything was
wrong. Fulke said he felt we'd come to the end of the road.

We went away on holiday, and when we came back her horses were still
there! She said she'd decided not to leave after all! Fulke told her, 'I think
it's probably for the best that you do.' It was a shame.

As trainers and jockeys came and went over the years, some lasted
little more than a few months, and in the case of the jockeys maybe just
one race, before being assessed and dismissed. Not all were discarded
in short order, though: some, like Bryan Marshall, Charlie Smirke,
Gordon Richards and Tommy Carey, all managed to survive and thrive
for some while. They seemed to empathise with her, somehow 'clicked'
with Dorothy's complicated character.

John Hislop, who rode for her shortly after the war, learned how
working for Dorothy was like handling a highly-strung racehorse.
One day he was riding her horse Kinsale. Dorothy had two horses
running on the card, but the first of them, the Charlie Forester-trained
Explorer, ridden by Tommy Gosling, had been beaten, and she was
not best pleased. She had backed both horses to win in a double, but
also individually.

When I entered the parade ring, she at once addressed me: 'I hope you're
going to win for us, Mr Hislop, and get me out of trouble. Did you see
the last race? My jockey rode a dreadful race – he should have won.'

As usual she was wearing her old, blue-grey woollen coat – it was worn re-
gardless of the temperature, and was covered in lucky charms of various sorts.
She was in a highly excitable state, chain-smoking and making periodic,
derogatory references to the unfortunate Gosling's efforts.

When the 'Jockeys up' signal was given, the lad leading Kinsale brought
the horse towards us, whereupon Miss Paget barked out, 'Don't bring him
here! We were unlucky when the horse came here in the last race. Take him
to the other end of the ring.'

Since Kinsale had a great deal in hand he won easily, and Miss Paget
was delighted.

Most popular of all of her riders with Dorothy was the jump jockey
Dave Dick. In fact, he was one of her very favourite people, full stop.

'Of course, she hated men,' is how Dave's widow, Caroline, began
her description of Dorothy and Dick's relationship, a refrain that recurs
throughout this story. 'But she liked my husband. And Dave liked
Dorothy, too – he wouldn't hear a word said against her.' Dick would
talk with Dorothy about her horses for hours on end, something not all
her previous jockeys could be bothered with. Such patience meant that,
when he needed support against officialdom, Dorothy would deliver
in spades. 'When he was injured she was incredibly kind to him,' says
Caroline – 'she made sure he had the best doctors, the best hospitals and
treatment. There was no expense spared.'

In November, 1952, Dick was seriously injured at Cheltenham when,
partnering Prince of Denmark for Dorothy, he was forced into the
running rail, agonisingly trapping his ankle. At that time the rails were
sharp and metallic. His left shin bone was smashed and his calf seriously
lacerated, and he was ruled out for the season. While he was convalescing
in hospital, Dorothy insisted he should be surrounded by every conceiv-
able luxury. Dick received Fortnum & Mason hampers on a daily basis,
and telephone messages were relayed by her staff almost hourly.

Meanwhile, Dorothy eviscerated Cheltenham's management. 'Her
sympathy for her injured jockey was only equalled by her fury at the
Cheltenham executives,' wrote Quintin Gilbey, 'for their carelessness
and criminal disregard for the safety of the men whose job it was to

ride around their track'. When Dick was released from hospital after a month, Dorothy insisted he should take legal action for negligence against the Cheltenham authorities, and fully supported him in doing so. She later described herself as being 'completely satisfied' when the matter was settled out of court for £5,000.

'She was a very kind and misunderstood woman,' Dave Dick would say of Dorothy. 'I enjoyed riding for her and she always treated me well. She did live in style, though – when she arrived at a hotel, half of Fortnums would arrive with her!' Indeed, she once sent a Bentley packed with food from, as usual, Fortnum & Mason to Dave's cottage, arriving shortly afterwards in her own Bentley.

Their relationship was not always smooth-running, of course: there was an occasion at Worcester when Dorothy was so anxious to discuss a ride Dick had given one of her horses that she sat outside the jockeys' changing room on her shooting stick waiting for him to emerge. He didn't, and it subsequently transpired he had exited via a back window and swum across the nearby river to avoid a discussion with her. 'My father's riding days were long before I was born,' says Dick's daughter Katherine (known as Daisy), herself an accomplished rider, as an Olympic bronze-medal-winning three-day eventer, 'but he did say that he had huge respect for Miss Paget. They got on extremely well. Perhaps she appreciated his way of calling a spade a spade. He never minced his words, and was blunt and honest!' 'She only seemed to respect those who showed no fear of her,' agreed the triple champion jump jockey Terry Biddlecombe, 'and Dave Dick was one of them.'

Perhaps part of the reason Dorothy was so pro-Dave Dick was that he was an excellent source of betting information for her. 'I had a good talk with Dick,' reads a message from Francis Cassel to her in April 1952: 'I asked him if he had any tips for tomorrow. He said you must back Caribou and save on Evian. In the 4.40 have a little bit on his father's horse, Red Oxide, each way.'

Cassel had not always been a supporter of Dave Dick, once briefing against him to Dorothy that he had orchestrated a gamble on one of her horses which he had ridden, but which had been beaten. As a result Dorothy wrote to her trainer's wife, Diana Nicholson, that 'I am more than satisfied with D. Dick. However, I wanted to check up with you before Cassel's snowball became a snowman.'

The reply she received was adamant: 'I do not find Dick unsatisfactory, though yesterday I do think he rode a bad race, but all jockeys do that occasionally. Dick needs a firm hand and is inclined to do silly things, but there is no harm in him and we consider him not only a first-class jockey, but the best.'

The bloodstock agent James Delahooke says Dave Dick

was always involved in [Dorothy's] plots. She was always involved in scheming, which in those days an awful lot were. But when there was a big freeze one year there had been no racing for weeks. A car pulled up outside Dave Dick's home. Miss P. got out and walked into the house, handing over an envelope full of white fivers to Dave: 'Scheming money, Dave,' she said. 'Scheming money…'

Dave's widow Caroline recalled how he had told Dorothy that in her horse Mont Tremblant, still at that point a novice, who had just won at Kempton, he detected a glimpse of greatness, and that he could win a Cheltenham Gold Cup.

'Nonsense,' Miss P. told him. 'Novices don't win Gold Cups.'

So, when Mont Tremblant duly went to Cheltenham for the 1952 Gold Cup – and won it with Dave Dick aboard – he told Dorothy as he dismounted, 'There you are, what did I tell you? He's won the Gold Cup.'

Quick as a flash, Dorothy came back at him: 'But who entered him for the race?'

'That was lovely,' says Caroline. 'She could be a real star. Dave wasn't overawed by her. He'd say what he felt, and she appreciated that. She was a strange, eccentric woman, but they got on really well.'

A postscript to this story comes from Francis Cassel. 'Dick asked me if you had said anything about the little present for [riding] Mont Tremblant,' Cassel wrote to Dorothy. 'What he would like would be to take perhaps £35 off his ordinary 21% [of prize money as his riding fee] and use that for the watch. I imagine you would really like to do this, so shall I buy a gold watch for him and ask you to write a little message on the back?'

A further example of the healthily robust dialogue between owner and jockey came over Mont Tremblant's brother, Lanveoc Poulmic. Of the pair Dorothy preferred him, indeed, but Dave, Caroline says, 'thought he wasn't up to much, and once told Dorothy so – 'He's the biggest **** that ever walked a racecourse.' Dorothy just chided him gently: 'I think we can forget the adjective.'

One day Dorothy set eyes on Dave's new pride and joy, which he had always coveted: an XJ120 Jaguar – in green. She came straight to the point: green was unlucky, she told him, and if he kept that car he would never ride for her again. It had already been far from a day to remember for Dorothy: she had had four short-odds runners all beaten into second place and, according to the trainer-turned-writer Michael Pope, she went one step further. 'Dorothy Paget flounced off the course with her entourage. When she got to the car park she instructed one of her team to get into Dave's [green] car and drive it home. Bewildered and tearful, the poor lady did as she was told.' Dick turned up shortly after, to find his car missing, and reported the theft to the police.

He managed to scrounge a lift home, to find a telegram from Miss Paget telling him she had 'removed the car because of its colour and that it would be replaced with a blue one in the morning.'

Another jockey who got on well with Dorothy, this time riding for her on the Flat, was Charlie Smirke, who in 1957 married one of Dorothy's most trusted lieutenants, Ruth Charlton, known as 'Toots'. During his career Smirke would ride four Derby winners, the last Hard Ridden in 1958, and he had been riding for Dorothy since at least 1935, when he won the valuable National Breeders' Produce Stakes at Sandown in her famed blue and yellow colours. A mark of his good relations with the owner, perhaps, is the former *Daily Mirror* tipster Bob Butchers' remark that 'It is a wonder Dorothy Paget did not sack Charlie Smirke when that cheeky chappie was seen to put his arm around her ample waist in the Newmarket parade ring!'

The year 1948, wrote Smirke, was 'undoubtedly the most successful [year] during her career as an owner – of the 60 victories gained for her, I was associated with more than half – and not one was unexpected.' 'She was an exciting personality to ride for,' he recalled. 'One could never be certain after motoring 100 miles or more to a race meeting, whether she might have changed her mind during the night and instructed the trainer not to run her horses.' He described a typical Dorothy Paget arrival at the racecourse:

> A meticulous time-studier, she had worked out the car journeys between her home and the various racetracks to a matter of minutes, if not seconds. It was never surprising to see her arrive with her retinue of secretaries, in the parade ring at the moment that the trainer was preparing to give me a leg up into the saddle.
>
> A hurried, last-minute conference, and the bet might be doubled or halved, and the secretaries would go scampering off to the bookmakers and the telephone kiosks as I made my delayed way down to the start.

Smirke confirmed her betting habits – 'she would have £5,000 or more on one of her horses' – and said she 'appreciated a direct summing-up before a race.' For him there 'couldn't have been a better patron' for a jockey 'who has seriously studied his horses and the form book'.

'She could be cross if the result went against our preconceived ideas,' he added, 'but she was never vituperative to the jockey in defeat – unlike so many other women whose colours I have worn.'

One of Dorothy's regular Flat jockeys was to become her last Flat trainer.

The multiple champion jockey Gordon Richards had had a good relationship with her as a rider, as is illustrated by one particular incident. In 1939 he was riding Dorothy's horse Captain Payne for the trainer Fred Darling. Captain Payne had hitherto been a little disappointing, but he had cost 15,000 guineas and Darling liked him, and now thought he had worked the horse out and told Dorothy it was the proverbial good thing for the Cork & Orrery Stakes. 'Her first bet was £10,000,' writes Paul Mathieu in his history of the Beckhampton racing stable, 'and she fired similar salvoes round the ring up to post time.'

However, Captain Payne had evidently not been told he had to win, and indeed he didn't. In the unsaddling area Dorothy demanded several times of jockey Richards, 'Where's Mr Darling?'

Eventually Richards stirred himself to answer. 'I wouldn't be quite sure, Miss Paget, but I've a pretty shrewd idea he's up on the stand cutting his throat.' 'To her credit,' Mathieu records, 'Paget responded with a roar of laughter.'

Well though it reflected on Richards, the incident may have been the beginning of the end for Darling's relationship with Dorothy. He had already made it clear to her retinue that he would not respond to telephone calls after 6 p.m. – he would take the phone off the hook when he retired for the night.

One night Dorothy sent a member of staff to Beckhampton, who arrived after midnight, hammered on the yard door and demanded to know why the phone had been continuously engaged when Dorothy was endeavouring to call Mr Darling. Outraged, Darling decided the time had come to sever the relationship, and notified Dorothy that unless she collected them by 10 a.m. the next morning her horses would just be turned loose on the downs, and instructed his head lad Norman Bertie to ready the animals for departure. A few minutes before deadline the next day a fleet of horseboxes arrived to remove her squad for pastures new.

By 1955, the Beckhampton stables had a new tenant. Gordon Richards had set up as a trainer, and Richard Baerlein of the *Guardian* and *Observer*, still remembered for his forthright advice to readers to back the mighty Shergar to win the Derby – 'Now is the time to bet like men' – was staying with him on 'the evening Dorothy Paget rang up to ask him to look after her horses.' Richards did not jump at the idea as so many would have done. 'He told her he wanted 24 hours to think it over. He hardly had enough boxes, he was not sure his other owners would like the idea, and she had the reputation of ringing her trainers at 2 a.m.'

Eventually Richards did decide to team up with Miss Paget. 'Gordon becomes No. 15 on the long roll of custodians of the blue and yellow brigade,' observed John Porter in *Racing Review* in March 1955, pointing out that the widespread belief that Dorothy engaged more trainers than anyone before or since was not in fact true. 'I sincerely hope Miss Paget has not scented a new target in the 28 trainers of [American owner] Mrs [Elizabeth Arden] Graham.'

It would prove to be the best decision both Richards and Dorothy had taken, however. Initially her horses made up around a third of his string, but she soon settled down to leave all her horses in one place at last, in turn establishing Richards in his new profession, which so often has proved a step too far for former big-name jockeys in the racing industry they love. Dorothy certainly trusted Richards, and it was one of her horses, The Saint, who gave him his first winner as a trainer at Windsor. After the race, Richards gave her due credit, and the pair shook hands in public, a moment recorded in the 'little and large' photographs which, in Paul Mathieu's words, 'suggested she was sizing him up for one of her gargantuan middle-of-the-night snacks.' At this stage of her life it is prob-able Dorothy weighed at least twenty stone.

The following year, 1956, Richards entered into the jockey 'transfer market' to persuade the top Australian rider Scobie Breasley to join him at Ogbourne Maizey in Wiltshire, where he'd already moved his oper-ation and half his yard's residents were now owned by Dorothy Paget. She took to the new stable jockey, albeit she wasn't going to let either of them know, and would regularly demand of Richards when they met up at a racecourse, 'How is the wretched Breasley? Has he got a cold today?' To Scobie's amusement, she'd also tell him: 'Now, Breasley, do not cut it too fine this time.'

Breasley became British champion jockey in 1957, and believed Dorothy dubbed him 'wretched' and 'the miserable Breasley' because she thought he 'looked cold and unhappy' in the English climate. 'She really was a strange lady. I don't think it is any secret that she didn't like men very much.' But when Breasley got injured, Dorothy again showed her generous – and quixotic – side, telling Richards not to run any of her horses for the next few weeks until Breasley was fit again! Sir Gordon tactfully explained that such a move would not be very benefi-cial for the horses, and persuaded her to reconsider.

Despite her good relationship with Gordon Richards, whom she had taken to calling 'Moppy', Dorothy never visited his yard – Richards speculated that she didn't even know where it was. This fitted the pattern: never visiting Ballymacoll, just one trip to Fulke Walwyn's stables. When the two of them did meet up she would try to provoke Richards with some outrageous comment, but Richards, said Quintin Gilbey, would merely 'smile and say, looking her straight in the eye, "Miss Paget, you know you don't really mean that," causing her to laugh and agree.'

They got on so well, in fact, that she even added bets for him on to her account, settling up with him at the end of each season. 'I never want a better owner,' Richards often said of her, 'and she was the best loser I have ever known.'

In the same year that Dorothy switched her Flat horses to Gordon Richards, 1955, she also selected a new trainer for her National Hunt horses. At the suggestion of Dave Dick, in June she sent two horses to Prestbury, near Cheltenham, to Herbert Charles Denton Nicholson, known to all and sundry as 'Frenchie'. Again there was a Golden Miller link. Frenchie had ridden him for her as early as February 1937 when they won a selling chase at Birmingham. Dorothy had once given him the sack as her jockey, something she'd obviously either forgotten or forgiven. 'We knew only her reputation when she sent her horses to us,' Frenchie's wife Diana told *The Times'* Alan Lee. 'Plenty of people thought she was crooked, but I came round to believing that was an attitude born of jealousy in some minds, and a lack of understanding in others.'

Soon 30 of Dorothy's horses were at the Nicholson stable, something of a problem for a yard with 25 boxes. 'She was an owner of such unlimited means that she made many of our landed gentry seem like smallholders,' observed Frenchie's son David, who went on to have a successful training career himself, during which he was widely known as 'the Duke'. David rode for Dorothy as well, and his wife Dinah told the authors that, 'If Dave Dick rode a horse in a big race that David had been riding, and it won, she'd always make sure David got a "present" as well.'

David Nicholson remembered Dorothy as 'a large, obese woman, with a gargantuan appetite, [who] was also a diabetic, did not trust racecourse catering and preferred to take her own hampers of food.' A doctor's note found among Martin Pipe's collection of Dorothy's papers also concluded she had diabetes, which was probably a consequence of her obesity. The excessive eating which led to the obesity is, as we have seen, very possibly had a psychological cause, emerging as a conscious or unconscious way of momentarily blocking out negative emotion, or even in some people to amplify negative feelings.

Dorothy's erratic waking hours soon became an issue for yet another of her trainers. They were 'not welcome news for my father, who liked to be tucked up in bed early every evening when he returned from the pub,' noted David Nicholson. 'He knew of her habit of ringing her trainers late at night, and sensibly refused to install a telephone extension in his bedroom.' 'Frenchie wouldn't tolerate Dorothy's peculiar habit of wanting to ring everyone late at night,' said Dinah. 'Once he made that obvious, she stopped doing it. It was almost as though she would make unreasonable requests of people to see how far she could go before they would stand up to her. I think she was a bit of a lost soul.' Also less than welcome was the embarrassing requirement for the Nicholsons to pass comment on horses being trained for Dorothy by Gordon Richards!

It wasn't only trainers whose lives could be turned upside down by Dorothy Paget; their wives could also be affected, and Frenchie Nicholson's wife Diana found she was caused 'no end of work', specifically because the owner demanded a detailed rundown of the chances of her horses winning. 'Every time we had a Paget runner she was expected to go through the form of every horse in the race and comment on their chances in percentage terms,' explained David.

Sometimes it would take my mother two hours to complete her homework on a race. The evening before they ran she would be required to ring Miss Paget's secretary Miss Williams with her views. I suppose she had a Christian name, but we never did learn what it was. Everything was black and white in [Dorothy's] eyes. There were no grey areas. If you told her once a horse needed soft ground, then she believed it always wanted soft.

He saw for himself how Dorothy punted: 'Those closest to her often hinted that her standard 'banco' bet was £10,000 – a quite staggering amount in the 1950s. If the horse was considered unbeatable – double banco. £20,000 in one go.'

However, for all her foibles, David, and the rest of his family, were fond of Dorothy. 'She never failed to remember people's birthdays, sent Christmas boxes for all the family and lads, and would arrange tickets for Wimbledon or the International Horse Show at the White City.' When David organised a local raffle in aid of Cancer Research, Dorothy donated every prize, but insisted that 'they should be said to have come from Golden Miller.' Her good nature was also illustrated when her horse Prince of Denmark got a little jumpy with his lad Chris Middleton and smashed his watch and tore his jacket. Dorothy heard about it, rang the Nicholsons to ask why no one had let her know, and told the Nicholsons to buy the lad a new watch and suit at her expense. 'No one in the family,' concluded David Nicholson, 'would allow a word against her.'

Fourteen

GAMBLING WITH HER
FINANCIAL EMPIRE

You bet Dorothy was a keen gambler. This is her membership card to London's swanky Les Ambassadeurs, frequented by some of the highest rollers in town.

'No other figure is quite as outstanding as Miss Dorothy's,' recorded an awed London *Evening News* as early as 1934, 'when her enthusiasm is taking possession of her and big money is flying to the right and left of her.' For Dorothy Paget was quite probably the heaviest gambler the world of horse racing has ever seen. 'With the possible exception of Joe Sunlight, a Russian émigré who became an architect and built the then-highest building in England, as well as being a Liberal MP,' declared Geoffrey Hamlyn, the *Sporting Life*'s experienced observer of the racecourse betting scene, 'Dorothy Paget lost more money on the British turf than any man or woman before or since.'

Hamlyn had Sunlight's turnover 'in the region of £5,000 a day for over forty years', yet although Dorothy's racing career lasted only from around 1930 until 1960, 'her stakes were considerably higher' (and while Dorothy settled her accounts 'on the nail' Sunlight might make his bookies wait for months). Only Terry Ramsden, a fearsome punter said to have gambled away some £58 million during the 1980s, and Dorothy's contemporary Mrs J. V. Rank, may have run her close. At one point serious fears were expressed that her gambling might bring down the whole of her financial empire.

Evidence that she was either a classic compulsive gambler, or entirely oblivious to financial reality, dates back as early as July 1939, when a shocking letter marked 'Private' arrived from her legal advisers, Allen & Overy.

Dear Miss Paget,

There have been further very large drawings on your account last week.

The position is getting quite impossible. Your present accounts are over £50,000 in debit, and I must see you immediately.

I think there is very good reason to suppose that you have been swindled on occasions on your betting.

I have heard, because people know that I act for you, rumours of this on several occasions and now have some confirmation.

At any rate, it is quite clear you cannot go on on the basis you have been doing, and, as I have said, I should like to see you at once.

Five months later, Dorothy received another equally unwelcome, and devastatingly honest, letter from her long-serving and trusted employee Mme Fregosi:

Dear Miss Paget,

I do feel it is my sacred duty to point out to you that to-day apparently you have lost £7,250.

Actually, as you only get 3/- in every pound you have to find over £40,000 to pay your Bookmakers.

Can nothing or nobody help me to make you understand what a serious position you are putting yourself in with this terrible gambling? I have pointed out that you will within a year or two be absolutely broke unless you decide to go easy. Is it not possible these times to limit your bets? I remember Brisco [sic] said that perhaps three times a year one could go Banco.

I am sure I am more upset about losses than you are yourself, and the reason is because I know how serious it is. I know very well at the bank there is very little money, how I am going to meet these accounts I do not know. It is difficult to know where the money is coming from. The money you have in America you cannot bring over here, and the same thing applies to what you have in France.

GROSVENOR 1602.

8.BALFOUR PLACE,
W.1.
December 6th. 1939

Dear Miss Paget,
      I do feel it my sacred duty to point out to you that to-day apparently you have lost £7250. Actually as you only get 3/ in every £ you have to find over £40,000 to pay your Bookmakers. Can nothing or nobody help me to make you understand what a serious position you are putting yourself in with this terrible gambling? I have pointed out that you will within a year ortwo be absolutely broke unless you decide to go easy. Is it not possible these times to limit your bets? However small your bets are you will still be a loser. So why not start now. With perhaps an occasional extra bet when you are pretty sure of your horse. I remember Brisco said that perhaps three times a year one could go Banco.
      I am sure I am more upset about your losses than you are yourself, and the reason is because I know how serious it is. It is terribly serious. I know very well at the bank there is very little money, how I am going to meet these accounts I do not know.

      Some time ago Mr. Overy wrote me and he wrote you that we were to manage everything on £5000 per month. This was for all your houses, stud Farm, all the trainers, and your personal needs. Here in one day you have lost over 6 weeks money, and yesterday you purchased a horse for £2000. It is difficult to know where the money is coming from. The money you have in America you cannot bring over here, and the same thing applies to what you have in France. Another thing do you realise that you have lost to-day as much as you spent in France during the four months you were there. Surely this must convey something to you.

      Last year you lost in gambling only over £137000. This year up to date £80,000. This makes over £200,000. Actually with the income taxe it means nearly ONE MILLION. Never have you had a winning year in the past 6 years. So why increase your stakes as you do?

      I hope you will think this over very carefully,

        Yours sincerely,

Another thing, do you realise that you have lost to-day as much as you
spent in France during the four months you were there. Surely this must
convey something to you.

Last year you lost in gambling over £137,000. This year up to date
£80,000. This makes over £200,000. Actually with the income tax
it means nearly ONE MILLION. Never have you had a winning year
in the past six years.

I hope you will think this over very carefully.

M. M. Fregosi

As Mme Fregosi had worked for both Dorothy's sister Olive, and her
mother Pauline, this message must have given Dorothy considerable
pause for thought. Occasionally setbacks led her to tone her betting
down, but one run of losers prompted a magnificently futile attempt at
belt-tightening. 'We must economise,' she once told staff. 'From tomorrow we will do without grapefruit for breakfast.'

So where did her gambling bug come from? Dorothy's father Almeric
enjoyed backing his own horses, albeit for modest stakes. In 1922 his colt
St Louis won the 2,000 Guineas, and there was some suggestion that day
that he may have been involved in a betting coup, albeit inadvertently.
'I really do not know how St Louis came to be so well backed for the
Guineas,' wrote 'Hotspur', Sidney Galtrey, in the *Daily Telegraph*. 'It was,
I believe, something of a mystery to Lord Queenborough. Some folk
were wise before the event, and richer afterwards.' It sounds as though
Mr Galtrey believed Lord Q. may have been 'put away' by his trainer.
Had he later relayed this suspicion to Dorothy it may have informed her
early aggressive attitude towards her own trainers.

She was soon dabbling in greyhound racing, introduced into the UK
in 1926, and had runners at White City, London's first greyhound track,
whose first meeting, in June 1927, attracted a crowd of 10,000. Her
involvement proved short-lived, even though her dogs Darky Joe and

Evil Ways were winners, but then from 1929 through to 1932 she developed her interest in motor sport, on which betting was possible, albeit the markets were probably too small to absorb the kind of wagers she would become well-known for at the country's racecourses.

The novelist Peter de Polnay remembered playing bridge with Dorothy in Aix around the outbreak of the war, but back in 1932, she and Gordon Selfridge, the department store owner and a notable gambler, had been at a gambling party in December at the London home of Lady Weigall, where chemin de fer, roulette and bridge were on offer. According to Quintin Gilbey she was already a 'hardened gambler' at London's card tables by her mid-twenties, and the first record of her gambling for serious stakes is in late 1933, when the *Daily Express* was reporting that Dorothy had 'won £1,160 in a single coup' at a private party of the Duchess of Sutherland's she had gone to with her sister, where it was 'after 4 a.m. before the doors closed.' 'No excitement that money could buy could equal the joy they find in the hazard of a game of chance,' wrote the *Evening News* in 1934 of Dorothy and Olive, 'because of the interest of the hazard itself.'

When that headstrong hunter Bridget ran away with her during a hunt and she asked Alec Law to take the animal in, he soon won a race with it, and she found herself in horse racing. Now here was a sport in which Dorothy could allow her gambling instincts, as it were, free rein. Money was to be no object – when one trainer asked how much she was prepared to pay for a specific horse, she told him, 'Don't ask bloody silly questions. I said, buy him!' Once racing became Dorothy's all-consuming gambling passion, other bets didn't get much of a look in.

At the outset Dorothy seemed to be a profitable punter: one estimate suggested that by the end of the 1931/32 season she had won over £60,000 from the betting ring. But already a reckless streak was manifesting itself. Philip Gribble owned horses at Basil Briscoe's stable, where Golden Miller was housed, and on one occasion he and Dorothy were at Lingfield, and

> *I mentioned that a certain horse was rather fancied. I said I should have a fiver on it. It ran second. I apologised to Miss Paget and she was most gracious, saying it was a near thing – and that she had had £2,000 on it. This made me very chary of giving views to Miss Paget in the future. I did not want money risked too lightly.*

In April 1933 Gribble's Slieve Donard was a fancied 100/8 shot at Newmarket. 'Briscoe had arranged to stake £2,000', he recalled, 'Miss Paget £4,000, and I had butted in with a miserable £500. The whole amount was invested at an average of 8/1, starting price 7/1. The stable stood to win £52,500.' Dorothy's retained jockey Rufus Beasley was riding and, after a close finish, 'in our opinion won by nearly half a length.' Beasley rode his horse into the unsaddling enclosure 'into first place – and to his astonishment he was relegated to second place. Our good stuff was blued,' complained Gribble colourfully, who was adamant that 'even *The Times* racing correspondent said the next day that the judge must have been looking the wrong way.'

One of the earliest and biggest gambles on a Paget horse was also one of the least explicable – and there is little proof that she was even involved.

Her colt Tuppence had performed poorly in his three races before the 1933 Derby but, as an expensive 6,600-guineas purchase, and with Derby winners in his bloodline, he was allowed to take his chance. A week before the big race Tuppence was available at 250/1 – one bookie was happy to accept a bet on the horse winning of £1,000 to a punter's cigar; another took £1,000 to 2d: odds of 120,000/1.

However, on the day of the race a huge gamble developed on the horse, which dropped from 200/1 to 10/1 fourth favourite, apparently as a result of a 'public' gamble by small-money punters after a rumour went around (almost certainly unfounded) that Dorothy had dreamed the horse would win and backed him accordingly. The 'dream' had a nightmare outcome as Tuppence straggled home in 19th place.

'In the matter of betting Miss Paget was the easiest and kindest of friends,' said Philip Gribble –

> *fair, straight and reliable. We made a pact. She had the better horses and the larger string, but I, with fewer and cheaper horses, won quite a lot of races; so we agreed to share information on the understanding that I, as the smaller punter, should always be allowed to get my money on first. I knew if Miss Paget fancied a runner, and I knew how much she was going to stake. This information enabled me to make some very shrewd wagers, and more than one bookmaker wanted to close my account.*

As for the horses she owned and then bet on, Quintin Gilbey believed 'She had no great love for horses as such, but a real affection for certain individual animals. Dorothy regarded her horses in the same way as a gambler at a casino regards his pile of chips.' Her trusted lieutenant Sir Francis Cassel rather bears Gilbey's opinion out in a conversation he had with the BBC's Julian Wilson after she died. 'You must remember that Golden Miller was asked to do remarkable things,' Cassel told Wilson. 'If Miss Paget was in trouble [betting], the Miller was the horse she looked to to get her out. So he was never treated like a good horse.' This comment goes to the heart of the relationship between owners and their charges, and is often regarded as an insult to an owner, since he or she is the one paying a hefty amount of money to have their runners fed, sheltered, trained, treated for injuries and entered in races. All too often it seems to be the trainer who regards him- or herself as effectively the horse's owner, determining where and when it should run, even if usually in consultation with the owner.

In her heyday Dorothy became notorious for risking huge sums on her 'banco' bets – £10,000 – and even 'double banco', on confident tips from her trainers. Gordon Richards' wagers 'were on a modest scale,' notes Paul Mathieu,

but they gave her an indication of his confidence. If he wanted £10 on, she confined herself to a 'tiddler'. If he said £25 she loosed off one of her 'banco' bets: £10,000. If his bet was £50 – his limit – she thumped down a double banco…She added Sir Gordon's bets to her own, and the pair settled their account at the end of each season.

A standing instruction for her usual bet of the day was to stake enough on it to make her a profit of £20,000. This caused a sensation once when she backed a certain horse which she had expected to be a 1/2 chance – which would have meant she'd have had to stake £40,000 to make that profit. But her bookmaker telephoned her secretary to inform her that the horse was now 1/8, so did she want to go ahead with the transaction – as she would now have to risk £160,000 to make the anticipated £20,000 profit? Miss P. instructed the secretary to 'Inform him I consider his question a piece of gross impertinence.'

Apparently she showed few signs of nerves as she awaited news of her mega-bet, possibly the biggest wager of the twentieth century. As the race-result tape machine she had installed clicked into action, it revealed that the odds had been landed. Dorothy 'gave a beaming smile,' recorded Quintin Gilbey, 'and dealt out fivers to everyone in the vicinity.'

Losing a big sum, on the other hand – at least earlier in her betting career – was not something she bore lightly. Dorothy's chaser Roman Hackle won the Cheltenham Gold Cup for her in 1940, but when the jockey Ron Smyth took a tumble from the horse at the same course and broke his collarbone, all thoughts of sympathy from the owner soon vanished: 'She'd lost her money and she was so mad she never even asked me how I was,' he told the *Guardian*'s Chris Hawkins in 1991.

To Geoffrey Hamlyn Dorothy was 'the most eccentric, the most extravagant, the most anti-social and the most successful' owner of his time. Another observer described her as 'betting like a Chinaman, eating like Henry VIII, and living at night, like Winston Churchill.' Hamlyn saw at firsthand how her extravagant betting did not always go her way. Ruth Charlton, one of her senior members of staff,

> *was kind enough to give me lifts from stations to racecourses in the Midlands and the North. In modest return I was able to introduce her to suitable rails bookmakers who welcomed Miss Paget's mammoth wagers.*
>
> *One such day we arrived at Worcester, where I introduced her to the late Jack Woolf, a genial Birmingham layer who at the end of the day expressed his gratitude to me: 'Thanks very much, Geoff. I won £85,000 off her.'*

Dorothy could be quite a superstitious punter. She had one particularly odd way of deciding how much to stake on one of her horses, writes Jamie Reid in *A Licence to Print Money*: 'If someone rang her up on the morning of a big race day and their telephone number was 3403, she would want exactly £3,403 on one of her horses that afternoon.' She always took precisely nine freshly sharpened pencils to the races with her, to assist her to find her winner. Finding Christmas presents for her wealthy employer a problem, one year her racing secretary Ruth Charlton gave Dorothy a gold pencil. She duly added the gift to her usual bundle of nine – and promptly started backing more losers than before. After a few months, at a racecourse with Ruth one day, Dorothy told her, 'I've lost £20,000 today – and it's all because of your bloody pencil. You can keep the bloody thing!' And she handed it back, to resume her nine-pencil custom.

'For Dorothy Paget, backing horses was an obsession,' said David Nicholson.

> *Gambling ruled her life. She bet fortunes, and although she hated losing, the vast fortune she left behind in the ring became part of racing legend. If we thought her horse had at least an each-way chance in the race we were to tell her the degree of her bet... Some of her horses were quite useless, but she refused to sell them just in case someone else happened to win a race with one of them.*

Another story often recounted about Dorothy is that, as a result of her unpredictable sleeping schedule, she was permitted by William Hill to place bets on races which had already been run that afternoon. He may have allowed such behaviour because he knew her to be a consistent backer of losers, and scrupulously honest with it, and, despite the outcome of the races already being known, that she would be very likely to lose over any given period of time.

Francis P. M. Hyland unearthed an occasion when this system backfired on Dorothy. On Saturday, 6 June 1953, Dorothy 'rose as usual, studied the form and decided on her selections, one of which was Pinza'. Pinza was joint favourite for that day's running of the Derby at Epsom, and she had decided that his jockey, Sir Gordon Richards, might well end the famous jinx that had seen probably the greatest rider of his or any other generation failing to win the race that would complete his legacy. Before the call could be made to place her bets, however, 'one of her many secretaries forgot herself in her excitement and told Miss P. the great news about Sir Gordon winning the Derby at long last.'

'Why did you tell me that?' Dorothy rebuked the secretary. 'Pinza was my nap of the day and now I can't back it.'

According to a bookmaking source, in 1948 William Hill allegedly stopped two of Dorothy's horses in races at Wye and Sandown. On each occasion the stopped horse was favourite, and ridden by Bryan Marshall. And each time she had gone for a 'double banco' bet.' There were no enquiries into either race, and nothing was ever proved. In 1949, Ron Pollard was clerking for William Hill at Taunton, where Dorothy had placed a 'large bet' on a favourite. 'A message came down the line,' Pollard recalled subsequently, 'for me to give a certain jockey £100: "He knows what it is for. He will be parting company," I was told from Hill's London office. The horse did not win, for the jockey did indeed part company from his mount.' Dorothy, alleged Pollard, had been 'the victim of a sting, and I fear that I was the distant "someone" who played his part in ensuring that a particular favourite did not win.' By July 1952, Dorothy owed William Hill alone £12,781 13/6d.

But there may have been more occasions when others were keen to ensure her horses didn't win when they were heavily backed. Also in 1948, she was expecting a big showing from her Explorer, heavily backed with plenty of her own, and public, money, but with 31 rivals to beat, for the Cambridgeshire at Newmarket. Doug Smith, the future five-times champion Flat jockey, had the ride. He was alarmed to be approached 'and told that it would be made well worth my while if I ensured that Explorer did not win. £4,000 was mentioned.'

A stunned Smith refused point-blank to countenance any such action. But 'the go-between did not seem to be willing to take no for an answer, because he said that he would speak to me again two days before the Cambridgeshire.'

Approached again, Smith 'repeated that I should be doing my utmost to win.

"Never mind," replied the go-between almost casually. "You won't win, anyhow."'

Explorer did not win. The horse 'was a spent force at the Bushes and faded out to finish eighth…I cannot see that Explorer showed signs of having been doped,' mused Smith. 'I am at a loss to account for the go-between's confidence that Explorer would not win.'

Dorothy herself, as she became more experienced in her gambling and racing exploits, was not averse to pulling the wool over the eyes of interested observers as to which of her horses were actually 'trying', and occasionally she turned the tables. Quintin Gilbey described an occasion when she and Fulke Walwyn duped bookies and punters by permitting Bryan Marshall to ride one of her hot favourites, in the knowledge that their other runner, with a little-known but trusted jockey on board, was much better fancied. It duly won. 'The public don't pay my training bills,' was Dorothy's defiant riposte, 'and bookmakers are quite capable of looking after themselves.'

Such ruses, however, eventually got her into trouble. She was not at the races at Goodwood in July 1952: Francis Cassel was looking after her interests, and telling her jockeys that 'unfortunately she is not very well and not able to be present.' Her absence seems to have been rather more politic, though, as Cassel was called in to see the stewards on Dorothy's behalf, with them making it clear it was her they really wanted up before them. The Senior Steward, a Major MacDonald-Buchanan, gave him a dramatic message to relay to his employer: 'He says that every horse that runs in a suspicious manner has a black mark and comments beside it in the Jockey Club book. Your horses have got any number of these black marks and comments, and the Stewards are very worried by their running.' They were well aware of Dorothy's standing in the racing world, they told Cassel, and that 'if it came to a showdown and unpleasantness with you it would rock racing to the founda-tions.' 'These were his actual words,' emphasised Cassel, adding that the stewards felt Dorothy

could be relied upon to look into this yourself, with the object of your horses not receiving so many black marks in the future... You were the

object of today's meeting. That is why you were bombarded with letters
from Weatherbys asking you to attend. Obviously this little lecture about
black marks was not made on the spur of the moment but has been
brewing possibly for weeks.

The issue Cassel identified was clearly closely related to the ploy she'd
cooked up with Fulke Walwyn.

I don't believe that 'Runs' with Marland [one of her lesser jockeys],
and then a 'Go' with Gordon [Richards] is really a paying proposition,
because it is too obvious. Far better to have a good second jockey who
you can have a go with, and a little on if it looks dangerous. Far better
to do its best at a good price when you have a chance of winning, than
constant runs with all the bother of the Jockey Club stewards.

The stewards had identified a race in which Marland partnered a horse
called No Nonsense, where 'all the Stipendiaries seemed to be watching
No Nonsense and nothing else', as a prime example. They had called in
Marland, who, said Cassel, had proved 'a rotten witness, mumbled and
shook', and been given a caution. 'My advice,' concluded Cassel, 'is to be
very careful with 'Runs'…

Just how Dorothy was betting at that time is illustrated by another
memo from Cassel to Dorothy: 'Most of the money you have lost has been
on a lot of frittering bets when you have had no runners and been bored
with the racecourse. Obviously you must have your fun, but I think one
ought to know where the losses occur if they do'. The year of the Goodwood reprimand, 1952, gives a striking picture of her betting activity.

At Salisbury that year Dorothy lost a six-figure sum in just one
afternoon, remembered Fulke Walwyn's wife Cath, when she had gone
to see her promising two-year-old Wilna run in a race Fulke had told
Dorothy would warrant a maximum double-banco bet:

She arrived – late as always – at Salisbury that afternoon, and went
mad when she discovered Fulke had withdrawn Wilna because the
ground was too firm. Dorothy believed the going was not a problem
because her secretary Barbara Allwright, who had walked the course
in five-inch heels, had told her the going was suitably good.

Fulke would not back down, and told Dorothy that she would jeop-
ardise their relationship if she insisted on running Wilna. For once,
she accepted his decision, albeit with bad grace. She walked away with
Mrs Allwright telling her that she should not have given in.

The upshot of this spat, recalled Cath, was that 'Dorothy got into a complete mood and ended up punting like I don't know what, and losing
£100,000 in that single afternoon.' 'She betted like a drunken sailor,'
confirmed Francis Cassel, 'and lost £25,000 in bets I did for her. God
knows how much she lost with other people.'

However, she was not losing elsewhere. A typed record shows that
between 1 January and 29 July 1952 she made a net win across her
various accounts of £51,354 11/-. Indeed, in April Cassel wrote to con-
gratulate her on her 'first big betting triumph – you have knocked them
out and they cannot afford to go on betting with you.' He was referring
to a letter from the bookmakers Scotland & Co. of London W1, advis-
ing her that 'All commissions must be given not later than fifteen minutes
before the advertised time of the race in which the horse(s) are engaged.'
Dorothy's rage shows her in-depth understanding of betting markets. 'You
must make it quite clear that unless we can make a compromise, I cannot
bet blind like that. Obviously this letter means they intend to lay it off.
They probably want £4,000 on and then get at the jockey or something.'

An account of her attendance at Alexandra Park on 28 July paints a
lively picture. 'I thought we were off at 8 a.m.', Ruth Charlton wrote to
Olili, 'but no – 1.40.

We drove up at Ally Pally in good time for the 2.30 [in which Dorothy had £6,300 riding on the 2/5 Danehurst]. He was the best of a poor lot. Although he made all the running it wasn't a very impressive performance.

The 3.00 we had that good-looking but devil, Supremacy. He was useless. I can't believe he could be so bad. [That was £600 wasted.]

The 3.30 we had Straight Cut [carrying £2,800]. This was the most wonderful race. Half a furlong out Ronson headed us, and then Gordon [Richards] battled away and got Straight Cut just ahead. Gordon rode like a demon and kept Straight Cut in the lead to win by a short head.

[There was £3,300 on Blue Express] who looked the pick of the field but somehow wasn't much fancied. He won like a good thing, anyway.

Then came the last – such a good-looking boy, Good Deed [with £3,900 on him]. The old boy led all the way to win comfortably.

A lovely day only marred by you not being there. I went back home to my nest, exhausted but satisfied. All my love darling.

Toots.

The four-timer had made it a profitable afternoon for Miss P.

By 25 September, however, Dorothy's betting fortunes had changed. 'This week has obviously been a stinking one,' admitted Francis Cassel,

and we now owe: 'Luton' [one of her bookies] £10,430; Hill £4,555.

I only have £10,200-odd to meet these bills.

It is not as bad as it looks because you are still up in the region of £25,000 on the year, even after paying these accounts. We shall get it back in time.

By 4 October that prediction was looking somewhat optimistic. 'This has been a terribly bad fortnight,' reported Mr Cassel:

*as black as any we have known in steeplechasing. Not only have all
the bets gone down, all the jockeys absolutely hopeless, the trainer does
not seem to know whether he is going or coming, but in addition I
have successfully lost my honour as a gentleman.*

*By now we must be down to plus about £17,000 on the year, which
makes me weep when I think you were up £51,000 at the end of July.*

At the end of 1953 Dorothy received a 'Private Report' on her betting:

I think it would be helpful to show you how you do:

1948:	*Loss. £108,000*
1949:	*Loss. £88,000*
1950:	*Loss. £87,000*
1951:	*Win. £12,000*
1952:	*Win. £18,000*
1953:	*Up to Christmas. Loss. £24,000.*

Fifteen

AT HOME WITH DOROTHY

Dorothy bought Aggie the donkey on a whim – she became best friends with the retired Golden Miller and Insurance.

In 1938, a young woman by the name of Hermione Llewellyn, who had been working most recently for the Governor-Designate of New South Wales, was told that a Miss Dorothy Paget was looking for a secretary. Vaguely aware that Miss Paget was a racehorse owner, Hermione wrote to apply, and duly attended an interview at Balfour Place, Mayfair, clad in her best apple-green overcoat.

She was invited in by 'a smiling butler', then welcomed by three 'charming elderly women', who informed Hermione that Miss Paget was currently asleep and might not wake up until the next day, but Hermione must stay for lunch in case her potential employer woke up and wished to see her. 'They told me that my hours would be from noon to midnight, my pay £12 a week,' and insisted she would have to dispose of her overcoat because Dorothy thought green was an unlucky colour. At midnight she was permitted to leave, on condition that she returned at noon next day – but when she arrived back, Dorothy was still asleep.

Then Dorothy woke up, and announced that she was leaving immediately for Sandown races, 'and we were all to go too.' One of the elderly women, Mme Orloff, explained that 'Dorothy was very shy and would want to look at me through field glasses before she might consider taking me on.'

Hermione never got close to Dorothy at the track, witnessing her watch her horse lose, have a 'quick talk' with her trainer, and then speed off home. 'Regardless of traffic signs, very fast and brilliantly, she reached her front door, shot out of her car, left the engine running, dashed to the lift and vanished upstairs.'

Nevertheless, Hermione was told, 'You have the job. She liked the look of you.' Her new colleagues told her about Dorothy's 'wonderful' work on behalf of Russian refugees – the three ladies who had first greeted her said they had 'escaped with their lives but little else' from Russia.

Hermione was astonished by DP's size and 'ugliness. She looked bloated and about to burst'. Two months into the job, she was summoned to see her employer:

> Up in the lift I went and found her in bed in a huge room.
> A big table laden with marvellous food was wheeled in just
> behind me. Stupidly I said, 'Oh, Miss Paget, if you have a
> lunch party, I mustn't stay long.'
>   'Guests?' she said sharply. 'Certainly not. That's my lunch.'

There was an awkward silence. Then Dorothy asked Hermione whether she had a boyfriend, and she explained that she had recently become engaged. 'She was horrified. She said her Russians loved me, my work was excellent, and this was a catastrophe. "Go away, go away. This is dreadful news and I must think." I turned at the door and was stunned to see she was crying.'

Hermione was due to marry in January 1939, and gave notice. Her departure upset not only Dorothy but 'her Russians' too, who told her she was making Dorothy 'sad, perhaps ill'. Hermione 'one day forced myself to leave. I felt as if I'd deserted the Russians, but also that I'd escaped from a prison.'

On her marriage, Hermione became the Countess of Rathfurly. She retained bittersweet memories of Dorothy and her bizarre household.

Perhaps because I'd known sadness in my own family, it did not take me long to realise that Dorothy was a dreadful tragedy. She was clever, quite young, immensely rich and marvellously generous to those she recognised as unfortunate.

But she was abnormally shy and hid herself day and night from the world she belonged to. Sometimes humble, often arrogant, she would stay awake for several days and nights on end and then go to sleep, perhaps for several days and nights.

In between waking and sleeping she ate enormous meals of luxury food which were kept ready round the clock so as to be instantly available should she demand them.

...she had made herself into a monster. Her Russian refugees, her horses and her food were her only interests. By nature shy, her appearance had made her want to hide. Now she was a recluse.

The same year that Hermione Llewellyn was taken on by Dorothy, another young woman applied for a job with her, giving rise to one of the most widely recounted of all anecdotes about Dorothy Paget. The most reliable version of the story appears to be the one told to Caroline Ramsden, the daughter of the chairman of Manchester racecourse.

In 1938, explains Ms Ramsden, Dorothy wanted to employ a racing secretary, and was tipped off by Daisy Walker, who rode showjumpers for her, that a friend of hers, Miss Ruth Charlton, would be ideal for the role. An interview was arranged at Paddington Station, where Dorothy would be arriving from Newbury races before being driven home.

Ruth arrived, to be greeted by a frock-coated and top-hatted station master, who told her that there would be a delay as one of Dorothy's cases had been left behind at the races, but that it was being sent up on the following train, after which Miss Paget would see her.

'Well, what do you have to say for yourself?' was Dorothy's opening gambit when the interview finally began, followed by, 'What's your typing speed?' and 'What about languages? Do you speak German? French? Russian?'

By now assuming that she was failing the interview, and having been left waiting for so long on a chilly railway concourse, Ruth was beginning to feel unwell. 'Please don't bully me. I can see I'm not suitable, and anyway, I don't want to work for you.'

Dorothy was not taking no for an answer. 'I'll see you on Monday. You'll find my bark is far worse than my bite.'

Ruth developed fully-fledged flu, and took to bed at her sister's house. Soon the house began to resemble a florist's as bouquets of flowers arrived from Dorothy, along with a note: 'Get well – see you soon. Dorothy Paget.'

Ruth decided to give the job a try, and was soon firmly ensconced as Dorothy's racing secretary, rapidly discovering Dorothy's foibles but finding, unexpectedly, that she had a sense of humour and could take a joke. 'Stories in which she was ridiculed made her laugh till tears rolled down her cheeks,' recalled Ruth – at parties Dorothy would call on Ruth to tell them.

Further first-hand accounts of life with Dorothy reveal the extraordinary reality of her way of dealing with everyday events, and the bizarre activities and daily routines in her household. There was the time in the early thirties, for example, shortly after deciding to transfer her seven racehorses to Basil Briscoe's stables at Longstowe, when Dorothy decided she would like them to be brought to the home she rented in Balfour Place in London.

She had arranged for the horses to be stabled overnight in a nearby mews, but when they arrived in their horseboxes, supervised by stableman Stan Tidey, he was ordered to take them out one by one and jog them up and down the foggy street, past parked and moving vehicles alike.

Even back then, seeds of the ultimate state of Dorothy's Hermits Wood home were being sown, as Gregory Blaxland reported that she was accumulating a hoard of sporting and racing newspapers that 'filled her bedroom, obliterating everything from view except the upper part of the bed and some priceless Fabergé boxes on the glass top of a table.' These teetering heaps of the *Sporting Life*, which she bought in multiples and seemed unable to throw away, were not to be touched by the staff who cleaned and tidied around her. When a new 'tape machine' came on the market that would receive all the racing results from around the country and spool them out on an endless ribbon of thin, white paper tape, Dorothy had one installed in her bedroom, and would be glued to it for hours at a time.

Food, too, could be left untouched for hours. The racing writer Ivor Herbert, who knew Dorothy's Irish trainer and stud manager Charlie Rogers, wrote in *Winter Kings* that

> *She would call for food enough for 20 at varying dark hours, pick at it and leave it. Sometimes she would simply fancy a boiled egg and bread and butter. Two would come up, be disregarded, then two more would arrive also to be ignored, until by dawn her room gleamed ovoidly with cold, vain eggs.*

Dorothy's staff came and went, with a long-serving few maintaining an almost military-like discipline and order. 'Miss P. runs the establishment as if it were an army,' one newly arrived secretary wrote home, 'and she were working out a plan of campaign.' She added: 'Miss P. has a lovely speaking voice. Although she is so rich this is a very ordinary house and the furniture isn't nearly as nice as ours at home.' Dorothy's favourite piece of furniture was a tiny mahogany stool that went by the name of Tootsie. 'She was a tremendously strong woman and didn't tire easily,' a former member of her staff remembered after her death. 'But whenever she did want to relax she used to say, "Bring me Tootsie" – and put her feet up.'

Shortly after Dorothy moved into Hermits Wood early in the war, Molly (real name Mary) Fountain began working in the kitchen there. She was still there in 1960 when her employer's sudden death put her and the rest of the staff out of work. Molly's daughter and son were both taken to work with Mum and became great fans of Dorothy – although they learned to keep out of her way when she made it clear that they should make themselves scarce. 'She didn't really want children around making a noise,' remembered her daughter Janet.

> As I got a little older and would play outside during the summer months, Dorothy would sometimes look out of the window and tell us to 'Bugger off', but without any real anger. She saved the F-word for adults who upset her, but she tolerated us, and was a wonderful person – everybody who worked there liked her.

Janet still has the silver spoons and Irish linen tablecloth Dorothy gave her as a wedding present. Dorothy did a great deal for the village of Chalfont St Giles and its inhabitants, Janet believes – 'she was very generous in many ways' – and is 'aggravated' that today there is nothing in the village to indicate that Dorothy ever lived there.

The *Daily Express*'s high-profile columnist Nancy Spain evoked some nice details of Dorothy and her lifestyle in Buckinghamshire:

> She had exquisite little hands – no rings – and she shuffled cards like a master. Her intimate staff were never less than eight in number. They rose in time to serve their mistress. They went to bed when she

did. Sometimes they were on their feet without sleep for 30 hours,
or expected to go on sleeping for 24.
The house was run on a system of dictated memoranda.

Other small details Ms Spain noted included Dorothy wearing blue and white silk striped men's pyjamas in bed, and calling for assistance from her room by means of a 'beautiful little blue and gold enamel bell on a long flex.' She collected gold French snuff boxes, added Spain, as well as 'nut boxes for cigarettes, many of them jewelled.'

Dorothy referred to her establishment in Bucks as 'The Cattery' or 'Pandemonium Palace'. The grandest staff lived at Hermits Wood; the rest were at Pollards. Among the longest-serving members of staff was Dorothy's racing secretary, Ruth Charlton, who was universally popular with the other staff, though she and Francis Cassel slightly rubbed each other up the wrong way, as both claimed to be overseeing their boss's racing interests.

Sir Francis Cassel was never an employee, although Dorothy often treated him as one. Independently wealthy and an occasional concert pianist, he had met Dorothy when he found some of her private papers lying around at a racecourse, and returned them. She valued his racing knowledge, and when she wanted the benefit of it was not worried about interrupting anything he was doing. On one occasion, aware that he was giving one of his Albert Hall pianoforte performances, she sent a note by messenger to his dressing room at the interval: 'Give me your tip for the 3.30 at Wolverhampton tomorrow. I must have it right away. D. Paget.' That he forgot about what he should have been concentrating on to ensure she got it perhaps explains the review he got from the *Guardian* for a performance at Manchester's Free Trade Hall:

Wrong notes, but not as many as this, can be forgiven in an exciting or
original interpretation. I have never heard so many wrong notes in the
course of one evening of public performance.

Cassel apparently spoke in falsetto tones and addressed everyone as 'Darling'. 'To hear them talking you'd think she was a man and he was a woman,' confided one of Dorothy's secretaries in a letter to her parents. Quintin Gilbey doesn't beat about the bush: 'He was no more attracted to women than Dorothy Paget was to men.' In a 2001 obituary of his brother, the *Daily Telegraph* noted some of Francis' eccentricities:

> *He claimed to have taught his horses to speak French and German, and to count to ten backwards. He was sometimes seen wearing a cloak and white tennis shoes in the town centre at Luton, where he once intervened successfully in a deadlocked bus strike.*

The well-entrenched chief secretary, Annette Williams, had a room on the ground floor of Hermits Wood, and worked signing cheques, sending and receiving messages, memos and instructions. At Pollards Wood was Mrs Haase, with her husband; she oversaw the other secretaries. Miss 'Truey' Clarke was a more than competent mechanic, an excellent driver, and doubled up as horse show secretary. One anonymous source is adamant that Dorothy insisted on a style of dress from her female drivers – often recruited from the services – which involved a military-style uniform incorporating boots and breeches, but no underwear.

Molly Fountain's daughter Janet still vividly remembers Robert the butler,

> *a tiny man, well groomed, short-tempered. Dorothy would yell for him at the top of her voice and he'd rush upstairs where Dorothy's pet bird – a macaw, I think, but we called him 'Robert the Parrot' – would mimic what she'd shout at him – such as 'Bugger off' when she wanted him to go. It made Robert get so annoyed when the bird swore at him!*

Then there was Mr Hall, the gardener and odd-job man, who was rarely allowed to cut the lawn during the day, when Dorothy was asleep. As a result the lawn was high and unkempt, as it was difficult to cut the grass at night when it was dark. Hall had other uses, the racing journalist David Ashforth was told during a visit to Hermits Wood in 1980: 'A trip to the races was preceded by a flurry of notes and instructions, including one to Hall to stand in the middle of Nightingales Lane to ensure that Paget's chauffeur-driven Rolls-Royce made an unobstructed exit.'

The head chef was Mrs Hackemer, whose overnight counterpart was Mrs Styche. In her later years, Dorothy would frequently demand fish and chips, to the frustration of her talented cooks, who preferred greater culinary challenges.

A message to Mrs H. about pre- and during-theatre food showed how particular Dorothy's orders could be:

A tender Irish stew in two dishes with nine pieces of meat ready so that I can eat at any time after 4.30 p.m. Iced coffee must be ready 5.30 p.m. also theatre sandwiches made up – sardines, chicken and ham with lettuce. Very important about lettuce.

Next came the long-serving, elderly, reliable, and trusted ladies Hermione Llewellyn had encountered: Mesdames Djakelly, Fregosi and Orloff. Mme Fregosi had been a trusted secretary to Dorothy's mother Pauline in New York before leaving to marry, returning when her husband died to become a secretary to Dorothy; Mme Orloff was a paid companion Dorothy had known since schooldays in Paris. This was an era when it was far from unknown for members of the upper classes to employ paid 'companions' of the same sex to accompany them on holiday trips and to functions, and generally enjoy their leisure hours with.

Then there were Dorothy's close friends and associates, all colour-coded in memos in Dorothy's bizarre communications shorthand like something out of a spy novel. 'Pink' was Olili de Mumm, extremely popular with all and sundry, who had a room close to Dorothy's on the first floor of Hermits Wood. 'Blue' was Mrs Irene (pronounced 'Ireenee') Robbins, a talented musician: they had met as young ladies when Dorothy was dabbling with music. Irene would take her niece, now Liz Kahn, with her to see her friend, and Liz remembers Dorothy sitting up in bed at 2 p.m., having originally gone to bed at 3 or 4 in the morning, and as 'unbelievably generous – she gave me *ten pounds* for my birthday and at Christmas', as well as presents 'always tied with beautiful blue and yellow ribbons – her racing colours'. Liz particularly remembers one holiday with her aunt and Dorothy when she was about twelve in Portmarnock in north County Dublin. 'I rode one of Dorothy's ex-racehorses on the sands there. I was a reasonable rider but was along-side a jockey, who challenged me to a race on the sands – but I got run away with, and we ended up charging towards some rocks and I only just managed to ride the horse into the sea instead to stop it.' After Dorothy's death, Liz bought several things in the sale of her possessions, and still has Dorothy's curtains hanging up, and a statuette of her four dogs.

And then there was 'Yellow'.

Barbara Allwright had arrived at Dorothy's in 1949 in her twenties. She was apparently extremely attractive. Soon Mrs Allwright – Mrs A., as she was always called – and her son Alan had caught Dorothy's eye, and within a matter of weeks, according to Quintin Gilbey, the two women were 'inseparable'. 'It was not Mrs Allwright's skill at the wheel which first attracted the notice of her mistress,' murmurs Gilbey.

Whatever it was, Barbara was soon upgraded from Pollards Wood to a bedroom on the first floor next door to Miss P. Dorothy even deigned to visit Mrs A.'s parents on her way back from the races one day. 'As Dorothy loathed meeting strangers, this was a tremendous feather in

Mrs A.'s cap,' noted Gilbey, 'but did not increase her popularity with other members of the Hermits Wood household.' Surprisingly enough, though, Barbara's sudden promotion – she had quickly become a paid companion – did not appear to cause Olili any alarm.

'Olili was on friendly terms with Mrs A., but three are a crowd,' mused Gilbey, suggesting that Mrs A. would sometimes find herself the odd one out when the other two conversed in French in her presence. But, he added unequivocally, Barbara and Olili were 'the two people [Dorothy] loved…Everyone supposed that Dorothy would leave [Mrs A.] and Olili the bulk of her fortune.'

Not everyone approved of Barbara's elevation. 'I can't quite make out Mrs A.,' wrote one secretary. 'Mrs A. often goes on as if she were the boss and Miss P. her secretary.' But none of the gossip and back-biting from house insiders seemed to dent Dorothy's feelings towards Barbara. She not only paid to send her son Alan to college, but also 'promised a house to Mrs A., as she was always called,' wrote Gilbey. Eventually, he says, they found one, and shortly before her death Dorothy even stayed there with Mrs A. for a few days.

It was famously said of Dorothy that she always voted Conservative because 'I dislike being ruled by the lower classes' – not that anything in her eventful life suggested that she was or ever could be conservative by temperament! Thanks to Truey Clarke, who was inspired to commit the event to paper for posterity and talented enough to make it a vivid scene of life à la Paget, we are able to observe her in October 1951 heading off to vote in what was now the Buckinghamshire South constituency.

'It was about 8 p.m. when I was told that Miss Paget was going to vote,' wrote 'T.M.C.':

Molly said, 'You are to fetch Mrs Haase in the Jaguar now to warm it up. Miss Paget will be going at 8.25, and you and Mrs Haase will be going in the Lagonda.'

I had just commenced my dinner. I said, 'There is time to finish the game and beat the Spaniards, too, Miss Paget will not go until 10 to 9.'

I went on with my dinner, but I was not left in peace. Molly fluttered round like an agitated moth. 'Miss Clarke, she will be ready before you know where you are,' she said.

I grumbled, 'Oh all right, I will fetch Mrs Haase now and finish my dinner when I come back.'

Molly appeared again. 'Miss Paget wants a voting pencil.'

I took the box of Horse Show pencils to Miss de Mumm – 'Miss Paget will want a choice of pencils,' I said. 'She always does.'

We waited outside in the cars, and at 10 to 9 I was wearing a smug, 'I told-you-so' expression. Shortly afterwards, Mrs Allwright came flying back from Staines in the Tiddler [one of Ms Paget's smaller vehicles].

At about 4 minutes to 9 Miss Paget arrived at the front door and walked unhurriedly to the car. I was to lead the way, and shot off. Soon we were at the Poll.

When Miss Paget got out of the car, I thought she looked extra nice somehow, and her hair sort of looked just right. It was not until later that I learned that underneath this prepossessing exterior lurked a pyjama jacket…

Miss Paget, Mrs Haase and Mrs Allwright went inside the Polling Booth. Miss Paget marked her paper, and, fortunately, Mrs Allwright spotted a suspicious move – yes, we might have known: Miss Paget had 'repeated', she had given 'her' candidate, Mr [Sir Ronald] Bell TWO crosses, to make sure.

Another paper was obtained, and this time all was well.

As Miss Paget came out of the Polling Booth, the clock was striking 9. She gave an impish grin: 'It's just like Weatherbys, isn't it?' she said.

Tales of motoring adventures with Dorothy are legion. One celebrated trip by the Paget entourage to Manchester races by train saw Dorothy and Ruth Charlton 'finishing the journey in a 12-cylinder Lagonda which she had just bought,' says Caroline Ramsden, who had the story from Ruth, 'her chauffeur, Harry Jackson, bringing the car to a pre-arranged rendezvous.' Dorothy duly relegated Harry to the back seat and took the wheel but 'the car made a sudden dive towards the kerb.' Dorothy felt the steering had gone; Ruth feared a puncture. Even though her chauffeur was no farther away than the back seat of the car, Dorothy demanded of Ruth, 'Ask Harry if he thinks we've got a puncture.'

'Harry, have we got a puncture?'

'No, miss.'

'Tell him to get out and see.'

'Miss Paget says, get out and see.'

Harry got out, as did Ruth, and 'sure enough, one tyre was so flat that the metal rim was touching the ground.'

'Tell Harry to change the wheel as quickly as he can.'

Harry couldn't.

'There was no garage in sight,' Ruth related to Caroline Ramsden, 'only a small village shop with a young man of about 19 or 20 in charge, who vouchsafed the gloomy information that, as it was a Bank Holiday, all the local garages were closed.'

Parked outside the shop was an Austin Seven. 'Whose car is that?' demanded Dorothy. Informed that it was the young man's car, she told him: 'I have to get to Manchester. I'll hire it from you; you can come with me and drive it back.'

'I've promised to take Mum for a spin.'

'Your Mum can have a spin another time. Get into the back, Ruth. Tell Harry to follow us to Manchester as soon as he can get that tyre changed.'

Vanquished, the young man got in the back of his own car while Dorothy, 'who was very generously proportioned, squeezed herself into the driving seat.' Off they set for Manchester, stopping only to fill the car up.

'I don't expect your car's ever been driven as fast as this?' Ruth asked the lad.

'No.'

'Ruth, don't gossip,' warned Dorothy.

Arriving in Manchester and seeking directions to the racecourse, Dorothy opened the car's sun roof and stood up through it to demand of a nearby policeman: 'Racecourse?'

Eventually they arrived at the course where, Ruth told Caroline Ramsden, 'the rest of the party was assembled on the steps of the Club Stand, keeping an anxious look-out for the enormous, unmistakeable Lagonda.' Once they realised it was Dorothy and Ruth in the anonymous Austin they flocked around in surprise.

Ruth always carried a substantial cache of cash around for emergencies such as this, and Dorothy told her, 'Give me £75.' Ruth counted it out and handed it over, and Dorothy handed it to the young man. 'Thank you very much indeed. Go carefully on your way home. Don't drive as fast as I did.' This is the genesis of the apocryphal story that Dorothy always took two Rolls-Royces to the races, in case one broke down en route.

Yet another story from Ruth Charlton went back to the war, and found her behind the wheel of a Humber owned by Dorothy, whom she was driving to Cheltenham.

As they drove out of High Wycombe the car's engine seized up. Ruth headed for a nearby AA box, for which she had a key with which, in those days, members of the organisation could access a phone to call for assistance. Ruth planned to call Dorothy's residence to arrange for the Lagonda to come to the rescue. However, as she headed back to the stricken car it was to find Dorothy waving down a passing vehicle. The driver must have been local as he recognised Dorothy, who told him:

'I want to get to Cheltenham.' Coincidentally that was where the car's driver and passenger were headed, too, but Dorothy had no intention of sharing the car with its owners. Instead, she took it over and drove off in it on her own, leaving them to wait with Ruth in the Humber until the Lagonda arrived and they could follow on behind. Once they were all assembled at Cheltenham, Dorothy asked Ruth to hand over £100 cash from her handbag, which she thrust at the owners: 'I'm most grateful to you – please accept this. I'm afraid I had an accident with your car. I didn't realise the windows were made of talc; I'm afraid I put my hand through one of them.'

Another eventful trip to the races – this time Hurst Park in 1952, when Dorothy's Mont Tremblant beat one of the Queen's horses – taxed the patience of the anonymous writer and fellow staff member Mrs Falk.

First, Dorothy's post mortem with Fulke Walwyn after racing had finished went on for so long that both Mrs Falk and her colleague fell asleep and were subsequently banished to the 'loo'. Then, when it finally came time to leave,

Miss P. was not in a mood to go home, and just before Uxbridge roundabout we sat in a convoy in the moonlight for a long, long time, during which my love for the Tiddler went through a very strong test! The wind whistled through all the gaps in the sidescreens, there was nothing on the radio and I rolled myself into as tight a ball as possible and took a very poor view of life in general!

'All the same,' the author gamely concluded, 'these excursions are great fun usually and I don't believe any of us would miss them for the world. Think how dull life would be without the "blue and yellow" and all it means.'

Then there is this hair-raising, or even hair-streaming, tale from December 1951 of Dorothy putting a Healey demonstration car through its paces. One of her staff – presumably Truey Clarke, the chauffeuse – had gone to collect it from the Cotswold Gate Hotel, leaving Dorothy's Humber 'in temporary exchange'.

> *I made fairly good time in the Humber. It was quite a thrill, taking over a strange car in the dark, but I was soon away. I did the trip to Hermits Wood in 1 hour 10 mins – 56 and a half miles – and having done 113 miles since dinner I thought I had not done bad.*

Next morning she and Dorothy were to drive separate cars.

> *At 9 a.m. the cars were at the front door and we were off about 10.30 a.m. to Windsor racecourse to see some gallops.*
>
> *We had a most wonderful run to the tacecourse; there was practically no traffic, and Miss P. set a very fast pace in the Tiddler, as she wanted to see whether the Healey would keep up. I just managed to hold her and I think it was one of the most exciting runs I have ever had. The Healey went like a gun, and it slid the corners beautifully.*
>
> *We arrived very quickly at Windsor after this epic run, and what fun it was to see Miss P.'s horses going round the parade ring, and no race crowd there but us.*

They swapped cars for the return journey.

> *I was under instructions to try and pass Miss Paget if I could. Of course it was asking too much of the Healey, as this time IT had the 'top weight', and being 16 hp against the Tiddler's 25 it really was not fair.*
>
> *I could not resist the invitation to pass Miss P. I swept by and she could not catch me, and then I slowed down and just as she was going to pass me, I pulled away again. It was GREAT fun!*

After all this Mr Toad-like careering across the country, 'Miss Paget decided she did not like the Healey sufficiently well to buy it as it felt under-powered after driving the Jaguars.'

Another of Ruth Charlton's traffic-related duties was to go on a 'recce' the day before Dorothy was to go racing, to check out the route, find out if there were any roadworks in the way, and if so, in those days before a sat nav could find an alternative route, 'chat to the workmen, giving them £2 each, asking them to keep a lookout for Miss Paget's car and see that it had a clear run.'

A trip to one of Dorothy's favourite events, Wimbledon fortnight, produced a 'very important' note to her transport supremo, Truey Clarke, showing just how like a military campaign her instructions could be:

Five-seater Jaguar and Lagonda at front door at 11 a.m. Definitely tune radios both cars to Home Service. Also have right-hand window of the Tiddler open.

Meet me at 1.45 where I unload, having with you loo ladies, programmes, and loo ladies' cushions. Also their buns. Have these on your arm and DO NOT STIR. Teacase remains Lagonda.

Unsurprisingly, sometimes Dorothy's staff flagged, even lost it a little, in the effort to keep up with Miss P.'s insatiable demands. In December 1951, Truey Clarke had complained about being overwhelmed by her task of keeping the Press Book in which all mentions of Miss P. were collated.

It has got completely out of hand, I just cannot cope, I simply don't have the time. I have packets and packets of cuttings, and piles of newspapers waiting, and it worries me to death. I do not wish to complain but there are people who have much more time than I do and I should appreciate some help.

A week later she wrote to Miss P. again, this time to lead off about having to walk her dog, Sabu. 'I must say,' declared Miss Clarke,

that knowing I had other things to do I should have thought you could ask Miss Rankin to do this. She is doing absolutely nothing but read the papers. She has not even bothered to see if Sabu is still shut in the shed. I do not like 'telling tales' like this, but I don't like unfairness, and I don't like unwilling people.

Was Truey the unidentified employee Dorothy fired off a memo to, pointing out that now dear 'Sabu has taken to lifting his leg in the house, this must be stopped forthwith'? If she was, then her response could not have been more tart. 'Have you ever tried to stop a dog lifting his leg? Sabu does not ring me up and tell me when he is going to do it.' Sabu's breed is unknown, but during David Ashforth's visit to Hermits Wood he inspected a shed in the grounds 'fitted with a heated floor for the comfort of Paget's Great Danes.'

By and large, though, it seems domestic problems at Hermits Wood were eventually resolved with good humour. A document among Dorothy's papers headed 'Xmas Lists of Xmas 1951' shows what a generous woman she was in private, even if she did not go out of her way to tell the world. During that festive season she handed out gifts to contacts, suppliers, staff and tradesmen, including 'cigars' for the Bovingdon [aerodrome] Commandant, £5 for 'Nice Man Tickets', flowers for Mrs Hyman, a hamper for Mrs Allwright.

There was apparently much confusion and deliberation that Christmas, however, over whether Olili would come over from Germany for it. 'If you obstinately refuse to come for Xmas will you promise to come Boxing Day, then at least you can cope with Cheltenham,' ran a telegram from Dorothy on 12 December. 'Please do your utmost as everything quite impossible over here. Fond love.'

Two days before Christmas came the reply Dorothy didn't want:

Very, very sorry darling, made a blunder. Utterly miserable. But
can only arrive Victoria 8 a.m., Friday 28th. Can I please be met
Chalfont station around 10 a.m. Friday. Very Happy Christmas,
wish I was with you. God bless.
  Love Olili.

On Christmas day itself, another private memo reveals, Dorothy was 'unfortunately feeling not at all well' – possibly pining for her friend. The staff 'had a very enjoyable party in the afternoon, but,' Truey Clarke admitted, 'I could not help thinking of Miss Paget, all alone upstairs.'

Eventually Dorothy appears to have cheered up enough to call the staff up to 'the Dining Room upstairs' to hand out Christmas presents. 'This was great fun,' wrote Miss Clarke, 'and first of all we had a glass of champagne with Miss P., more or less on the landing! Then we all went in the "Work Room" and received our presents from Miss Paget. I was delighted with my clock and very thrilled to have one of the coveted Stud Books, bearing my initials – that will be a real treasure to have.'

Dorothy and Olili seem to have been reconciled by New Year's Eve, which was seen in at Pollards. Truey Clarke's account of the occasion confirms what a happy, united household Dorothy Paget ran. 'We commenced the ritual of preparing the punch,' she wrote,

a delicious and mellow brew – known as Witches' Brew ... while
Miss P. paced agitatedly up and down, continually consulting her
Ermeto [a Swiss brand of watch], as she feared we should be late,
but we were in plenty of time, and let the New Year in at precisely
the right moment.
  This brew, concocted by Mrs Haase and Mrs Thomas, really induced
us to let ourselves go, and the party was very merry. On sober reflection it

*is almost impossible to say what we did. We pulled crackers, we danced
Scottish reels to the radio – or attempted to! We played dice on the floor
– but we did not quite manage to get Miss Paget to join in in this,
although she was definitely interested.*

*Mrs Haase sang a little, and we joined in, then Miss Paget said she
was hungry.*

They made short work of an 'excellent cold buffet' prepared by Mrs Haase.

*We were all very merry and happy and it was a lovely party. I did not
notice the time when we got home, it was pretty late, and then I was
sent back to Pollards to get something we had left behind, so I finally
got to bed at 5.15 a.m. but I felt very happy and fresh as paint!*

*Thank you Miss Paget for another very lovely day. Believe me, they
are all very much appreciated.*

Perhaps the funniest, albeit most scurrilous, vignette of the incorri-
gible, maddening spirit that was Dorothy Paget was composed in 1953
by one Jim Lawrence, who sent it to an unknown member of staff with
a note, 'I hope only you and Miss Paget see it', and requesting it be
sent to the Hotel Metropole, Wengen, in the Swiss Alps – presumably
where Dorothy could be found at the time. Entitled 'Great Chalfont
Disposal Sale', it ostensibly offered for sale via auctioneers Weatherby
& Christopher ten 'Lots' of horseflesh. The various Lots clearly depicted
certain members of Dorothy's entourage, but one of them in particular
appears instantly identifiable:

*Lot 7: by STRAIGHT DEAL out of RACING BENTLEY.
Slightly unpredictable mare but winner of many races. Does not
like being left by herself out in front. Apt to fret when off the
racecourse; apt to fret on the way to the racecourse; apt to fret*

on arrival at the racecourse. Has not yet shed her 1940 winter coat. Needs careful handling, also special racing plates, and runs best in gaiters in cold weather.

Sixteen

COMING TO THE LAST

Dorothy's final resting place – alongside her parents but kept at arm's length.

In September 1958 Dorothy had to enter St Mary's Hospital, Paddington for an operation. It seems to have involved her neck: 'I depend a lot on my meals to steady me,' she declared to her surgeon, Mr Dickson-Wright: 'what is the last time I ought to eat? I would want a proper lunch.' In her absence, much-needed decorating and tidying at Hermits Wood was progressing apace: 'snowcemming has been completed to your side of the house,' she was informed – 'Pandemonium Palace will need to be renamed Purity Palace!' But the St Mary's doctors had some bad news for her, confirmed her good friend Irene Robbins:

> Dr Kemp confirms that you have mild diabetes. He does not want to put you on a diet as he realises this would be very difficult for you to carry out. If you follow his very simple instructions it should not be necessary for you to go on a diet, anyhow.

Dorothy was told to cut out as much as possible sugar, bread and potatoes, and all starchy food such as porridge, sweet biscuits, cakes, cereals, chocolates, spaghetti, bread. That all of these were itemised suggests they were no strangers to Dorothy's usual diet. Another of Dr Kemp's demands would have chilled Dorothy's very soul: 'He would like to see you lose between three and four stone. This is absolutely essential for your health.'

Some things, though, just had to carry on as normal. A memo from the very next day lists 'Doncaster and Bath bets: Darlene 830/400 – Lose £1,230; Ben Alligin 280/190 – Lose £470; Fangio 830 win – Lose £830.' 'I think you should try to come home and not linger a day longer than you can help in hospital,' Francis Cassel wrote to her,

> otherwise they are sure to find something else wrong with you
> – they always do! On the same day I reckon once the surgeons have
> tasted blood they cannot be restrained and if you wait there long enough
> they will find a good reason for removing everything except the shell!

Earlier in the year, Dorothy had been fitted with dentures by her long-suffering dentist, Dr Ackner, insisting as always on his final appointment of the day, and an empty waiting room when she finally arrived, complete with a table laid out for tea. She was not fond of them, and kept them in a small box in one of her cars, entrusting one of the secretaries to remind her to insert them.

The following spring something happened to disturb the usual flow of everyday life at Hermits Wood. The day after Valentine's Day, Dorothy was demanding,

> Report at once if Mrs Allwright telephones or if she comes here, and
> find out unofficially (only 'mauve' and 'blue') if she, Mrs A., has
> telephoned Miss de Mumm since last Friday when the bust-up occurred.
> This is most important that I know this, as when I telephone Miss de
> Mumm I do not want the fact that Mrs A. is at Peacehaven to rattle
> Miss de Mumm.

Details of the 'bust-up' are tantalisingly unavailable.

Maybe still preoccupied with whatever was causing her such uncertainties, Dorothy still seemed out of sorts in October when, in response to a note from 'W', presumably a member of staff, telling her: 'I have had a phone call to say that there is no change in my mother's condition. She is still not conscious. The chances of recovery are extremely remote,' Dorothy snapped back, 'Naturally I am very sorry, but your mother was damn lucky and at the moment with all my worries I wish the same could happen to me. I am too ill to take control.'

Her racing interests, meanwhile, seemed to be dwindling. During the 1958/59 National Hunt season she won just six races, worth £1,333. In March 1959 Cannobie Lee, a 45/1 chance, was her final Grand National runner. The horse fell. A memo dictated in August sees her becoming nostalgic, even a little philosophical, looking back twelve years to when

> I was beaten a short head in the Gimcrack Stakes. My jockey objected, but I knew he would never get the race as it was against [the Royal trainer] Boyd-Rochfort and Black Tarquin – a sad day that I will never forget, though I left the course a winner, nevertheless. The horse was Birthday Greetings, born on my birthday.

Something had clearly been stirred within Dorothy – as though she had lowered her defences, unusually revealing a little of her deepest thoughts. 'It is one of the stories for my autobiography,' she added, 'if I ever have time to write it!'

She was also contending with the now-knighted Sir Thomas Overy, who had 'quite rightly sent me several irate letters querying Pollards Wood expenses', and conducting something of a purge of unnecessary expenditure.

Under no circumstances whatsoever is electric light to be left on outside or inside after staff has gone to bed.

I walked round my property one lovely sunny morning at 5.30 a.m. and was disgusted to see, disgusted, every bedroom window sealed, and the electric light on outside.

Windows are to be left open – and I could not care less if anything was stolen – there is nothing of any value anyway.

I am clearing up many unsatisfactory messes in Hermits Wood and will continue to do so at Pollards.

Dorothy really wasn't herself, as the tirade from an unidentified member of staff in response to an upbraiding over the unauthorised erection of a garage on her property shows. Clearly this was someone confident enough of their position in the household to risk standing up to her employer:

I am sorry if you have had upsets, but please don't take it out on ME.

NOW. Let's get to this electricity nonsense which I gather has been going on in your mind since I went away in March. I am writing to Sir Thomas about this and many things.

Then the correspondent breaks off into something of a rant:

Your memory of good deeds is no longer with you, I am very unhappy to note – because I don't want praise for anything I may have tried to do – but I certainly don't want unjust kicks provided and made by others supplying false information – and if you can't check in the nicest manner, then what the hell is the whole thing about?????

Where was I?

when I came here the water boiler had been so badly knocked about during the occupation of the house that it was eating fuel – which I was obliged to supply myself.

And now we get a bitter unveiling of the culprit:

Things went satisfactorily and smoothly until Mrs Allwright came and complained bitterly to you that she couldn't have enough baths.

Your message was: 'I am not going to lose my very nice Mrs Allwright and her son for the lack of water – so make it better.'

And another thing: Dorothy's language:

As for the 'laughing stock' – don't you think it would be nice if we draw a veil over all these expressions – you cannot really think or mean what you write lately. If you do, then the 'YOU' I thought I knew, past brickbats and all, doesn't exist... and that makes me sad – very, very sad.

This really does suggest a Dorothy acting out of character and upsetting long-standing allies for no apparent reason. Around this time a number of staff seem to have been leaving or threatening to leave, some seeking monthly salaries rather than weekly wages, and Dorothy was struggling to find enough night staff. On top of all this, was she worried and distracted by worsening health? It no longer seems to be a happy house. Or is the problem an unhappy owner? 'I do hope you have slept well and are feeling calmer', wrote a friend from Maidenhead in November. 'Please try not to worry so much otherwise you will not be fit to take some of your cars on the Continent next year!'

On 12 December 1959, Admiral's Lodge, ridden by David Nicholson, won a Windsor juvenile hurdle – Dorothy's last winner on an English racecourse. On 30 January 1960, by which time she was rarely seen at the races, Fortescue won at Naas in Ireland. It was to be her very last winner.

On 8 February 1960 Dorothy complained of feeling unwell, but perked up and ate one of her usual gargantuan meals, probably washed down with her favourite Malvern water (un-iced) and tea, and finished with a Turkish cigarette from her gold cigarette case puffed through a holder. According to Francis Cassel, 46 at this time, she was by now being looked after by a nurse, though this may have been her maid, May. Barbara Allwright and Olili were heading to London on a shopping trip and planning to stay overnight in town. Olili asked Dorothy whether she'd prefer it if she returned that evening. 'Don't fuss' was the response.

At 7.30 p.m., Dorothy rang Sir Gordon Richards to ask about her yearlings. Richards told her they had something to look forward to, and recalled her being thrilled. In just under a fortnight she would celebrate her 55th birthday. Around 4.30 the following morning Dorothy's secretary Miss Williams was said to have looked in on her and found her poring over the *Racing Calendar*. 'We must get these entries off first thing,' Dorothy told her. An hour or so later, her maid found she had died in her sleep.

The death certificate confirmed the cause of death as coronary thrombosis and arteriosclerosis. Dorothy's chaser Cannobie Lee was due to run at Newbury that day, but was withdrawn from the race. But he would run in the forthcoming 1960 Grand National – according to Sir Peter O'Sullevan 'one of her last bets is known to have been on Cannobie Lee to win £12,500 in the National'. Its owner listed as 'The Late Miss D. Paget', trained by Frenchie Nicholson and ridden by his son David, the horse refused at the 22nd fence.

Shortly after Dorothy's death, on 12 February, *The Times* ran a piece entitled 'A Friend Writes':

Dorothy Paget is dead.

She was neither beautiful nor intelligent. But she was kind and generous.

As a young girl she was sent to a finishing school in Paris, run by a very remarkable White Russian Princess. During her stay there she could not do anything to help the destitute Russians, but looked upon the finishing school as their refuge. In fact, it could only accommodate very few of them.

When she became of age she was able to put her plan into prac-tice. She built a house there that was finished at the start of 1927 at Sainte-Geneviève-des-Bois. At first, this institution catered for forty old ladies and gentlemen; in a few years, Dorothy was able to put up 200 of them. It was entirely free, everything including clothing was provided.

Then came the war. In 1939 a fund was organised to provide what Miss Paget thought would be adequate funds for the war years. Alas, this fund did not last over 1941. The old people suffered greatly. There were no more Christmas trees, no more evening parties with wonderful presents and Russian music, and above all they had lost their best friend and confidante.

With these old people she was neither awkward nor shy and they worshipped her.

The ultimate failure of this special one [charity] affected Miss Paget deeply. She became more remote, less accessible to her relations and friends.

Miss Paget was not illiterate. She read a lot and at odd times. But now that her great plan had failed, the Turf seemed to be her only real distraction.

It seems certain that the friend who wrote this heartfelt, insightful appre-ciation was Olili. No one was better placed to have seen for herself the emotional truth of her companion's life.

Olili had already also responded to a *Sporting Life* obituary by Len Scott. Headlined **THE POOR LITTLE RICH GIRL**, it had described her glory as 'mostly reflected', her chief claim to fame as having been 'the richest unmarried woman in Britain', her dream of winning a Derby…cut down to a second-class Derby', and noted that 'Most people were broke in 1931 – during the period of the Great Depression; Miss Paget paid 6,000 gns for that yearling colt who would become the notorious Tuppence.' 'We shall reminisce about her bad manners, enormous appetite and extraordinary clothes,' concluded Scott heartily. 'And we shall miss her!'

Olili's letter to the *Life* condemned its obituary as 'most undignified'.

> *No one can expect Mr Scott to know that Miss Paget did not inherit her fortune until she came of age. Nor can he know, when he says 'her profession was to avoid publicity', that the publicity Miss Paget avoided was for the innumerable charities on which she spent much of her income.*
>
> *He also cannot know that since Miss Paget had to cut down on helping to relieve distress she spent much time giving pleasure to people whom the world had treated none too kindly.*
>
> *She never wanted fame but she loved a good horse. She had an extraordinary knowledge of pedigrees, though she would say humbly, 'The experts know much more about it than I do.'*
>
> *I personally would be interested to know what kind of Derby Straight Deal could have won in England in 1943 or whether to Mr Scott, Gainsborough's World War I Derby victory was also second-class.*
>
> *Where Mr Scott is right is in saying, 'We shall miss her.'*
>
> *Yours, etc.,*
>
> *Olga de Mumm*

Sir Peter O'Sullevan's verdict, without the emotion of friendship and personal loss, comes across as unillusioned but fair.

> *Without doubt she was a very curious woman. But even when she died there was no outpouring of grief. For many people it was almost a relief she was gone. In fact it is probably to people's credit that in death she was not suddenly made into this wonderful character.*

Two other tributes struck a pensive note. 'In an off moment,' noted the *Daily Telegraph*, 'she said she "hated meeting people, but hated being alone".' 'She was terribly shy and gauche and lived by night,' reflected Cath Walwyn. 'She has become something of a figure of fun, but actually hers was a sad life.'

Dorothy's funeral took place at 3 p.m. on Friday, 12 February, at St Mary's Church, Hertingfordbury. Perhaps feeling it was what Dorothy would have expected, Truey Clarke drove some of Dorothy's closest friends from Hermits Wood to the church in the Jaguar at speeds of up to 100 mph. 'She weighed 24 stone and stood over six foot,' Nancy Spain wrote subsequently in the *Daily Express*. 'The four pallbearers were unable to lift her coffin. They were reinforced by four chauffeurs.' The funeral procession included a string of her racehorses.

Dorothy's sister, Lady Baillie, did not attend, according to *The Times*, but her cousin Jock Whitney, the American Ambassador, did, as well as her trainers and jockeys. Barbara Allwright is not on the list of mourners published by *The Times*. The vicar was assisted by the Russian Orthodox Bishop of Sergieve, representing the Russian Home, which sent the largest wreath, some three feet high. Many of the other wreaths were in Dorothy's blue and yellow racing colours'; daffodils lay on the coffin, which was draped in blue satin. As the coffin was carefully placed into the grave, Olili was seen to almost lose her footing. She managed to regain her balance and composure, and walked away slowly and unaided. Sir Gordon Richards was seen to linger at the graveside.

Dorothy Paget died intestate. 'Everyone supposed that [she] would leave [Barbara Allwright] and Olili the bulk of her fortune,' wrote Quintin Gilbey, 'but once again she procrastinated until it was too late.' 'For years her lawyer had been trying to persuade her to make a will,' wrote Ruth Charlton, 'and she had got as far as naming people to whom she would like to leave bequests, but his last letter to her on the subject was found, unopened, after her death.'

Frustratingly, even Ruth doesn't name those Dorothy may have included.

The fortune she left, at just over £3.5 million (over £73m in 2017), the largest in England for two and a half years, was largely swallowed up by death duties of £2,778,073 – 'enough to pay for a Victor bomber, or two and a half de Havilland Comets', calculated the London *Evening News*. The residue passed to her sister, Lady Baillie, with whom she seems by the time of her death to have been barely on speaking terms. 'The weakening of share prices', the *Guardian* reported in April, 'was explained by the first sales for death duty from the £3,500,000 estate of Miss Dorothy Paget, one of the largest estates to come into the market for some time.' Dorothy had, though, it seems, made arrangements to leave the five Gold Cups won by her great horse Golden Miller to Cheltenham racecourse, for which they are now looked after by the Cheltenham jewellers Martins.

In the interim, Lady Baillie had been 'granted letters of administration' over her sister's estate and, acknowledging that 'I know nothing about horses', agreed that the racehorses could continue to compete until the string could be dispersed at sales. So they did, with several of her jumpers racing at Birmingham on 22 February. Many of Dorothy's horses were bought by Sir Michael Sobell, whom Gordon Richards also persuaded to take over Ballymacoll, and leave Charlie Rogers in position. A promising chaser she owned called Desert Fort, at the time of her death recovering from a leg injury so severe the vet had advised putting the horse down, was given to Frenchie Nicholson's wife Diana. 'After three months,' reported her son David, 'Desert Fort was led out to the nearest paddock to gallop round the field. Miraculously the treatment had worked,' and the horse even raced again, winning the Hurst Park National Trial two years in succession. In January 1974 Dorothy's yellow and blue racing colours were once again seen on a racecourse, now belonging to her great nephew, David Russell, when his Night And Day won a handicap hurdle race at Wincanton.

Olili died in Germany the year after Dorothy, at the age of just 51. In 2006 Hermits Wood was demolished and replaced by a block of flats.

Shortly after Dorothy's death, a journalist called Richard Viner wrote an affectionate piece about her 55th birthday celebrations, which she had not lived to enjoy, and to which he had been invited – though had he been suffering from the slightest ailment, he conceded, the invitation would have been cancelled, however short the notice: it had happened to him before.

'She could not bear anyone near her with a cold. She was terrified of catching one'.

If all had been well, though, Viner would have turned up for a night at the theatre, decked out in a dinner jacket, and met fellow invitees who 'would probably have consisted of Sir Francis Cassel, the pianist, possibly a half-sister and her husband, and one or two secretaries', either or both of whom would have brought with them 'the invariable bag, weighed down with a Thermos of tea, of soup, sandwiches, chocolates, medicines, additional scarves (she always had these brought along in case there was a draught) and paper handkerchiefs.'

Dorothy, driven by Barbara Allwright, would almost certainly have turned up late – 'she liked to arrive after the curtain had risen so that she might go to her seat unseen. She never left until it was all but empty.' One of her secretaries would have had the task of reconnoitring the shortest route to the nearest lavatory, and preparing the attendant for Dorothy's visit with a generous tip to ensure there would be no obstacle to her entry.

After the theatre would come a visit to a night club – she 'took a childish delight in cabaret,' said Viner, 'especially conjurors'. There might well then be food to be consumed – 'I remember one supper party at the Café de Paris. I ordered Lobster Armoricaine. She ordered Lobster Newburg. When the waiter served us she took one look and said, "That's what I wanted. You have this." And promptly changed our plates.

'I would not say her vast wealth brought her great happiness,' pondered Viner. 'In the end it only bought her the luxury of solitude. She lived rather like a tortoise, a shy, retiring, self-conscious tortoise, barricading herself from the world…like most of us, her own worst enemy.'

Dorothy was laid to rest within reach of, but separated from, her mother and father, under a rather plain tombstone, nowhere near as ostentatious as the memorial to her parents. Her sister Olive opted to be cremated, and to have ashes scattered at Leeds Castle, and their baby sister lies in America. In 2017, both monuments were in a worsening state of disrepair. The church confirmed that nobody undertakes maintenance on them apart from the church volunteers who cut the grass around them.

POSTSCRIPT

There are two enigmatic postscripts to the story of Dorothy Paget. Unlikely, even outlandish, they may seem, but the sheer unknowability of so much in the life of this very private person might explain how such rumours arise, and also why such odd tales are difficult to dismiss or disprove conclusively. Nature, as they say, abhors a vacuum.

The first refers to a suggestion – passed on by not one but two credible sources – that perhaps Dorothy's demise was encouraged or hastened. A particular member of Dorothy's household, so the story goes, had been given to understand that their employer had made arrangements for them to be made a substantial beneficiary of her will. 'I know that pressure had been put upon [Dorothy] by a certain individual to make a will,' Dorothy's first biographer Quintin Gilbey claimed, 'and she is alleged to have said that she was giving it her consideration.'

Impatient to collect on that deal, runs the theory, this individual found the opportunity to bring it forward presenting itself when Dorothy suffered her heart attack that night. Rather than immediately calling for medical assistance, the perpetrator instead ensured there would be no possibility of that arriving, by smothering the source of the potential windfall.

Amongst the 'evidence' produced to substantiate this seemingly
unlikely allegation is the 'fact' that when Dorothy's body was eventually
discovered, all the drawers in the room had been turned out, shelves
clearly searched, papers disturbed, in an effort, so goes the theory, to
find the will which the culprit feared might otherwise be discovered and
disposed of in order to avoid any of the 'rogue' conditions being enacted.

No will, however, was ever found.

Or, at least, none was ever produced.

The second 'revelation' is an infinitely more recondite, improbable, and
intriguing tale.

A few miles from the centre of High Wycombe a late-middle-aged
lady opens the door of a well-kept house and says, 'I suppose you've
come to hear his story…'

Others have heard this story too; most have been far from convinced.
One no-nonsense racehorse trainer called it 'utter nonsense', and dismissed the man whose story it was to tell as 'a chancer', 'purely a public-
ity-seeker', 'uneducated' and 'a complete fake'. Another respected racing
figure, the former clerk of a major racecourse, agreed: 'A rogue'. He was
after cash, no doubt.' When you read the story you might well agree.

But the unprepossessing, softly-spoken, now elderly gentleman in his
seventies who tells it has an unshakeable belief in its truth. As far as he is
concerned, he is the son of Dorothy Paget. Although he is happy for his
details to be made public, it has been decided not to name him here, lest
the interest aroused might disrupt the rest of his family's quality of life.

This is his story.

His 'parents' are Doris and William. Doris worked for Dorothy as
an assistant cook, also helping out at Hermits Wood when Dorothy
gave parties for local children, particularly at Christmas. William joined
the army in 1914 on forged papers as a 15-year-old and ended up in

the King's Own Royal Rifles, seeing action in France. Subsequently he worked as a groom in Newmarket and later as a French polisher. A couple of his places of work were connected to Almeric Paget.

The Son, as we shall call him, believes that he was born illegitimately to Dorothy and his aristocratic father at Leeds Castle, after she only discovered she was expecting seven months into the pregnancy. Neither Dorothy nor the father wanted, or was able, to wed, so he was placed with Doris and William to become his foster or adoptive parents.

An illegitimate boy was born on Saturday, 18 January 1941 to a corsetiere named Paget, living in Bristol. His birth certificate appears to indicate that he was adopted. Our man believes this may well have been him, and that the certificate was actually created by Dorothy, using false names and a false address. In order to facilitate our man being fostered by Doris and William, the employees falsely registered his birth as being on Thursday, 11 December 1941. They were able to do so, having lost a child of their own, born prematurely on this date, which they had secretly disposed of. They had other children of their own, and there does seem to be no good reason why they would have taken on someone else's illegitimate offspring unless it would have been made worth their while.

The Son has a number of what he considers to be genuine memories of times when his real mother, and occasionally his father, visited him. They do not, though, seem to have maintained any sort of long-term relationship following the birth of the boy. When he was four years old Doris took him, and her own legitimate daughter Rosemary, with her to work, where he met Dorothy 'on many occasions'. Doris ceased working for Dorothy in 1947 or 1948.

Doris and William were living in High Wycombe – and Dorothy made the short trip from Hermits Wood to see him 'several times', usually, he believes, accompanied by her sister Olive, who he is convinced was his godmother, or her trusted secretary Ruth Charlton. He 'didn't really know who she was', but was told to call her Aunty Dot or Dorothy. When he was nine he was selected for the part of Dwarf in the school pantomime, and 'two big black cars and Dorothy arrived with an entourage. She sat next to Doris in the front row.' In January 1952 he was rushed into a local Amersham hospital for an appendix operation. Dorothy visited him three times while he was in hospital bringing him, he remembers, oranges. (Before you scoff at this, remember how popular she was with other children who have appeared in this book, and that Dorothy's staff were incredulous at how she doted on Barbara Allwright's son.) His natural father also visited. 'The sister told me I had a visitor. I remember a pinstripe suit. He was very jovial and asked how I was getting on, and told me, "I'm your father. Always remember I came to see you."'

In 1953, the Son was set to leave Downley School, and Dorothy wanted to send him to private school. He refused to go, and instead attended the local Mill End Secondary School. A year later he fell off the roof of a barn, suffering a serious head injury, and was transferred to Oxford's John Radcliffe Infirmary where he underwent four operations during the next three weeks. He remained in hospital for four months, during which time Doris and Dorothy were regular visitors. To recuperate, he was moved to Wellesley House Convalescent School in Broadstairs in Kent. Dorothy took him down by train, worrying that she might not see him again. He didn't get on with some of the other boys there and ended up in a kind of 'solitary confinement', only for his natural father to intervene and have him removed. Eventually, he returned to Doris.

Once recovered, he went on to play football for Wycombe Schoolboys. Dorothy came to watch a game, he says, along with her entourage, attracting some attention, and being recognised by the spectators. 'She shouted at me once, "Don't head the ball"'.

He finished school in 1957 and joined Airmec Ltd in High Wycombe, experiencing some difficulty in getting a National Insurance number. On a couple of occasions, says the Son, he and one of his brothers cycled the few miles to visit Dorothy's home, with the intention of asking his birth mother some questions. Each time they were 'met by secretaries, who wouldn't let us see Dorothy and warned us, "Don't make waves."' In 1960, he married his sweetheart. He hadn't at this point told his wife-to-be his story. In fact, it wasn't until his daughter was 27, in 1990, that he finally told his family about his background.

His wife and children believe him. His daughter understands that there are problems with the story. Some parts of it don't quite seem to add up – but then, which of us can remember with complete clarity what happened to us when we were children over half a century ago? 'There were things which happened during my childhood that I'd never understood. When Dad told Mum and I, the story initially seemed far-fetched but, yes, I did believe him, and still do.' She believes her father was conflicted between wanting to get on with his life, and knowing that something intrinsic to who he was was being withheld from him.

What triggered him to start looking into his background was initially just a query of his tax status. He was asked a lot of questions, undergoing investigation, and believed the person asking them had information about him which he didn't have himself. He wanted more details. He still thinks that the authorities know only too well who he is.

But he seemed to be frustrated and diverted at every turn as he tried to delve into his background. I think it stressed him. He thinks that the 'Establishment' knew that, should it ever come out that he was Dorothy's son, it would be seen as a 'disgrace' for his blood family.

I don't think it has been about the money to which he'd clearly be entitled that drives him – just the potential satisfaction of knowing he's been right all along.

When Dad dies, maybe part of me will feel that I have to carry on trying to find the truth on his behalf.

Armed with his supporting evidence that he was the child of Dorothy Paget, in early 2011 the Son eventually took his case to a solicitor. Given that by then he was over 70 years old, had his only reason for claiming to be Dorothy's son been somehow to make a claim on her estate, or to suggest that he had been provided for by a trust, one might have thought he would have made such a move much earlier.

The solicitor gave his thoughts on his situation. He was unconvinced by his production of a birth certificate the son had obtained in 1990:

> *I think you may be wrong about this being your true birth certificate. It seems to me very strange that your mother, having gone to all the trouble of fabricating a completely false address, job, place of birth and Christian names, and registering the birth as far away as Cardiff, should then give her correct surname.*
>
> *It also seems to me unlikely, if you were in fact adopted by William and Doris, that they should then have falsely registered you as their own son many months later. It remains perfectly plausible that your mother, being anxious to conceal the fact of your birth, arranged for William and Doris to bring you up as their son.*
>
> *You are certain of your true parentage because you say William and Doris did not make a secret of it, and because you were visited on several occasions by both your true parents, who both confirmed that you were their son.*

Addressing the question of Dorothy's will, the solicitor notes that 'You believe that there may in fact have been a will' – which, of course, is the suggestion from a number of other sources – 'but it would be quite impossible to prove that now.

If you are Dorothy Paget's son and only child, then under the rules relating to people who die without making a will, you would have been entitled to her entire estate.

However, the grant was obtained by Dorothy's sister, Lady Baillie.

In order to obtain the grant, Lady Baillie must have sworn an oath stating that she was Dorothy's next of kin and that Dorothy had no children.

You say that she was perfectly aware of your existence and hence told a deliberate lie.

You believe she did this under heavy pressure from certain figures. You think that she created a trust for your benefit. You never received any cash from this trust but you believe that it was used to assist you discreetly on various occasions such as when you received private medical treatment.

The solicitor accepts that Lady Baillie did create a trust fund in May 1960,

*in other words, at the same time as she obtained a grant of administration to Dorothy's estate…called The Staff Trust Fund No. 2. You believe that this trust was deliberately named in such a way as to be misleading and is actually the trust of which you are a beneficiary … One of the Trustees was named as 'Albert William ******'.*
*'You believe that your 'father', William George ******, was the second trustee, though his Christian names are incorrectly stated.*

The solicitor points out that one of the people who obtained the first temporary grant of administration to Dorothy Paget's estate was Mr Albert William, 'who is there described as a solicitor. It really does seem very likely that the same Albert William ****** was the second trustee.'

The solicitor then deals with the obvious point of whether Doris and William had any solid evidence to support the Son's case: 'I understand that any paperwork "your parents" may have possessed concerning any trust in your favour has long since been lost.' He notes that DNA tests could be a way forward, but that

> *it seems unlikely in the extreme that the necessary samples would be given voluntarily. Nor do I think any court would be willing to order them.*
>
> *You have the distinct advantage, which many people in your position do not, of knowing for certain who your true parents were because they both acknowledged you. To be honest, I think that you should be satisfied with that.*
>
> *My advice has to be that you should simply drop the matter. To investigate thoroughly could easily cost you several thousand pounds with no guarantee of any satisfactory result. I cannot recommend chasing an old phantom with little prospect of success – spend your time and money enjoying the rest of your life.*

This analysis was written in 2011. The Son still clings to the story.

There is a separate coda to the story. In 2008, a house-clearing company went to a property in the South Bucks area where an elderly woman had lived, but recently died. The man and woman who set about the clearing job discovered in the garage a huge cache of papers in suitcases and trunks. There were letters, photographs, scrapbooks, newspapers and other material – even a locket. 'At home that evening,' said the house clearer, who came to the authors' attention through an article in the *Racing Post,*

> *I had a look on the internet to find out how and why I recognised the name Dorothy Paget, which had been on many of the letters I found. When I read about her I thought that perhaps there would be people interested enough in this kind of material to want to buy it. I brought*

the material back, sorted it into different sections, and eventually
contacted auction houses. I remember the name of the deceased person
being Mrs Barbara Brown, but couldn't be absolutely sure.

Dorothy did have many secretaries over the years, but a Mrs Brown does not appear to have been among them, although there was a Barbara, Mrs Allwright.

Unprompted, the house clearer revealed that, when he looked through some of the letters he found, he recalled seeing a reference to Dorothy having a son. He remembered the name mentioned. It was one of the Son's Christian names.

Much of the material sold at auction by the house clearer was purchased by Martin Pipe, who has yet to file and read all the thousands of documents, memos and letters. But several lots were not bought by him.

Just as the Son has been unable to prove the truth of the Story, so is it not possible conclusively to disprove it. No living distant relative of Dorothy is likely to agree to a DNA test; the Son says he has never considered hypnotism or regression to try and extend his fleeting memories of his birth parents.

So was there actually a secret Dorothy known to only a tiny number of people – Dorothy the mother?

'How could that be true?' That's the reaction from virtually everyone who has been told the Story. They seem to 'know' it could not possibly be true because, even if Dorothy Paget was not a lesbian, then at the very least she hated men. But if she didn't 'hate' men, perhaps she was bisexual, or why not asexual? Or, indeed, as the name of a horse she once owned and probably named herself, might indicate – Celibate?

Perhaps Dorothy's initial serious experience of a male with sexual allure was Sir Henry 'Tim' Birkin. When their sponsorship deal failed to work out, and Birkin shortly after met a tragic end, Dorothy may have felt that the love of her life was already lost to her.

The timeline of the Son's story is plausible. There is no doubt that a one-off liaison between Dorothy and the alleged father was possible, given that they certainly moved in the same circles. Nothing in what are known to have been Dorothy's movements at the relevant time would rule it out. Whether there would have been any physical attraction is another matter, but a combination of location, opportunity and desire might have produced the claimed result. Parties at Leeds Castle, as we have seen, could certainly have created such circumstances. Both father and mother are very likely to have regretted their actions, and chosen to allow others to cover the matter up and make the necessary arrangements for the innocent product of their actions to be brought up by others. Given Dorothy's history of broken and disappointing relationships she would probably have felt the need to see her child on occasion – few mothers deprived of a close relationship with their offspring can ever have fully come to terms with it.

That Dorothy Paget was his mother the son genuinely believes, even if he has convinced himself of that over the years out of a need to feel he knows his own background. He keeps her photograph and a handwritten letter by her in a display in his house. Neither he nor we will ever know for sure. But neither can we conclusively rule out the possibility.

What, ultimately, are we to make of Dorothy's character and life?

In an effort to try to understand how and why the name of Dorothy Paget eventually became synonymous with eccentricity, misandry, and over-indulgence in the public perception, Graham Sharpe enlisted the help of former Times racing writer and psychologist, John Karter. The authors are very grateful to him for the painstaking and thought-provoking psychological profile he has produced:

POOR LITTLE RICH GIRL

A psychological profile of Dorothy Paget

By John Karter

People love to put other people in boxes. We like to think that we know someone's character, how they function, and what makes them tick. In most cases, these boxes take no account of the individual's subjective reality or their personal worldview; they are based on expectations of what we regard as normal parameters of human behaviour.

These expectations can be broken down further into what are known as filters. These include gender and all the stereotypes that go with that filter; generation and age; nationality, ethnic background, skin colour; and education and manner of speaking.

If someone deviates from these perceived 'norms' they are put in boxes marked 'eccentric', 'oddball' or 'weird', which is a convenient way of dismissing who they really are as a person, what is important to them individually, and their distinctive or specific way of being in the world. We engage in this form of human classification or 'tagging' because it makes us feel safe and in control. If we can predict how other folk will behave, and know their limitations and their capabilities, we can file them away in our minds as tick-boxed and sorted. In essence, we do not have to worry about them, because in thinking that we know all about them we do not feel threatened.

That is why when someone like Dorothy Paget arrives in our midst, manifesting a lifestyle and behaviour that does not conform to our expectations of how someone with her background, gender, and personal circumstances should behave, it makes us feel uncomfortable. Her nonconformist, maverick qualities shake up our cosy little world by making us question our own way of being in it, including the way we relate to others, our day-to-day living habits, our values and our priorities. We think we have our lives sorted and under control and suddenly someone comes along and shows us that people don't have to conform to any pre-set notion, that in essence you can do what you damn well please, which is unfamiliar and threatening. Dorothy is out of the box and because we cannot pop her back in again and shut the lid, she is attacked and labelled in various ways because that is our natural form of defence against the kind of perceived threat she represents.

So, for example, Dorothy's apparent aversion to men, which appears to have had no basis in fact, other than her preference for associating with women, was distorted to fit the widely-held but blinkered view that if a woman is not in a relationship with a man she must be a man hater, sexually frigid, a lesbian or a combination of those three things. The truth is, of course, far more complex than that, as indeed are the personal circumstances that led to Dorothy also being labelled, amongst other things, 'eccentric', 'cranky', 'bizarre', 'rude', 'domineering', 'arrogant' and inhabiting a 'peculiar world.'

Those demeaning labels defined her throughout her life in the eyes of the public, and yet they were based purely on assumptions born out of her larger than life behaviour, her unconventional lifestyle, and her individual preferences for forming relationships. The people who judged her in this way were focusing purely on shallow, external observation rather than any attempt to dig deeper and find out about Dorothy's true character and what underpinned her behaviour and her way of being in the world. In his laudable efforts to look beneath these assumptions, Graham Sharpe has shown that she was in fact a generous, compassionate, enthusiastic and passionate woman. So, the question one must therefore ask is: how did these misconceptions come about?

The obvious place to start when looking for reasons why an individual manifests particular character traits, behaves in a certain way, and has their own emotional template and way of relating to others, is to examine their childhood, their upbringing and their relationship with their 'primary caregivers', usually their parents. In Dorothy's case this immediately throws up a wealth of material that goes a long way towards explaining why she became the person she grew up to be and why the 'inner woman' was very different to the public image.

As a simplistic way of summarising her upbringing and the effect it had on her, you could say that Dorothy was a typical 'poor little rich girl'; poor in this case meaning well-catered for in material terms, but emotionally impoverished and lacking in the proper parental nurturing, affection, and guidance that a child needs in order to develop into a psychologically healthy, well-rounded adult (I am aware that these terms are themselves open to question in terms of subjective validity). To say that Dorothy's high-flying, high-profile parents led the kind of busy, 'buzzy' lives that left little room for parenting in any real sense could in itself be seen as an assumption, but there is sufficient evidence to enable us to draw that conclusion.

Given her parents' own preoccupations with their high society way of life and in her father's case his naked political, social, and commercial ambitions, plus the fact that her mother's health was consistently poor, Dorothy would almost certainly not have received the attention and, equally importantly, the discipline a child needs for healthy development. Discipline is a form of love which a child needs to make her feel safe because it lays down boundaries. Without boundaries a child feels out of control and insecure. I have little doubt that this was a major factor in Dorothy's rebellious behaviour which led to her being expelled from six schools by the time she was 15. Furthermore, children whose parents are high-flyers feel under enormous pressure to make their mark on the world in a similar way. Some find that pressure too much too handle so they opt out, rebel, or exhibit extreme behaviour.

Add to this the fact that Dorothy inherited a fortune at the age of 11 (albeit that she could not access the money until she was 21) and also that her mother died when she was the same age, and it becomes clear that she had an enormous amount to deal with and make sense of when she was an immature girl still trying to establish her place in the world. Anyone of that age would struggle to deal with those pressures, but Dorothy had another major issue to contend with as well – a strained and distant relationship with her father.

A girl's father is her first love: he provides a model of 'maleness' and what it means to relate to a man. Her adult relationships with men will be underpinned by this template. Dorothy's stormy, emotionally barren relationship with her father clearly explains why she avoided close personal relationships with men during her adult life, although the suggestion that she was a man hater was surely given the lie by her close association with the racing driver Tim Birkin, which obviously meant a lot more to Dorothy than just a professional alliance.

The author John Welcome suggests that Dorothy's father longed for a son and after being landed with five daughters vented his disappointment on Dorothy. Welcome paints a vivid picture of the animosity between them, which was clearly initiated by her father, when he writes: 'In her minority, she and her father conducted a sort of running warfare interspersed with short truces.' Knowing that her father would have preferred a son, would have had a hugely negative impact on Dorothy because in essence what he was saying was that he would rather she hadn't been born. Dealing with that running emotional sore was bad enough, but Dorothy had to cope with a lot more from him during her formative years.

Racing writer Clive Graham confirms Welcome's suggestion that her father wanted a son and says that he used to make fun of Dorothy in public. Worse still, he forbade her to cry in case it upset his wife's delicate health. That must have heaped enormous pressure on Dorothy: not only could she not show any emotion, which is essential to healthy psychological development, but she might also have felt that she was in some way responsible for her mother's death. In this context, it is fascinating that she formed such a strong attachment to Princess Mestchersky (sometimes written as Meshchersky), the principal of her finishing school, who forced Dorothy to submit to discipline and became a mother substitute.

Five years after her mother's death, Dorothy had to contend with the arrival of a step-mother in the form of her father's second wife. There is not sufficient evidence to suggest that she was the archetypal wicked step-mother but it was no secret that she and Dorothy did not get along. And if we need confirmation that her father was a 'cold fish', more interested in his own advancement than his family's well-being, it presented itself in a fairly bizarre way when he locked his second wife out of the house because he considered her an impediment to his career.

Given this background of emotional deprivation and pressures of many different kinds, you do not have to be a psychological genius to work out why Dorothy's ways did not conform to what people regarded as normal and why she manifested such an unconventional lifestyle and behaviour, which led to her being labelled her in such harsh and disparaging ways. However, in terms of the sneering and downright nastiness that Dorothy endured throughout her adult life, much of it media driven, there was almost certainly a psychological phenomenon known as 'projection' going on as well. Projection is a common, everyday device whereby we project or locate characteristics or traits that we find unacceptable about ourselves into other people so that we can rid ourselves of the negative feelings those unacceptable character flaws engender.

For example, a bored wife who has a secret longing for an affair, might accuse her husband of flirting with every woman he meets when that is what she would really like to do with other men. The same mental mechanism is at work when people stand outside law courts hurling abuse at murderers and rapists. What they are really doing is telling themselves: 'I could never be evil or sadistic like that.' The truth is that we are all capable of many things that we would not own up to, a principle summed up by the psychologist and philosopher Erich Fromm when he wrote: 'There is nothing human which is alien to me.

Everything is in me. I am a little child, I am a grown-up, I am a murderer, and I am a saint.'

So, when Dorothy was tagged by the kind of vicious labels mentioned earlier – one writer dismissed her as 'A bad-tempered lump of a woman' – those insults say far more about the people who made them than Dorothy herself. Yes, she could be demanding, capricious, and idiosyncratic, but look beneath the public image and you will find a woman with a heart of gold, who liked helping people as much as she liked to get her own way. In the end, you can hardly blame her for that. You could even say that it represents a pretty well-balanced epitaph.

John Karter is a psychotherapist with the United Kingdom Council for Psychotherapy and was also the Racing Correspondent for The Sunday Times *and* The Independent, *and Racing Editor of* The Times, *for whom he also wrote.*

APPENDIX

PAGET FAMILY TREE

Lewis BAYLY
(Anglican Bishop)
died 1631

|

Nicholas BAYLY
born before 1631

|

Nicholas BAYLY
1684–1741

|

Sir Edward BAYLY
1st Baronet of Plas Newydd
1684–1741

|

Sir Nicholas BAYLY
2nd Baronet of Plas Newydd
Lord Lieutenant of Anglesey
1709–1782

|

Henry PAGET
Born Henry Bayly
1st Earl of Uxbridge
10th Baron Paget
3rd Baronet of Plas Newydd in Anglesey
1744–1812

|

Henry William PAGET
1st Marchess of Anglesey
2nd Earl of Uxbridge
1768–1854

|

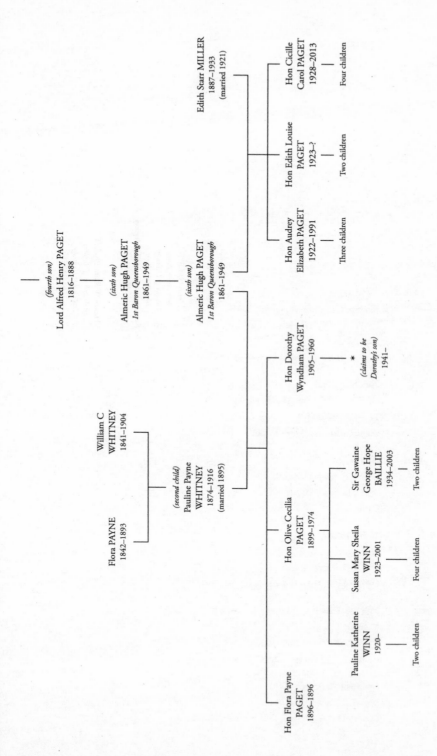

Flora PAYNE
1842–1893

William C
WHITNEY
1841–1904

(second child)
Pauline Payne
WHITNEY
1874–1916
(married 1895)

(fourth son)
Lord Alfred Henry PAGET
1816–1888

Almeric Hugh PAGET
1st Baron Queensborough
1861–1949

(sixth son)
Almeric Hugh PAGET
1st Baron Queensborough
1861–1949

Edith Starr MILLER
1887–1933
(married 1921)

Hon Flora Payne
PAGET
1896–1896

Hon Olive Cecilia
PAGET
1899–1974

Hon Dorothy
Wyndham PAGET
1905–1960

Hon Audrey
Elizabeth PAGET
1922–1991

Hon Edith Louise
PAGET
1923–?

Hon Cicille
Carol PAGET
1928–2013

Pauline Katherine
WINN
1920–

Susan Mary Sheila
WINN
1923–2001

Sir Gawaine
George Hope
BAILLIE
1934–2003

*(claims to be
Dorothy's son)*
1941–

Two children

Four children

Two children

Three children

Two children

Four children

Researched and created by Anita Brown

GOLDEN MILLER RACING RECORD

1930 **1st September**
Southwell – Farnsfield Hurdle (2m)
UNPLACED (25/1) behind Bucksome Lady. 17 ran (At this point owned by trainer
Basil Briscoe)
Carried 10 st 4 lbs and ridden by Tommy James

29th November
Newbury – Moderate Hurdle (2m)
THIRD (100/6) behind Black Armstrong. 21 ran (Now owned by Philip Carr)
Carried 10st. and ridden by Bob Lyall

1931 **20th January**
Leicester – Gopsall Hurdle (2m)
WON (4/5 fav) 20 ran
Carried 10 st 2 lbs and ridden by Bob Lyall

26th January
Nottingham – Annesley Hurdle (2m)
WON (5/6 fav) 24 ran
Carried 10 st 12 lbs and ridden by Ted Leader

21st February
Newbury – Spring Chase (2m)
SECOND (9/4) to Rolie 10 ran
Carried 10 st 5 lbs and ridden by Gerry Wilson

8th April Flat race
Warwick – Spring Handicap (2m)
EIGHTH (7/1) behind Little Blackbird. 11 ran

Carried 8 st 11 lbs and ridden by Bobby Dick

16th April Flat race

Newmarket – April Stakes (1½m)

FOURTH (3/1 fav) behind Craig Park. 8 ran

Carried 9 st 4 lbs and ridden by Jack Leach

12th October

Chelmsford – Witham Hurdle (2m)

WON (4/11 fav) 6 ran

Carried 11 st 10 lbs and ridden by Billy Stott.

(Now owned by Dorothy Paget)

22nd October

Sandown – Norbiton Handicap Hurdle (2m)

THIRD (9/4 co-fav) behind Clydesdale. 14 ran

Carried 11 st 9 lbs and ridden by Ted Leader

30th October

Manchester – Irish Hospitals Hcp Hurdle (2m)

THIRD (3/1) behind Knuckleduster. 13 ran

Carried 12 st 1 lb and ridden by Mr R – Bobby – Mount

11th November

Chelmsford – Chelmsford Hurdle (2m)

WON (4/11 fav) 6 ran

Ridden by Ted Leader

4th December

Newbury – Moderate Chase (2m)

WON (11/10 fav) later disqualified for carrying incorrect weight; Forbra awarded race. 11 ran

Carried 10 st 5 lbs and ridden by Ted Leader

30th December

Newbury – Reading Chase (2m)

WON (4/5 fav) 7 ran

Carried 10 st 12 lbs and ridden by Ted Leader

1932

20th January

Newbury – Sefton Chase (2m)

SECOND (8/11 fav) behind Parsons Well. 15 ran

Carried 12 st 5 lbs and ridden by Ted Leader

27th January

Gatwick – Brook Chase (3m)

WON (4/6 fav) 3 ran

Carried 11 st 3 lbs and ridden by Ted Leader

1st March

Cheltenham Gold Cup (3m 3f)

WON (13/2) 6 ran

Carried 11 st 5 lbs and ridden by Ted Leader

19th March Flat race

Liverpool – Maghull Plate (1m 6f)

SECOND (4/1) behind Free Fare. 8 ran.

Carried 9 st 5 lbs and ridden by Harry Beasley

28th March

Manchester – Lancashire Chase (3m 4f)

UNPLACED (9/4 fav) won by Huic Holloa.
15 ran

Carried 11 st 10 lbs and ridden by Ted Leader

1st December

Kempton – Middlesex Handicap Chase
(2m 4f)

WON (6/4 fav) 8 ran

Carried 12 st 2 lbs and ridden by Billy Stott

10th December

Lingfield – Open Chase (3m)

WON (4/9 fav) 5 ran

Carried 11 st 4 lbs and ridden by Billy Stott

1933   19th January

Hurst Park – Mitre Hcp Chase (3m)

WON (6/4 fav) 8 ran

Carried 12 st 7 lbs and ridden by Billy Stott

4th February

Lingfield Park – Troytown Chase (3m)

WON (2/1 fav) 9 ran

Carried 12 st 10 lbs and ridden by Billy Stott

7th March

Cheltenham Gold Cup (3m 3f)

WON (4/7 fav) 7 ran

Carried 12 st and ridden by Billy Stott

24th March

Liverpool – Grand National (4m 4f)

FELL (9/1 fav) at the 24th fence. (This is
disputed by some sources who argue that the
horse unseated his rider) Kellsboro' Jack won.

1932 Gold Cup trophy

1933 Gold Cup trophy

34 ran

Carried 12 st 2 lbs and ridden by Ted Leader

25th November

Lingfield – Open Chase (3m)

WON (8/11 fav) 5 ran

Carried 11 st 8 lbs and ridden by Gerry Wilson

27th December

Kempton Park – Gamecock Hcp Chase (2m 4f)

SECOND (4/7 fav) to Thomond II. 8 ran

Carried 12 st 7 lbs and ridden by Gerry Wilson

1934 **18th January**

Hurst Park – Star & Garter Hcp Chase (3m)

THIRD (1/2 fav) behind Southern Hero. 9 ran

Carried 12 st 7 lbs and ridden by Gerry Wilson

6th March

Cheltenham Gold Cup (3m 3f)

WON (6/5 fav) 7 ran

Carried 12 st. and ridden by Gerry Wilson

23rd March

Liverpool – Grand National (4m 4f)

WON (8/1) 30 ran

Carried 12 st 2 lbs and ridden by Gerry Wilson

26th December

Wolverhampton – Penkridge Chase (3m)

WON (1/4 fav) 10 ran

Carried 11 st 5 lbs and ridden by John Baxter

1934 Gold Cup trophy

1935 **7th January**

Leicester – Mapperley Chase (3m)

WON (7/100 fav) 6 ran

Carried 12 st. and ridden by Gerry Wilson

22nd January

Derby – Breadsall Chase (3m)

WON (7/100 fav) 8 ran

Carried 12 st 7 lbs and ridden by Gerry Wilson

ww16th February

Sandown Park – Grand International Hcp Chase (3m 5f)

WON 6 ran

Carried 12 st 7 lbs and ridden by Gerry Wilson

14th March

Cheltenham Gold Cup (3m 3f)

WON (1/2 fav) 5 ran

Carried 12 st. and ridden by Gerry Wilson

29th March

Liverpool – Grand National (4m 4f)

UNSEATED RIDER at 11th (2/1 fav)

behind Reynoldstown. 27 ran

Carried 12 st 7 lbs and ridden by Gerry Wilson

1935 Gold Cup trophy

30th March

Liverpool – Champion Chase (2m 7½f)

UNSEATED RIDER (Evens fav) at first; won by Double Crossed. 11 ran

Carried 12 st. and ridden by Gerry Wilson

6th December

Sandown – Arthur Coventry National Hunt Flat Race (2m)

THIRD (9/2) behind Free Fare. 4 ran

Carried 11 st 9 lbs and ridden by Mr J. H. Gordon

(Now trained by Owen Anthony)

30th December

Newbury – Andover Hcp Chase (2m)

WON (7/2 fav) 10 ran

Carried 12 st 10 lbs and ridden by Gerry Wilson

1936 **26th February**

Newbury – Newbury Hcp Chase (3m)

UNPLACED *(*Evens Fav) behind Hillsbrook (unseated rider,

and ran out five from home). 12 ran

Carried 12 st 7 lbs and ridden by Gerry Wilson

12th March

Cheltenham Gold Cup (3m 2f)

WON (21/20 fav) 6 ran

Carried 12 st. and ridden by Evan Williams

27th March

Liverpool – Grand National (4m 4f)

UNPLACED (5/1) behind Reynoldstown

(brought down at first, remounted, refused

at 11th) 35 ran

Carried 12 st 7 lbs and ridden

by Evan Williams

1936 Gold Cup trophy

14th April

Cardiff – Welsh Grand National (3m 4f)

THIRD (4/6 fav) behind Sorley Boy. 11 ran

Carried 12 st 7 lbs and ridden by Evan Williams

17th October

Wincanton – Lattiford Chase (2m 4f)

WON (1/3 fav) 8 ran

Carried 12 st. and ridden by Fulke Walwyn

11th November

Liverpool – Becher Chase (2m 4f)

SECOND (7/2 co-fav) to Royal Mail. 9 ran

Carried 12 st. and ridden by Fulke Walwyn

26th December

Wincanton – Sparkford Optional Chase (3m)

WON (1/5 fav) 6 ran

Carried 12 st. and ridden by Evan Williams

1937   **9th January**

Gatwick – Crawley Chase (3m) (E Williams)

WON (8/15 fav) in dead-heat with Drinmore Lad. 7 ran

Carried 12 st 7 lbs and ridden by Evan Williams

22nd February

Birmingham – Optional Selling Chase (2m 4f)

WON (2/9 fav) 7 ran

Carried 12 st. and ridden by Frenchie Nicholson

19th March

Liverpool – Grand National (4m 4f)

REFUSED (8/1 fav) at 11th behind Royal Mail. 33 ran

Carried 12 st 7 lbs and ridden by Danny Morgan

20th December

Sandown Park – Sandown Hcp Chase (3m)

UNPLACED (4/1 fav) behind Macaulay. 18 ran

Carried 12 st 7 lbs and ridden by Frenchie Nicholson

27th December

Wincanton – Sparkford Chase (3m)

WON (1/4 fav) 11 ran

Carried 12 st. and ridden by Sandy Scratchley

1938   **13th January**

Sandown Park – Princes' Hcp Chase (3m 5f)

WON (Evens fav) 10 ran

Carried 12 st 7 lbs and ridden by Frenchie Nicholson

18th February

Hurst Park – Hampton Court Optional Selling Chase (3m)

SECOND (4/6 fav) to Macaulay. 6 ran

Carried 11 st 10 lbs and ridden by Frenchie Nicholson

28th February

Birmingham – Optional Selling Chase (2m 4f)

WON (100/8 fav) 6 ran

Carried 12 st. and ridden by Frenchie Nicholson

10th March

Cheltenham Gold Cup (3m 2f)

SECOND (7/4 fav) to Morse Code. 6 ran

Carried 12 st. and ridden by Frenchie Nicholson

1939   **23rd February**

Newbury – Newbury Hcp Chase (3m)

UNPLACED (6/1 co fav) behind Antipas. 13 ran

Carried 12 st 3 lbs and ridden by George Archibald

**TRAINED by Basil Briscoe for all races until Sandown's 'Arthur Coventry' on December 6, 1935, for which Owen Anthony trained him, and for all his subsequent races

BIBLIOGRAPHY

Barrett, Norman (editor), *Daily Telegraph Chronicle of Horse Racing*. Guinness, 1995

Barry, Quintin, *Lord Derby and his Horses: A Tory Grandee and the Turf*. Red Horse Press, 2012

Beasley, Rufus, *Pilllow to Post: The Life and Times of Rufus Beasley*. Westminster Press, 1981

Beavis, Jim, *The History of Fontwell Park*. Jim Beavis, 2008

Bentley, W. O., *An Illustrated History of the Bentley Car, 1919–31*. George Allen & Unwin, 1964

Biddle, Flora Miller, *The Whitney Women and the Museum They Made*. Arcade, 1999

Biddlecombe, Terry, *Winner's Disclosure*. Stanley Paul, 1982

Bignell, Alan, *Lady Baillie at Leeds Castle*. Leeds Castle Enterprises, 2007

Birkin, Sir Henry (Tim), *Full Throttle*. G. T. Foulis, 1932.

Blaxland, Gregory, *Golden Miller*. Constable, 1972

Bloodstock Breeders' Review, 1932; 1935; 1945; 1953. British Bloodstock Agency

Brabazon, Aubrey, *Racing Through my Mind*. Vota Books, 1998

Breasley, Scobie and Poole, Cristopher, *Scobie: A Lifetime in Racing*. Queen Anne Press, 1984

Briscoe, Basil, *The Life of Golden Miller*. Hutchinson, 1939

Butchers, Bob, *Silks, Soaks and Certainties*. Blenheim Press, 2008

Cleggett, David, *Leeds Castle Through Nine Centuries*. Leeds Castle Foundation, 2001

Cottrell, John and Armytage, Marcus. *A–Z of the Grand National*. Highdown, 2008

Cranham, Gerry, Pitman, Richard and Oaksey, John, *Guinness Guide to Steeplechasing*. Guinness, 1979

Curling, Bill, *The Captain: A Biography of Captain Sir Cecil Boyd-Rochfort, Royal Trainer*. Barrie & Jenkins, 1970

Curling, Bill, *Royal Champion: The Story of Steeplechasing's First Lady*. Michael Joseph, 1980

Davies, Grenville, *A Touch of Colwick*. Pride of Place Publishing, 1994

Down, Alastair, *The Best of Alastair Down*. Racing Post, 2014

Eacott, Bill, *A History of Racehorse Training at Epsom*. C. W. Eacott, 2009

Fairfax-Blakeborough, J., *The Turf Who's Who 1932*. May Fair Press, 1932

Fitzgeorge-Parker, Tim, *No Secret So Close*. Pelham, 1984

Fitzgeorge-Parker, Tim, *The Ditch on the Hill: 80 Years of the Cheltenham Festival*. Simon & Schuster, 1991

Foulkes, Nicholas, *The Bentley Era*. Quadrille Publishing, 2008

Francis, Dick, *Lester: The Official Biography*, Michael Joseph, 1986

Fuller, Bryony, *Fulke Walwyn: A Pictorial Tribute*. Lambourn Publications, 1990

Galtrey, Sidney, *Memoirs of a Racing Journalist*. Hutchinson, 1934

George, Robert E. G. (aka Sencourt, Robert E.), *Heirs of Tradition*. Carroll & Nicholson, 1949

Gilbey, Quintin, *Queen of the Turf*. Arthur Barker 1973

Good, Meyrick, *The Lure of the Turf*. Odhams, 1957

Graham, Clive and Curling, Bill, *The Grand National*. Barrie & Jenkins, 1972

Green, Reg, *A Race Apart*. Hodder & Stoughton, 1988

Gribble, Philip, *Off the Cuff*. J. M. Dent, 1964

Hamlyn, Geoffrey, *My Sixty Years in the Ring*. Sporting Garland Press, 1994

Harman, Bob, *The Ultimate Dream: 75 Years of the Tote Cheltenham Gold Cup*. Mainstream, 2000

Hassell, James E., *Russian Refugees in France and the US Between the World Wars*. American Philosophical Society, 1992

Hay, Michael, *Blower Bentley: Bentley 4 ½-Litre Supercharged*. Number One Press, 2001

Hedges, David, *Mr Grand National*, Pelham, 1969

Herbert, Ivor, *Arkle*. Aurum, 2003

Herbert, Ivor, *The Queen Mother's Horses*. Pelham, 1967

Herbert, Ivor and Smyly, Patricia, *The Winter Kings*. Pelham, 1989

Hillstead, A. F. C., *Those Bentley Days*. Faber, 1953

Hislop, John, *Hardly a Jockey*. Marlborough, 1993

Holland, Anne, *Steeplechasing: A Celebration of 250 Years*. Little, Brown, 2001

Holland, Anne, *Stride by Stride*. Queen Anne Press, 1989

Hyland, Francis P. M., *Taken for a Ride*. Gill & Macmillan, 2006

Kahn, E. J., Jr, *Jock: The Life and Times of John Hay Whitney*. Doubleday, 1981

Kaye, Richard, *The Ladbrokes Story*. Pelham, 1969

Kenny, Paul, *The Man Who Supercharged Bond*. Haynes, 2009

King, Peter, *The Grand National: Anybody's Race*. Quartet Books, 1983

Knight, Lorin, *Scobie*. New Horizon, 1983

Laird, Dorothy, *Royal Ascot*. Hodder and Stoughton, 1976

Lee, Alan, *Cheltenham Racecourse*. Pelham, 1985

Lee, Alan, *Fred: The Authorised Biography of Fred Winter*. Pelham, 1991

Lucas, Pat, *Fifty Years of Racing at Chepstow*. H. G. Walters, 1976

Mackeson, Rupert (editor) and Onslow, Richard, *Great Racing Gambles and Frauds, vol. 2*. Marlborough Books, 1992

Magee, Sean (editor), *Freud on Course: The Racing Lives of Clement Freud*. Racing Post, 2009

Mathieu, Paul, *Beckhampton*. Racing Post, 2015

McGuigan, John, *A Trainer's Memories*. Heath Cranton, 1946

Mortimer, Roger, Onslow, Richard and Willett, Peter, *Biographical Encyclopaedia of British Flat Racing*. Macdonald and Jane's, 1978

Mortimer, Roger, *The Encyclopaedia of Flat Racing*. Robert Hale, 1971

Mortimer, Roger, *The History of the Derby Stakes*. Cassell, 1961; Michael Joseph, 1973

Munting, Roger, *Hedges and Hurdles*. Allen, 1987

Nicholson, David, with Powell, Jonathan, *The Duke*. Hodder and Stoughton, 1995

Oaksey, Lord, *Oaksey on Racing*. Kingswood Press, 1991

Oaksey, Lord and Rodney, Bob, *A Racing Companion*. W. H. Smith, 1992

O'Brien, Jacqueline and Herbert, Ivor, *Vincent O'Brien: The Official Biography*. Bantam Press, 2005

O'Connor, Bernard, *RAF Tempsford*. Amberley, 2010

O'Leary, Con, *Grand National*. Rockliff, 1947

Onslow, Richard. *Royal Ascot*. Crowood Press, 1990

Orchard, Vincent, *The Derby Stakes, 1900–1953*. Hutchinson, 1954

Pegg, Norman, *Focus on Racing*. Robert Hale, 1963

Peters, Stewart, *The Irish Grand National*. Stadia, 2007

Piggott, Lester, *Lester*. Partridge Press, 1995

Pitt, Chris, *A Long Time Gone*. Portway Press, 1996

Pitt, Chris and Hammond, Chas, *When Birmingham Went Racing*. CC Publishing, 2005

Pitt, Chris, *Go Down to the Beaten*. Racing Post, 2011

Pope, Michael, *More Fun and Frolics*. Sporting Garland Press, 1994

Plumptre, George, *Back Page Racing*. Queen Anne Press, 1989

Ramsden, Caroline, *Ladies in Racing*. Stanley Paul, 1973

Randall, L. John and Morris, Tony, *A Century of Champions*. Portway Press, 1999

Ranfurly, Hermione, Countess of, *The Ugly One: The Childhood Memoirs of Hermione, Countess of Ranfurly, 1913–39*. Michael Joseph, 1998

Reid, Jamie, *A Licence To Print Money*. Macmillan, 1992

Rickman, Eric, *On and Off the Racecourse*. Routledge, 1937

Rimell, Fred and Mercy, *Aintree Iron*. W. H. Allen, 1977

Robertson, William H. P., *The History of Thoroughbred Racing in America*. Bonanza Books, 1964

Robyns, Gwen, *Wimbledon: The Hidden Drama*. David & Charles, 1973

Rodrigo, R., *The Racing Game*. Sportsmans Book Club, 1958

Ruff's Guide to the Turf 1942, 1960, 1961. Sporting Life, 1942, etc.

Russell, Anthony, *Outrageous Fortune*. Robson Press, 2013

Saville, John, *Insane and Unseemly*. Matador, 2009

Sharpe, Graham and Bose. Mihir, *William Hill: The Man and the Business*. Racing Post, 2014

Smith, Martin (editor), *Kings, Queens and Four-Legged Athletes: the Telegraph Book of Horse Racing*. Aurum, 2011

Seth-Smith, Michael, *Steve*. Faber & Faber, 1974

Smirke, Charlie, *Finishing Post*. Oldbourne, 1960

Smith, Doug, with Willett, Peter, *Five Times Champion*. Pelham, 1968

Smith, Raymond, *Vincent O'Brien*, Virgin, 1990

Smith, Sean, *Royal Racing*. BBC Worldwide, 2001

Smyly, Patricia, *Encyclopaedia of Steeplechasing*. Robert Hale, 1979

Smythe, Pat, *Jump for Joy*. Companion Book Club, 1955

Smythe, Pat, *One Jump Ahead*. Cassell, 1956

Smythe, Pat, *Leaping Life's Fences*. The Sportsman's Press, 1992

Stanley, Louis T., *Newmarket*. W. H. Allen, 1984

Stevens, Peter, *History of the National Hunt Chase*. Peter Stevens, 2010

St John Williams, Guy and Hyland, Francis P. M., *The Irish Derby 1866–1979*. J. A. Allen, 1980

Tanner, Michael, *The Champion Hurdle*. Pelham, 1989 (revised edition, Mainstream, 2002)

Tavernier, David M., *Stories of the Rich and Famous*. Outskirts Press, 2012

Thompson, Laura, *Newmarket*. Virgin, 2000

Tote Investors' Who's Who in Racing 1939

Vassiltchikov, Marie, *The Berlin Diaries 1940–45*. Mandarin, 1990

Warner, Gerry (editor), *Who's Who in Racing 1947*. Warner's Racing Agency, 1947

Warner, Gerry (editor), *Racing Review Annual 1952*. Racing Review Publications

Wathen, Guy, *Great Horsemen of the World*. David & Charles, 1990

Watson, S. J., *Between the Flags*. Allen Figgis, 1969

Welcome, John, *The Cheltenham Gold Cup*. Pelham, 1973 (first published 1957)

Whelan, Richard, *Strategic Advance*. Matador, 2008

Willett, Peter, *Dick Hern: The Authorised Biography*. Hodder And Stoughton, 2000

Williams, Guy St John and Hyland, Francis P. M., *The Irish Derby*. J. A. Allen, 1980

Williams, Guy St John and Hyland, Francis P. M., *Jameson Irish Grand National*. The Organisation, 1995

Williams, Michael, *The Continuing Story of Point-to-Point Racing*. Pelham, 1970

Wilson, Jim, *Nazi Princess: Hitler, Lord Rothermere and Princess Stephanie*. The History Press, 2011

Wilson, Julian, *100 Greatest Racehorses*. Macdonald, 1987

Winn, Christopher, *London by Tube*. Ebury, 2016

Wright, Howard, *The Encyclopaedia of Flat Racing*. Robert Hale, 1986

ACKNOWLEDGEMENTS

Thanks to David Ashforth, for his unselfish encouragement to me to tackle a project I know he had eyed up himself in the past. Other journalists who weighed in with practical assistance and advice include Marcus Armytage, John Hanmer, Willie Lefebve, Sean Magee, Jim Mansell, Tony Paley and Alyson Rudd. Also thanks to: Harrow School archivist, Joanna Badrock; Amber Baillie, wife of Sir Adrian Louis Baillie, 8th Baronet, son of Sir Gawaine Baillie, 7th Baronet, and of Margot, Lady Baillie, who kindly provided rare photographs of Dorothy and her sister Olive; Kevin Barnes, who put me in touch with the house clearers who uncovered a treasure trove of Dorothy's private papers; Chester Beattie, Veronica Beeny, Betty Chantler, Ann Edgar and Jean Rountree, who all supplied some vital early hunting information; Daisy Berkeley, daughter of jockey Dave Dick; Alan Bodfish, for help with matters Bentley; Anita Brown, for her tenaciously efficient tracking down of the many branches of Dorothy's family tree, together with numerous vital documents; James Buxton, Tim Birkin's grandson; Graeme Calvert-Thompson, Rolls-Royce enthusiast, who painstakingly dug out long-lost details; Steve Carter of the Ashford Valley Hunt, who pointed me in a very productive direction; Richard

Charlesworth, for channelling the spirit of the Bentley Boys; William Church, assistant vicar at St Mary's Church, Hertingfordbury; our editor, Graham Coster, for finding the story among the plethora of material on a unique life we started with and stitching it into a coherent whole; bloodstock dealer James Delahooke, who believes Dave Dick deserves a book of his own; Jonathan Dimmer, keeper of the (Gold) Cups; the recently, reluctantly retired *Sun* racing reporter and legend, Claude Duval, who secured the authors an interview with former racecourse commentator, Cloudseley Marsham; Heather Falvey of the Rickmansworth Historical Society, for help with Dorothy's charitable donations; Isobel Haes, for Rolls-Royce information she wrote about in the Rolls-Royce Enthusiasts' Club magazine; Bentley guru Clare Hay; Nigel Hewston, Chairman of the Avicultural Society, to which Dorothy used to belong; Lucy Hughes, the Corpus Christi College archivist; John Karter, for readily accepting the invitation to unleash his racing, punting and psychotherapy insight on our subject; golf writer and roamer of the world Liz Kahn, current owner of Dorothy's curtains and niece of Dorothy's great friend Irene Robbins; Annie Kemkran-Smyth, for arranging access to the Leeds Castle archives; Paula Lavender, Headmistress' PA at Heathfield School; Willie Lefebve and his lovely wife Penny; Alan Lewis of the Brooklands Museum; Elizabeth M. Lloyd, General Secretary of the Royal Society of St George, who ferreted about in the archives to tease out details of Lord Queenborough's connections; Angela Macintosh, for recalling the days when Dorothy's Rollers came to stay during the war; Sir Rupert Mackeson, never less than entertaining, often scurrilously indiscreet about long-gone racing figures; the late Stanley Mann, a specialist dealer in and expert on Bentley motors, his son Oliver and wife Karen (who played Dorothy in the film, *Full Throttle*) and Stanley's archivist, Steve; Chris McNamee, who used to work for Tommy Carey; Paul Mathieu, for his encouragement; the late Bob McCreery, who felt Dorothy's reputation has been 'traduced' over the years; Marina Milmo, who was invaluable in helping make sense of Dorothy's instrumental involvement with the Russian Home; Ann Miller, the telephonist who connected Hermits Wood to the outside world; David Moore, Shelsley Walsh Hill Climb archivist; Dinah Nicholson, for memories of the days when Dorothy's horses were trained by members of her family; Nick Onslow, archivist of the East Kent Foxhounds, who provided details of the Mid-Kent Hunt; the much-missed Sir Peter O'Sullevan, who was generous with his thoughts about Dorothy to both authors; the Queen's photographer, Bernard Parkin, for the cartoon he created; Gordon Patrick, a one-time carol singer rewarded at Hermits Wood with mince pies and a 'few' shillings; Duncan Pearce – same initials, that's where the similarity ends; the patient staff at Pinner Library for helping to track down elusive books containing fleeting but important references to Dorothy and likewise to the shift at the *Daily Mail* cuttings library; Martin, Carol and David Pipe and family for letting me root through the invaluably fascinating treasure trove of Dorothy Paget memorabilia which he outbid me at auction to own – and also for feeding and watering me each time I turned up to disrupt the carefully randomly filed archives; Ron Pollard, for hinting at some of the less ethical elements of the racecourse during his bookie days; Sarah Prest and Richard Wilding of Weatherbys; Charlie Rennie Senior; Mercy Rimell, trainer's wife, who knew Dorothy personally; Anne Rolinson, for her memories of Dorothy's association with her father A. P. Hammond's horsebox business; Brough Scott, for finally coming round to the idea that there was a book in Dorothy Paget; champion jump jockey Peter Scudamore, who shared his father's memories of riding in the National for Dorothy; the Son, his wife and daughter, whose story was told freely and compellingly; Graham Snelling of the Newmarket Horse Racing Museum; Lowing Tripp, a family name for several generations, whose dad was one of Dorothy's blacksmiths; Ian Valentine, freelance journalist who imagined a road trip through France with Dorothy; Cath Walwyn, for tea and biscuits and recapturing the spirit of those days when she and Fulke had to cope with Dorothy the owner; Welwyn Garden City Museum; Janet Wilson, whose mum, known as Molly, worked in the kitchen for Dorothy Paget; and to everyone else whose enthusiasm for the project convinced us to keep the faith. Apologies to those who have inadvertently been omitted.

Graham Sharpe

I would like to thank everyone who supported and encouraged me throughout the writing process, particularly Mairead, my mum Eithne, brothers Austin and Mick, as well as Ken, Junior, Kaiser, Dan, Burkey, James, Murf, Don, Pedro, Der, Campbell and Daunty. Thanks to all those who subjected themselves for interview and/or summary grilling and I'd also like to thank Graham Sharpe for his unceasing work and enthusiasm – and contacts. A special word of thanks as well to Dan and Jo O'Sullivan and their wonderful staff at the Maryborough House Hotel in Cork.

Declan Colley

INDEX